# MUSHROOM

# MUSHROOM
## The Story of the A-Bomb Kid

By
John Aristotle Phillips and David Michaelis

WILLIAM MORROW AND COMPANY, INC.
NEW YORK 1978

**Library of Congress Cataloging in Publication Data**

Phillips, John Aristotle.
  Mushroom.

    1. Phillips, John Aristotle.  2. Atomic bomb.
3. Physicists—United States.  I. Michaelis, David,
joint author.  II. Title.
QC774.P44A33     623.4′5119 [B]     78-8411
ISBN 0-688-03351-2

Printed in the United States of America.

First Edition

1  2  3  4  5  6  7  8  9  10

*This book is dedicated to:*

Bessie and Aris                    Diana and Michael

Dean                                        The Big M

Frack                                            Frick

and Ross.


*And to our generation:*
*That we may make a difference in the world.*

## Acknowledgments

We would like to thank the following for their help during the preparation of this book: Big M, Bucky, Mark Carliner, Dean, Freeman Dyson, Bill Goyen, Halmeyer, Harper, Mike Heitner, Mrs. Harry, M. H. and Flora Irving, King Kool, Kelvin, Lala, James Landis, Bob Lasky, Sterling Lord, Washington Jefferson Lincoln, Robert K. Massie, Meg, Pearl, Peezner, Ross, Dan Seltzer, Cody Shearer, Ted, The Goddess Bovina, The Arctic Commissioner, van der Stoops, Sir Whoopee, and, finally, our parents.

# Contents

## Part 2

$$\rightarrow C^2F^2 \rightarrow$$

## Contents

### Part 3

### GC + Pimp → Personality = Whoopee

# Preface: Whoopee

*"Take it from me baby, in America nothing fails like success . . ."*
—Budd Schulberg in *The Disenchanted*

Once upon a mushroom, I was whoopeed.

"Whoopee" is a mass media action word. It describes the process which starts when an *Obscure Individual* does something Creative, Courageous, Frivolous, or Frightening ($C^2F^2$). The media decide that he will make Good Copy (*GC*). Using millions of newspapers, magazines, radios, and television sets, the media form a peephole through which the public can scrutinize him. The Public's Impression through the Media Peephole (*PIMP*) suddenly makes *him* more important than what he has done. The *Obscure Individual* is now a *Personality:*

*OBSCURE INDIVIDUAL* → $C^2F^2$ + *GC* + *PIMP* → *PERSONALITY* = *WHOOPEE*

Call me a Personality. I didn't want it that way. It just happened. If it happened to me, it can happen to anyone.

Whoopee has had a long history in America. War heroes have been whoopeed. Housewives have been whoopeed. Athletes, inventors, adventurers, astronauts, authors, magicians, quintuplets, mass murderers, and the girl next door have been whoopeed.

America makes whoopee best.

Charles Lindbergh was the King of Whoopee. Jackie Onassis is the reigning Queen. Muhammad Ali is the Clown Prince.

# MUSHROOM

You might be whoopeed tomorrow, or next year, or you might have been whoopeed yesterday. Most of the Princes and Princesses of Whoopee were whoopeed yesterday. Whoopee exists in the realm of the past tense. It is as spectacular and ephemeral as the dying arc of a firework on a summer night:

*Whoopee! . . . Ooooh! . . . Aaaaah . . .*

Whoopee is power. Whoopee is money and talent and beauty. Whoopee is sex. Whoopee is such an ingrown part of our culture that we can barely distinguish it from the feminine curve of a Coke bottle.

Whoopee alters the avenues of lives, the cross streets of history. People kill each other, and themselves, because of whoopee. Whoopee is written on some people's birth certificates. For others, it is engraved on their tombstones.

Whoopee is so powerful it can turn a poet into a businessman, a radical into a reactionary, or an athlete into a cripple. Whoopee can turn people into corpses.

We smoke whoopee. We eat whoopee. We read it, watch it, hear it, smell it, touch it, and taste it. We buy acres of whoopee and watch it grow. We invest in it, sell it, trade it, and lose it. But mostly we forget it.

Wherever you go in America, you will meet someone who was whoopeed—and forgotten: a World War II flying ace, a silent film star, a champion prize fighter, a novelist, a millionaire, or a bear. Smokey the Bear was put behind bars and whoopeed. Soon after his death, Smokey was replaced by Hootsie the Owl. Whoopee.

In the past, a ticker-tape parade was The Great American Whoopee. Thousands of tons of paper showered down upon Lindbergh, MacArthur, Armstrong, and Gertrude Ederle. But by the time they swept up the tape, the two million New Yorkers who cheered Miss Ederle up lower Broadway in 1926 had practically forgotten her. After she swam the English Channel and was given her parade, she was called "America's

Best Girl" by President Coolidge. She is now unrecognized, forgotten.

Public amnesia is the aftermath of whoopee. But the people who are whoopeed and forgotten don't forget. They remember what it was like to be given the best table in the best restaurant, the first-class tickets, the front page picture in *The New York Times*. They also remember the endless ringing of the telephone, the intruding reporters, the autograph seekers, and the hangers-on.

Whoopee is an ambiguous disease. Those who have it don't want it. Those who don't have it, seek it.

When Charles Lindbergh touched down at Le Bourget airfield in 1927, he looked out from the cockpit of his small plane and saw a "human sea" of Frenchmen surging toward him.

That human sea has swept down through the decades, shaping the tides and currents, leaving the wreckage of ships in its wake.

Millions of Americans have floated willy-nilly on the waves of whoopee. And some have gone down.

I was whoopeed. I could have drowned.

May 1977. I am having brunch at a restaurant in New York City. I finish my eggs and motion to the waiter. He comes over to my table.

"Could I have coffee and a piece of pecan pie, please?"

"I've been meaning to ask you," says the waiter, a pleasant blondhaired man in a blue apron. "Haven't I seen you somewhere before?"

"I don't think so," I tell him.

"Do you come in here often?"

"Never been here before."

The waiter thinks for a moment. "The newspapers? Have I seen you in the newspapers?"

"I doubt it." I begin to take great interest in a gob of béarnaise sauce on the tablecloth.

"Come on. Who are you?"

"I'm a hungry customer."

"No, *seriously.*" He smiles at me. "I can't remember why you were in the papers. What'd you do?"

"For starters I just ordered a cup of coffee and a piece of pie."

"Wait a second." The smile is broader now. "You go to Princeton or something, don't you?"

"Only when I can't get anything to eat or drink in New York."

"Wait a second. *You're* the guy who built an A-bomb, right? Am I right?"

"Not really," I tell him. He is unconvinced. "I never actually built a bomb . . . I designed one."

"What's your name? Hey, this guy built the atomic bomb," the waiter shouts to a colleague who is rushing off to the kitchen. The second waiter stops in his tracks.

"A goddamn A-bomb?" he calls back. "No shit. Like how long did it take you to build it?"

People are beginning to look over at me.

"I didn't *build* it. I designed it. In six months—less time than it takes to get a cup of coffee here."

"Oh, yeah, the coffee . . ." the first waiter says, turning to go to the kitchen. The second waiter asks me to autograph his apron.

"So you never like built it," says the second waiter. "What happened? You like chicken out at the last minute or something?"

"No, I just wanted to design it to show that if I could do it, so could a group of terrorists."

"So you didn't want a real live bomb like on your hands?"

"You must be joking."

The first waiter brings back the coffee.

"You forgot my pie."

"Sorry, I'll bring it right away. But tell me," he says, "where do you keep it? I mean where do you hide this bomb of yours?"

August 1977. I am submerged up to my armpits in the Beverly Hills swimming pool of movie producer Mark Carliner. Lifting the brim of my panama hat, I survey the elaborately landscaped gardens dotted with leering marble cherubs, and the huge white stucco mansion. I see Carliner walking across the terrace. He waves to me and I bring my arm out of the cool, blue water and wave back.

I reach for the telephone, which is silently drifting by on its own little inflatable raft. I pick up the receiver and dial David's number in New York. I imagine him working in a sweltering nightmare of cigarette butts and manuscript pages. The phone rings six times before David picks it up.

"David?"

"J.P.? Where are you?"

"In Hollywood."

"How is it?" he asks. "How's our favorite Personality?"

"Fine. I was just picked up at the airport in a limousine, and right now I'm sitting in the producer's swimming pool."

"Twinkle, twinkle . . ."

"Little star—very funny. How's the book? How's New York?" I ask.

"I'm being impaled on the broomstick of literary mediocrity. And as for New York, it's the same as when you left it six hours ago. Maybe a little worse. Son of Sam is still on the loose. The city hasn't recovered from the blackout yet. And the Puerto Ricans just bombed an office building down the block. Oh—and I just spilled cream soda on the first seven chapters. Other than that everything is fine. But how's the business end of it going? Have you signed the line? Are they going to make a TV movie about your life?"

17

"Don't know yet. I reassured Carliner in the limousine that I'll only sell him the rights if he gives me the lead. He wasn't too pleased, but he scheduled a screen test for Wednesday. My only problem is that I don't know how to act."

"That shouldn't be any problem. The 'T' in Television stands for time, not talent. You should fit right in."

"Thanks, I'll tell that to Carliner."

"I was thinking, J.P., maybe we should have a Hollywood chapter near the end."

"Great."

"Take some notes and we'll work on it when you get back next week."

"*If* I come back. They're giving me the royal treatment out here. I may never return."

"Promise?"

"Sure."

"Okay, well, I'm going back to my literary broomstick," says David. "Later, J.P."

"Much."

Pulling my panama over my eyes, I slouch down and feel the liquid cool rush up to my chin.

Everything is the book these days. As with all other things that I have ever done seriously, my recent existence has been dedicated to the book. The same can be said for David Michaelis, my best friend and roommate at Princeton, and the person I chose to co-author this book with me. To a large degree, we have *become* the book.

Over a year ago, when I was designing an atomic bomb, the same thing happened: I metamorphosed from student to terrorist to A-bomb. I was a walking, talking, A-bomb during the two months it took me to design it. The same thing happened when I was whoopeed as *John Aristotle Phillips—A-Bomb Kid—Tiger Mascot—Pizza Magnate—All-American College Kid of the Seventies.* Life was one long interview, and I became that kid in italics.

## Preface: Whoopee

My thirty-four-page junior independent project for the Princeton Physics Department outlined plans for a plutonium fission bomb similar to the device unleashed over Nagasaki in World War II. It demonstrated that a terrorist, with a background in college physics, a small amount of stolen plutonium and the wherewithal to construct the device, could pose a threat to world peace.

In the winter of 1976, after several sensitive pages of the report were deleted, my work was cited in speeches by Senator William Proxmire and Senator Charles Percy, who urged governments around the world to place stronger safeguards on the distribution of plutonium in the nuclear fuel cycle. In April 1977, President Carter announced that the federal government would no longer support the use of plutonium as a fuel source in the nuclear power industry.

I made my point about plutonium safeguards. But the media weren't finished making me. Newspapers and magazines continued running feature stories about my life as a Princeton undergraduate. Movie companies offered to buy the rights to "my story." I was asked to give lectures from Maine to California. Hundreds of different requests came from around the world: A woman in South Africa proposed marriage; a Texan wanted an autographed copy of my design to add to his gun collection; Pakistani officials just wanted the design without the autograph; and a woman in New York asked me to help her discover the source of a "psychic disorder." A Stanford student called me his "Honorary God," while a Georgetown coed called me a stud. Talk shows, game shows, speeches, and then this Hollywood producer called and . . . well, there I was in the swimming pool.

This is the story of a Great American Whoopee.

# Part 1

## The Obscure Individual →

*"We are now—in the Me Decade—seeing the upward roll . . . And this one has the mightiest, holiest roll of all, the beat that goes . . . Me . . . Me . . . Me . . . Me . . ."*
—Tom Wolfe

# Prologue:
# The Curve of the Earth

When I was a kid, I wanted to see the curve of the Earth.

The idea was irresistible: I imagined myself blasting off from my house in North Haven, Connecticut. I would soar upward without rockets or airplanes and I would climb higher. And higher. And higher still. There would be a vague, dizzy moment when the houses and trees would suddenly become miniature. But then I would feel fine. The air would be light, and the sun, hot and terrifying, would lead me up into the infinite blueness.

I imagined myself looking down at the world I had just been a part of, and there—yes!—there it would be: the curve of the Earth. In every direction, I would be able to see the colossal curvature of the planet. I would have a complete sense of its color. Its limitations. Its possibilities. Its impossible magnitude, now growing smaller every second.

I would continue climbing higher, no longer seeing just the curve of the Earth. At one moment I would look back and see something so beautiful, so awesome, that some untouched part of my mind would leave me forever: I would see the whole Earth, frighteningly blue and silent, and I would no longer be a part of that world.

And then I imagined myself falling upward into the unimaginable vastness of deep, inky space, on a journey forever.

Throughout elementary school I contemplated my curve-of-the-Earth fantasy. I sat in the back of the classroom while my head was up there in space. I could see the curve of the Earth better from the back of the room. I had time to think back there, but I knew that the teacher would call on me if I never raised my hand. So I raised my hand from time to time and she never called on me. The mathematics equations on the blackboard were a blur. The other kids could see the equations. But I could see the curve of the Earth.

My curiosity ate me up. I realized that there were no limits to the universe. Just infinite possibilities, infinite questions.

I hated elementary school. The teachers were narrow-minded. The questions they asked were mundane, uninspired. I wanted the universe and they gave me a rectangle with four sides. I could understand the space within the rectangle, but what about the space beyond the sides? I asked the teachers questions, but the answers they gave me were pat, solved: *Case closed.* I doubted pat answers.

I sat in the back of the class with the trouble-makers. They would make funny noises or throw erasers to disrupt the class and disturb the teacher. I would occasionally raise my hand to point out a mistake the teacher had made on the board. The trouble-makers would be momentarily silenced and the entire class would turn around to stare at me. Then the whole class would burst into hysterics. After about two weeks of this, my fifth-grade teacher called my parents in to tell them that I would never be able to handle abstract math. As my parents suspected, and I knew, it was the teacher who was having the difficulties with abstract math. She stopped calling on me and passed me into the sixth grade.

I remember a day when I was in the seventh grade. I was at home after school, standing in front of the bathroom mirror. I was studying my face. I was dissatisfied with it. My mother came into the bathroom. She knew what I was thinking. She took my face in her cool hands. She made me look her in the eye. It felt strange. "Johnny," she said, "you're a good-looking kid. And no matter what anyone else says, you can do anything you want." She told me that if I ever thought in terms of limitations others had set for me, I would be a limited person. My mother was right. She never allowed me to see my I.Q. score. It wasn't until much later that I discovered I had tested below average.

As I grew older, I learned to respect my mind. I resented the constrictions that high school placed on my intelligence. Why were most of the teachers dead set on making us feel like automatons? Why did some kids let themselves be treated that way? I rebelled. I seldom made it to school before lunch period. I wore my hair long and always dressed in faded jeans and T-shirt. There were a few others who wore the same uniform. They too were doubters. Together we published an underground newspaper, and I was branded a "radical" by the administration. But among my peers, I was considered more of a practical joker and less of a threat. When part of the stage collapsed opening night of the senior-class play, everyone was convinced that I had orchestrated it. From a cheering audience someone shouted: "Phillips did it!"

I really didn't do it.

In 1973 I went out to Berkeley in hot pursuit of "the Movement," which always seemed to recede just when I thought I could finally overtake it. It seemed as if I had always been tantalizingly close to that older, "in" crowd, first nicknamed the TV generation, and then the Flower Children, and, finally, the Woodstock Nation. Just a kiss away. But no matter how badly I wanted to join the Movement, like a little brother trying to keep up with his older brother's crowd, I knew that I would never be in the forefront. I was forever doomed to the mop-up squad.

By the time I got to Berkeley, the Movement had vanished. The few issues being protested were hand-me-downs.

# MUSHROOM

After the Vietnam War was over and Nixon resigned because of Watergate, the communal spirit of protest was somehow lost. The conflicts we saw every day were individual and personal, not national.

Berkeley was an endless party. The air was made incandescent by the perpetually burning lights of celebration. During my sophomore year, I joined a fraternity and was initiated by being made to swallow a live goldfish. Hubba, hubba. I drank beer and dated sorority girls. I was inspired by a professor of political science, and discovered a capacity for physics. But things were too comfortable. I wanted to work, I wanted to be challenged. My brain was slowly turning to oatmeal and I had to break out.

I wanted to go back east. Harvard was too snotty. Yale was too close to home. I decided on Princeton. Princeton was a new start, a fresh challenge. I would have to test myself against the ivy wall. The following September, I transferred to Princeton.

September was always my favorite month. After the summer, your body suddenly felt young and recharged. Women always seemed prettier with their suntans and new dresses. The air smelled new. You had a sense that life was beginning all over again. It always seemed ridiculous to me that the new year began on January first. The year really began when you bought a loose-leaf notebook with all that fresh, white paper and told yourself that this year, goddamnit, you were really going to *work*. You laced up a new pair of sneakers and stuck your nose in all those textbooks with the funny smell, and you realized that your slate had been wiped clean. Whatever you had done last year didn't make a damn bit of difference now.

During September 1975, my life was to begin again.

# 1
# Up Against the Ivy Wall

It is only after much argument and some innovative engineering that my parents and I manage to squeeze all my belongings into the station wagon for the trip down to Princeton. In customary fashion, Aris drives while Bessie rides shotgun and navigates. I am stuck in the backseat as an afterthought to the motorcycle helmet, desk lamp, stereo, record albums, hibachi stove, and twenty pairs of identically colored socks ("just in case you lose one"). I'm beginning to feel good about going to Princeton, and I merrily tap "Capitalist Pig," my cranky old typewriter which has the annoying habit of switching to capital letters in midsentence.

We swing onto the highway heading south to join a parade of similarly loaded vehicles, each car bearing one or more decals which proudly boast a collegiate destination. The parental pilots in the other cars appear relieved and proud: Mothers fussing with the wrong map, and fathers with their clip-on sunglasses and "I've-paid-five-thousand-dollars-for-this-so-you-better-goddamnwell-enjoy-it" expressions.

As we head down the New Jersey Turnpike, my mother launches into her annual speech, admonishing me to brush my teeth, take my vitamins, and write home, but not for money. When she begins warning me about the dangers of using university shower stalls without wearing my flip-flops, I decide it's time I dozed off. When I awaken a half hour later, we are driving up Nassau Street in the middle of Princeton.

It is a quiet, conventionally "pretty" town, with the campus on the left side of the street, and dozens of stores on the right side. Each shop seems to be a miniature version of

27

Brooks Brothers, or a quaint old tobacco shop. When I catch sight of Old Nassau Hall, the Georgian edifice that is supposed to symbolize the great glory of Princeton, I wonder if I'm trapped inside some Norman Rockwell painting depicting College Town, U.S.A.

Bessie is just now winding up her sermon with a spirited pitch for dressing warmly and eating three balanced meals a day. She turns now to look at me for emphasis.

". . . And please stay away from the junk foods, Johnny."

"Okay, Mom."

"And remember what I said about flip-flops in the—"

"Mom, I'm twenty years old now. I think I can handle the shower perfectly—"

"Here we are," my dad announces.

"The campus is beautiful!" my mother exclaims.

"Now this is an Ivy League school!" says my father, who, in addition to being a Yale professor, has an acute sense of the obvious. (He is the type of person who will observe, "It's raining!" after it's begun to pour and everybody else is dashing for cover.) "Which way to Little Hall?" he asks a fossilized security guard, who directs us to a long, stone-and-ivy building set beyond a manicured greensward near the middle of campus.

Parked in front of my dormitory, I extract myself from a tangle of bicycle spokes and clothes hangers and fall out of the car. A group of guys lazily throwing a frisbee on the green look over and continue their game. As I unload my things, a drama reminiscent of my freshman year at Berkeley proceeds around the courtyard: Parents of embarrassed freshmen are retrieving a forgotten stereo dust cover or a hiking boot from the trunk of a car. As they stand around saying their good-byes, trying somehow to prolong the childhood of their son or daughter, the parents have a distinct look of loneliness on their faces. The more lonely or tearful the parent, the greater the embarrassment for the freshman.

"Johnny, you left your flip-flops in the car," says Bessie, handing them to me.

"I thought you and Dad might need them for the shower at home."

"Don't be funny. Now, be sure to take your vitamins and your—"

"Mom, do we have to go through this again? . . . okay . . . I'll be careful . . . okay, Mom . . . yes, I'll remember . . . good-bye . . . bye, Dad . . . right, *vitamins* . . . good-bye! . . ."

As the station wagon pulls away from my mound of belongings and drives across the green, I realize I'm waving the goddamn flip-flops.

# 2

## 42 Little Hall

I stand in the doorway to my new room. The sounds of a fierce argument trail off. Five faces look at me.

"Please, gentlemen. Don't stop on my account."

The guy in the center of the room who has been talking the loudest extends his hand as he walks over to me. He has blond hair, athletic shoulders, and is wearing brown topsiders, corduroys, and the ubiquitous Lacoste shirt. He looks like the type who would immediately ask where I prepped.

"You must be the new guy from Berkeley. Kunst's my name. Franz Kunst. Class of Seventy-seven."

He says the last part as firmly as he shakes my hand. Emphasis on the "Class of '77."

"Hi, I'm John Phillips . . ."

"Class of Seventy-seven," he reminds me, smiling.

"Oh, right. I forgot."

"Don't worry, it'll grow on you."

Stepping into the living room, the first thing I notice is a huge orange-and-black banner hanging over the fireplace which reads: "GOD WENT TO PRINCETON." Draped above the window seat is another banner: "PRINCETON '77."

A tall, lanky guy who has been batting a tennis ball around with a hockey stick now steps forward smiling.

"Hi, John. I'm Jed Whitmore III . . . but my friends call me Whit."

"Pleased to meet you, Whit."

He seems like the quiet type, somewhat shy, trying to please. After a moment, Whit has nothing more to say. He seems uncomfortable without his hockey stick. He backs up somewhat awkwardly and resumes his game, firing the tennis ball into the fireplace. One of his shots ricochets back across the room, hitting a guy wearing baggy army-surplus pants and a "Princeton Ski Team" T-shirt.

"Wit! Wit! Wit!" shouts the guy, sitting on the couch, smoking a joint.

Possessing extremely bloodshot eyes and a broad smile, he extends his hand, not to shake mine, but to offer me the joint.

"My name's Scott Meadows," he says. "Wanna hit?"

"No thanks, later."

"I don't suppose this stuff is as good as the smoke you get out in Berkeley," he says with an apologetic tone.

"If you're the third roommate, who are those two over there?" I ask, referring to the guys who are beginning to take a refrigerator out the doorway.

"Seniors," mumbles Meadows, between drags on a minuscule roach. "They lived here last year. Most of the furniture is theirs. In the great Princeton capitalist tradition, they're trying to sell it all to us. Even this friggin' map." He points to an enormous National Geographic map of the world, which is glued to an entire wall of the room.

Meanwhile, Franz has jumped into action, barring the doorway to the hall.

"You aren't going anywhere with that icebox, guys," he announces.

"The hell we aren't," says one of the seniors. "We own it, pal. If you don't want to make a deal, someone else will."

"Okay, listen. We want the couch, the icebox, the fireplace screen, and the curtains—but *not* the map."

"Forget it," says the other senior. "It's a package deal. Everything for twenty-five bucks. *Including* the map."

This sounds like a fine deal to me, but apparently Franz is piqued that he will have to pay for something that is stuck to the wall and couldn't be removed anyway. He does have a point. Whitmore stays out of the argument and Meadows is too stoned to care.

"No deal," says Franz. "We aren't buying the goddamn map. If you guys paid for it last year, you were suckered. What do you think we are anyway—*freshmen?*"

Franz pronounces "freshmen" as if they were an inferior species of student. I imagine a bunch of pimply-faced kids stumbling around some ivy-covered dungeon in their flip-flops, being sold maps of the world by entrepreneurial upperclassmen.

"No map, no deal," says the first senior, grinning.

Like any good Greek, I love haggling over a deal or matching wits against a clever opponent. I can't resist. "Wait a minute," I say. "If we don't buy it, how are you guys going to get the map off the wall?"

"You've never heard of map-remover?" the senior asks.

I raise my eyebrows. Meadows laughs. Franz thinks for a moment. "Okay, okay. I've got a plan," he says. "We pay you twenty-five bucks for the icebox, the couch, the curtains, the fireplace screen, and *not* to remove the map."

"Good deal," says the senior.

Franz is proud of himself.

Jed Whitmore III pauses for a moment, shakes his head, and mutters something under his breath.

Meadows laughs excessively. "Anybody wanna hit?" he asks.

# 3

## Franz

"It was the principle of the thing," says Franz after the seniors have left.

"What do you mean the principle?" I ask. "What principle is there in paying someone *not* to remove your map . . . *our* map."

"Look, Phillips, you're new around here."

"What's the principle?"

"Figure it out."

"I don't get it?"

"Listen, Phillips, I'm no sucker," he says defensively. I decide to lay off.

"Does this kind of thing go on much around here?"

"Every year, it's the same old game: Upperclassmen going around suckering underclassmen into buying all sorts of crap. Freshmen are the most gullible. During my first year, some guys across the hall from me were suckered into buying the mantelpiece over their fireplace for thirty-five bucks."

"You're kidding." I take off my jacket and throw it on the couch. Franz leans over and reads the Pierre Cardin label.

"You've got a lot of class for a physics major," he tells me, taking a gulp of beer.

"I'll sell it to you, Franz."

Ignoring my remark, he continues: "When I heard you were a scientist, I tried to get you moved out of here."

"Really? You might try paying me not to move out."

"Very funny. You even have a sense of humor."

"Why'd you want me to move out?"

"I don't like grinds, but I can already tell you're no grind." As he says this, I grin. I knew that we would eventually find something to agree upon. A Princeton "grind" must be a relative of what was called a "nerd" at Berkeley. This is the infamous species of student whose natural habitat is the reference room of the library. Pre-meds are, generally speaking, the hardest-working and hence most feared of nerds, while pre-laws are the most obnoxious for their habit of dominating discussion during class.

"Grinds make me feel guilty," says Franz. "I don't go to the library more than a couple of times a year—you know, when things get really desperate. . . . I guess you have to be pretty smart to major in physics here, huh?"

"I'll find out soon enough. What's your major?"

"History. It's a gut major. I'm doing my Junior Independent Work on Walt Disney. How about you?"

"There's a professor named O'Neill in the Physics Department here who specializes in space colonies. I'm hoping to get him to be my advisor."

"Are you going to bicker?"

"Bicker? You mean those guys are coming back to try to sell us more stuff?

"No, I mean bicker at the clubs on the Street."

"What's that all about?"

"There are about a dozen eating clubs across campus on Prospect Ave. Some you can join just by signing up, but the others, like Cap and Gown, Cottage, Ivy, Tiger, Tower, and Charter you have to bicker at to be invited to join. They're private institutions, ya see."

"What does 'bicker' mean exactly?"

"You'll see. It's pretty awesome."

"Awesome?"

"The best club on the Street is Cap and Gown."

"That's your club?"

"Right. It's the only one of the Big Four that's coed. We've got a great bunch of guys. The food is terrific, we've got beer on tap twenty-four hours a day, and the guys are always rowdy."

"Didn't you just say Cap was coed?"

"Yeah. So what?"

"What about the great bunch of girls?"

"Princeton coeds don't have a great reputation in general. We've got some real bitches in Cap, I'll admit that. But I'll see to it personally that you get a bid to join. All you have to do is be yourself. Unless you're an asshole. In which case, be someone else. Fall bicker starts this week."

"What about Ivy Club? What are those guys like?"

"The Ivy man is no mere mortal," says Franz, affecting a thick British accent. "He's an aristocrat. A cut above the rest you know. He takes his meals by candlelight on crisp linen and is served by stewards. There being so few young men of adequate birth and proper station these days, Ivy is the smallest of the clubs with only fifty gentlemen permitted to sport the Ivy tie . . ."

"That bad, huh?" I laugh.

"Don't waste your time. They'd probably mistake you for a servant anyway."

"Did you bicker there?"

"Yeah." He folds his arms.

"What happened?"

"They busted my chops during bicker. Asked me all

sorts of asshole questions. A real bunch of turkeys."

"You mean you didn't get a bid."

"In a manner of speaking—"

The telephone rings. Franz walks over, picks it up, and announces: "Yankee dugout, DiMaggio speaking . . . Yeah, he's here . . . just a minute . . ."

Franz arches his eyebrows and makes a brief jerking-off motion in the air.

"It's for you," he says, grinning. "Somebody called Mary-Lay . . ."

# 4
# Mary-Lee

Mary-Lee O'Hara is a girl I met during the summer. I've never gone out with just one woman for a long time, but Mary-Lee is the only person in the "girlfriend" category at the moment. Her boisterous personality and Post Toasties charm make her the quintessential All-American girl and a hell of a lot of fun to be with. She is Pepsi-Cola, Patty Duke, and the pretty blond girl in the World War II movies who is waiting at the dock somewhere in New Jersey for her sailor boy to return home. In the last frame of the film, she is seen crying, but suddenly, the sailor comes running down the dock, they embrace, get married, and have lots of babies.

I'm really not the marrying type. But when Mary-Lee first learned that I was going to Princeton, she got very interested: going out with an Ivy League man, *crème de la crème,* all that crap. Apparently, it's a very big status symbol at the girls' college she goes to outside Philadelphia. I was, by turns, suspicious and amused, but at the end of the summer, I promised to invite her up as soon as I got myself settled.

I take the phone from Franz, who is now playing an imaginary violin and making low crooning sounds.

"Does your roommate think he's funny?" says Mary-Lee.

"He likes the sound of your voice."

"What's all this Mary-*Lay* stuff?"

"Franz is exhibiting his latent frustrations."

At this, Franz makes a big deal of crushing an empty beer can with one hand, which he throws across the room at me. I deflect it with the palm of my hand into the fireplace. Franz is impressed.

"Well? Aren't you going to tell me?" says Mary-Lee. "I mean how is it and everything?"

"I just got here an hour ago, but I think I like it."

"I knew you'd like it."

"How'd you get my number anyway?"

"I'm a smart little blond. Bet you thought you could ditch me, didn't ya, kid?"

"Don't be ridiculous."

"So when do I get to come up?"

"Lemme see. Today's Tuesday. Classes start tomorrow, and I've got bicker all this week . . ."

"What's bicker? Sounds nasty."

"I don't know. They say it's awesome."

"Awesome?"

"It's my ticket to three square meals a day at one of these hoity-toity eating clubs. Hey, why don't you come up and do this crazy bicker thing with me. After they take one look at you, I'll be sure to get a bid."

"Flattery will get you nowhere, Princeton boy."

"Can you spend the night?"

"Just like all Princeton boys—always trying to get into a girl's pants."

"I thought you were trying to get into my pants."

"Right! You're in the Ivy League for one hour and already it's gone to your head."

"Can you make it by five tomorrow?"

"I'll be there."

"Good. See you then."

"Bye, love," she says.

Franz is looking at me with a lewd smirk: "This Mary-Lay is a pretty hot ticket, huh?"

"Sure, Franz." I really don't think it's any of his business.

"Sounds pretty awesome."

"Yep. Awesome."

"You're lucky, what with all the dogs on this campus. I'm sure it'll be a real drag after Berkeley," he says.

# 5

# Berserkeley

Just now, my first two years of college at the University of California are getting moldy in memory land. I've been so involved in the here and now of Princeton that I haven't consciously paused to compare my past experiences with what I have found here. At least in the category of girls, I'm afraid that Franz is closer to the truth than even he suspects. The gorgeous, carefree California sorority girls will be hard to beat. But what's more important to me, for the moment anyway, is how I will stack up academically against the other students here. Can I cut the old mustard, as it were?

I know from physics at Berkeley that I can grasp difficult concepts with relative ease. But it is the pressure-cooker environment that has me concerned. I enjoy the rigorous and clear thinking which physics demands, and I do this well when I am left to myself. But destructive competition, ridiculous deadlines, and grade-grubbing are other matters altogether. My intuition tells me that Princeton is going to be one long one-hundred-yard dash.

Another thing on my mind is friends. Which is not to say I'm frantically searching the local personals columns for companionship. Usually, when I arrive someplace new, I make acquaintanceships—what others might call friends—easily. But the one thing I take very seriously is having one or more good friends whom I really click with. Franz, Whit, and Meadows definitely don't fit the bill. I could tell that right away. Sure, they're nice guys who mean well, but there are always lots of these around. I'm not being snotty when I say this. I'm just serious about good friends. Why should it be any other way?

And in the realm of serious friendships, my Berkeley experiences will also be tough to match. There was Flint Dille, the guy who lived downstairs from me in Bowles Hall during freshman year. Together we survived the trials and triumphed over the disappointments any college freshman encounters. The key to our survival, we discovered, was to remember how to laugh.

Sophomore year we moved out of Bowles Hall, Flint to become president of a recently revived fraternity, while I signed into the oldest, most established house on the street. By a twist of circumstance, I found myself rooming with Bill Stoops. Aside from possessing a first-rate mind and an incredible heart, Bill is one of the most popular people I will ever know. His popularity among the sorority girls in every house on campus resulted in an incredible, if hectic, social life for both of us. In many respects, Berkeley will be hard to beat.

Bill and Flint will always be my close friends. Countless alumni, drunken or otherwise, had impressed upon me the lasting nature of the friendships one makes in college. But it's probably because of what happened to the first friend I had at Berkeley that I cherish a good friend so much.

During my freshman year, I had a roommate named Teddy Jeffers. He was a friendly, open, naïve kid from a strict, middle-class black family. As a result of his generous and extroverted nature, he was always befriending the introverted or screwed-up, in hopes of helping them out. At seventeen, T.J. had never tried any drugs, was still a virgin and incredibly hung up about it. When he finally lost his virginity with a woman of impermanent affections, he became inordinately morose. Two days later, the drug dealer who lived down the hall from us convinced T.J. to drop acid. If Teddy wasn't wise enough to know that his temperament wasn't suited to LSD, the dealer certainly should've known.

T.J. tripped for five days straight. There was a large American flag hanging upside down in our room. On the first day, he ripped it down, took off all his clothes, and began wearing the flag around like a cape. His mood fluctuated between elation and deep depression. Sometimes he thought he was Captain America; other times he was Jesus Christ. The roles seemed interchangeable.

On the night of the third day, I woke up and saw him standing at the foot of my bed wearing a shiny purple bathrobe.

"Go to bed, T.J.," I told him.

"You're the devil, man. I'm gonna exorcise you," he said, making the sign of the cross in the air with a six-inch bowie knife.

The next day, I really began to worry about him. He hadn't slept or eaten in over forty-eight hours. I decided I had to get him to the university health clinic.

"T.J., I think you need some rest," I said to him, trying

to sound natural. You never know how someone will react when they're tripping. If I'd said, "T.J., I think you need a haircut," he might have stabbed me.

"Get away from me, man."

He was still holding the bowie knife.

"Why don't we go down to the clinic. They'll give you a tranquilizer or something."

"Don't need no tranc," he mumbled.

"It'll make you feel better."

"Is it cool, or ain't it?"

"It'll be fine."

"Okay, but be cool."

I walked him across campus to the clinic. Every few minutes, he would stop and ask me if I was going to let them hurt him. He was still wearing that crazy purple bathrobe. The nurse at the clinic was very discreet and didn't ask too many stupid questions. T.J. kept asking me if I was his friend, if it was cool. When the nurse led him away, I watched him disappear down a corridor, a shiny purple blot against the institutional green.

That afternoon, I was studying for a physics exam in the room. The door swung open and T.J. ran in crying. For a second he didn't notice me. He had the strangest expression I've ever seen on a human face: a combination of shock and naked terror. He looked as if someone had just gouged out one of his eyeballs and he was watching it roll across the floor.

"You!" he screamed, accusing me of God knows what. "They fucking locked me in a padded cell." He was out of breath.

"Whaddya mean? What happened?" I asked, trying to stay calm.

"Escaped, man. Be cool. I fucked up the motherfuckers."

"Did the doctor give you anything?"

"I ran, man, ran and ran and ran and ran . . ."

He started flailing his arms around as if he were running. Then he began to laugh. He was still wearing the shiny purple bathrobe. But I was beginning to weary of the whole episode. I had to do well on the physics exam, so I decided to study in the library. I told myself I'd done all I could, and I would deal with it—God knows how—after my exam.

I gathered my books together and started for the door. T.J. was standing by the window five feet away. It was open.

"Where you goin', John?" he asked accusingly.

"Library. I've got an exam."

"Don't leave me alone, man," he pleaded, terrified.

"Okay, okay, I'll study here if you want. But you have to keep the noise down. I'm beginning to go crazy myself." Even as the words came out of my mouth I regretted them.

"Hey!" he shouted. "I don't dig it when you get on my case like that—"

Then, all in one second: He climbed up into the window and pushed himself out. I heard myself scream, lunged for him, and somehow caught hold of his wrist.

He was dangling from the window, about forty feet above the parking lot. I wasn't sure I could hold on. His bathrobe had fallen off, and I remember seeing it fluttering to the ground like some bizarre, wounded, purple butterfly. I screamed for help. Moments later, Mike Andrews, who lived next door, and had heard the commotion, was standing beside me. He was screaming something into my ear that I couldn't make out. Finally we succeeded in pulling him back into the room.

T.J. was lying on the floor naked. There was something very strange and eerie about him. He wasn't saying anything, wasn't making a sound except for very heavy breathing. He didn't look like a man who had just jumped out a window. His face was calm and passive, but his eyeballs were flicking back and forth at a steady pace, as if he were watching a tennis match. While I kept him pinned to the floor, Andrews called the campus police.

# 6
## Old Nassau

Leaving 42 Little, I decide to wander around campus to get the lay of the land. I have an hour before I'm supposed to be at some honor code assembly. I walk down behind Little and find myself in another courtyard, facing Blair Tower with its huge Gothic archway. The campus has a carnival atmosphere. All around the courtyard students are sitting in the late afternoon sun drinking beer. Some fly kites, others chase dogs. Footballs crisscross the lawns. Someone goes to buy another case of beer. From a half-dozen open windows, huge stereo speakers compete for air space. One plays disco music, another reggae rock, and still others blare Patti Smith, George Benson, and the Beach Boys.

I see one guy sunning himself in tennis shorts, flipping through an organic chemistry textbook. He is listening to the Woodstock album. As the Country Joe and the Fish rag plays, he sings along: "One, two, three, what're we fighting for? Don't ask me, I don't give a damn. Next stop is Vietnam . . ." The guy sings the words happily, knowing that the next stop is medical school, not Vietnam. I think how much things have changed since the sixties. Instead of worrying about the draft, the most pressing thing on that guy's mind is probably deciding which eating club to join.

I walk on, climbing the stone stairway leading to Blair archway. A group of ten guys wearing identical T-shirts is standing in a semicircle under the arch singing the Princeton song, "Old Nassau." They're really belting it out; giving it the old college try. A crowd of students watches them and sings along. It surprises me how many people know the words. I don't think Berkeley even had a school song.

"Who are those guys?" I ask a girl.

"The Tigertones. A singing group," she says.

"Oh."

"Do you sing?" she wants to know.

"A little. Not really."

"I'm a member of the Katzenjammers. We're the only coed singing group. You should come audition for us this week."

"I really can't even carry a tune."

"We're holding open house tomorrow. Lots of beer. We have a great bunch of girls . . ."

"I've heard that before."

I continue on my tour. Under an elm tree, I pass a table piled high with orange-and-black beer mugs. A sign reads: STUDENT BEER-MUG AGENCY/CLASS NUMERALS IMPRINTED $2 EXTRA. I turn onto McCosh Walk, the long, tree-shaded path which bisects the campus. It leads me past Whig and Clio, two identical Greek-style temples that house debating societies, Murray Dodge Theatre (is there really a building under all that ivy?), and McCosh, which has more turrets, gargoyles, towers, and spires than Mad Ludwig's castle in Bavaria.

Seeing a shaded garden, I take a right, and after walking for some time, I see what looks like an Arabian bazaar at the bottom of the hill near the gymnasium. Clusters of students are milling around a series of tables set up by the various campus organizations to attract new members. The array of activities is mind-boggling. There are newspapers and literary magazines to work for and subscribe to, countless team sports to engage in, serious debate societies, humorous debate societies, Latin debate societies, beer debate societies, art museum organizations, theater groups, political organizations, ROTC platoons, religious affiliations, chess clubs, and press clubs. Even the alumni office has a table, already beginning the process of turning freshmen into loyal alumni.

This mawkish orange-and-black orgy has the quality of a Chinese dinner where you eat and eat, and twenty minutes later, can't remember what you had. I gorge myself, signing up, enlisting in, swearing allegiance to, and becoming a card-carrying member of countless organizations. (Why not?) At one point, a granite-muscled jock is plying me with beer in an attempt to get me out for lightweight crew. An ancient ROTC sergeant is making a pitch for helping out with the war effort. (What war?) As I'm being seduced by a slick campus politico into running for vice-president of the class on his ticket, two Playboy bunnies walk up to me. I've never seen a Playboy bunny in real life, and I wonder what the hell they're doing at Princeton. Selling subscriptions maybe. One of them giggles and the other says: "Wanna join the Triangle Club?"

"Sure," I tell her without taking my eyes off her body. "What's the Triangle Club?" Their giggles erupt into shrieks and more giggles when I reach forward and tweak one bunny's breast. "I knew they were fake. You two aren't bunnies." I laugh.

One of the girls stops giggling long enough to explain that Triangle is a musical comedy troupe.

"We're Triangle dancers," says the other. "We put on a huge spring show and right now we're recruiting for our fall touring company."

"Jimmy Stewart, Josh Logan, and F. Scott Fitzgerald used to be in Triangle," says the other. "Wanna audition? With your nerve you'd be a natural."

"Do you have a great bunch of guys, or a great bunch of girls?" I ask.

They pause, look at one another, and the first shoots back: "Neither. Triangle has a great bunch of egos."

An hour later, I'm sitting with a thousand other new students at the honor code assembly in Alexander Hall. The meeting starts with William Ruckelshaus of Watergate fame pontificating about the rewards of honesty. When he finally sits down, the Dean of the College gets up and says in three different ways that anyone caught cheating will be thrown out faster than yesterday's newspaper. The honor code is a system that requires all students to report anyone they see cheating in an exam. Accordingly, the professor leaves students alone in the room when the exam is in progress.

Most of what is being said doesn't interest me very much. I do not cheat, nor help anyone who does. But I don't like the part about reporting someone I see cheating. If I saw a good friend of mine cheating, I couldn't report him. I just couldn't. Therefore, to report anyone else would be clearly unfair, not to mention less than honorable. Furthermore, this business about removing the proctor from the exam room has nothing to do with reliance upon the honor of the students. The upshot is that fifty students are now acting as proctors where before there was only one. It's the collegiate version of hall monitors.

As I look around me, I wonder if other people share my reservations about this so-called honor code. Maybe I'm just an unprincipled, dishonorable wretch. When the Dean finishes his sermon, he is roundly applauded by the students. If I were going to cheat, I sure wouldn't want to do it in a room with these fanatics. Judging from their enthusiasm, they'd probably lynch a guy for scratching his epidermis in a biology exam.

Throughout the assembly, I've noticed a stooped-over elderly gentleman sitting on a piano. In contrast with the solemn administrators on stage, he is having a great time waving to students and tipping his orange-and-black cap. As a matter of fact, he is dressed entirely in the Princeton colors: His sport coat is striped orange and black, a pack of tigers runs across his tie, his pants are bright orange, and his shoes are black with orange laces.

This natty tiger-elf is now introduced to us as Freddie Fox, Class of '39, curator of Princetoniana and keeper of the tiger faith. We are reminded that Freddie once risked his life by climbing the bell tower on Nassau Hall to put a 1939 buffalo nickel in the gold ball atop the flagstaff. He is here to teach us the Princeton song.

Freddie regales the audience with anecdotes about "the old days," which leads him into a long harangue about Yale and "that institution up in Cambridge." We are encouraged to hiss loudly at the mere mention of our rivals. Freddie is getting pretty worked up by now. He whips out an orange-and-black handkerchief to instruct us in the preferred method of handkerchief waving during our song. It's all pretty archaic and I feel as if I'm being inducted into some peculiar religion.

As we go through a few rousing choruses of "Old Nassau," I survey the hall wondering if there's any close friend material in the crowd. Still too early to tell. Maybe someone will turn up during bicker. The song ends. Freddie is given a jubilant standing ovation. One word runs through my mind. As Franz would say: Awesome.

# 7
# Behind the Bicker Lines

The next evening, Mary-Lee and I are walking down Prospect Avenue. I have briefed her about the task at hand. With frightening dedication to the cause, she is dressed to kill. We pass various eating clubs on both sides of the street, the architectural styles ranging from Gothic to Colonial. A full moon turns the trees milky blue. It is idyllic.

Cap and Gown is the first club on my list. Inside, the parlor room is jammed with "bickerees" seeking a bid. Huddled together like soldiers on an assault craft nearing the beach, they smoke cigarettes and talk in hushed murmurs. Some are preening themselves in reflections from the windows. Others sit perfectly still on couches, their freeze-dried faces suggesting an advanced state of rigor mortis. The heat in the room is unbearable. The sound of a rock 'n' roll band plays off in the distance. In a room to the left, I can hear units from the first wave of bickerees being interviewed by club members.

Every few minutes, the mood in the parlor stiffens. A club member comes forth and selects one of the crowd for a five-minute interview. Since Cap is the only coed selective club, the girls are under the most pressure. As each girl is led away, the volley and thunder increase in the trenches off to the left. A rumor is passed around that any jerk with a nose and two nuts can get a bid. Franz appears. Mary-Lee introduces herself as "Mary-Lay." Franz is embarrassed. He whispers to me: "Don't worry about getting a bid."

"I'm not worried about getting a bid," I say. "What about this club of yours?"

"What about it?"

"Let's just say, if it were any phonier, it would win the Good Housekeeping seal of approval."

Franz is on the defensive. He digs in: "To hell with that. Give us a try. All you need to do is flatter one or two female members."

"He's good at that," Mary-Lee interjects.

"Let's go," says Franz.

Mary-Lee is sent off to reconnoiter the terrace. Franz leads me to the front lines. Along the way, I can hear the agony of the wounded in the trenches. Medics are sent for more beer. The rounds of questions slice the air with red tracers: "How do you like Princeton?" "What's your major?" "Aren't the people at Cap just great?"

In the harsh, uneven light of the battle, I see one of the enemy: a fair-haired girl wearing riding britches and high boots. She looks so uptight that she probably rides her horse sidesaddle with her legs crossed. She is grilling a short girl who wears too much blue eye shadow.

"Where do *you* ride?" asks the fair-haired girl.

Caught in the stark illumination of the overhead flare, the short girl is as good as dead. She dives in a foxhole and frantically searches for a grenade. She lobs one out at the fair-haired girl: "When I'm on the East Side I ride on the F.D.R. Drive, and when I'm on the West Side I take the Henry Hudson Parkway . . ."

Franz has led me into the thick of things. I'm facing a girl named Katie, ready for hand-to-hand combat. Her high-pitched voice and catty remarks crackle with the artillery fire. I circle her position and come in on a facetious angle from the rear: "Tell me, Katie, would I make a *great* Cap and Gown guy?" I ask.

"You might," she says. Then adds, "I mean you have the *potential*."

"What does it really take?"

"Actually, most of the guys in Cap are 'fish' who couldn't get into Cottage or Ivy," she confides. Her bayonet is glistening. "I'll tell you a secret," whispers Katie. "You should join Ivy."

"Why?" I whisper back.

"Because Cap girls go out with Ivy men," she says, touching my knee for emphasis.

This is undoubtedly the most damaging thing I've yet heard about Ivy. I decide I've had enough of this battle. Time to retreat to another front. I resolve to blow the top off the

enemy bunker before I go: "Katie, would you like to dance?"
I ask, smiling sweetly—oh, so sweetly.

"No, not really," she replies.

"That's too bad," I say. "Then I guess a blow job would
be out of the question?"

BAAA-WOWWWW!!

The enemy in the bunker lashes out with brutal retalia-
tion. Explosions surround my position. Bullets sing by me. But
the enemy is finished. Negotiating the dense terrain, I find
beautiful, blond Mary-Lee surrounded by a pack of slathering
GIs. I take her by the arm and find an escape route out to the
street.

The night is cool. The sounds of the artillery fade off in
the darkness.

"Who was that girl you were talking to?" asks Mary-
Lee.

"Someone named Katie."

"God, what a *bitch*," complains Mary-Lee. "At one
point she asked me if I was bickering at *her* club. When I
told her I don't go to school here, she said, 'That's too bad,
darling—then you're an *import*.'"

"She can't help it," I say. "She was born with her legs
crossed."

"I hope these other clubs are less pretentious."

"So do I. Maybe I'll have to cook rations by myself."

"Rations? What're you talking about?"

"Nothing. Forget it."

Cottage Club rears up in the moonlight, impenetrable
and huge. The muffled sound of the mortars echoes across
the broad lawn. Inside the crowded lobby, successive volleys
spit through the uproar. Battalions of brawny jocks wearing
jerseys and letter sweaters spray machine-gun questions at
the bickerees: "What sports do you play?" "Did you letter
in anything?" "Did you know that F. Scott Fitzgerald was a
member of Cottage Club?"

# MUSHROOM

A transport wagon carrying beer to the front careens by. Mary-Lee follows it to get us drinks. The machine guns rattle behind me. I've already got battle fatigue. Fine soldier I am. Must find the path of least resistance to another club. But the enemy has located my position: a slap on the back and a towheaded moron is telling me, "It's a pretty ballsy act to bring a girl over to a man's club during bicker, ya know."

"*This* is a man's club?" I ask incredulously.

"This is the Cottage Club, ya dink."

"You must be making some mistake," I say. "A cab driver just dropped me off here and told me to ask for Lucille . . ."

The towhead looks extremely insulted. "Well, she ain't here," he says. "Now scram! Ya whoremonger . . ."

I retreat from my position and fumble for a grenade. My pack is empty. The towhead is telling some other guy that I'm a freshman playing a practical joke. Mary-Lee returns with drinks and I turn her toward the door. The towhead is laughing loudly. We retreat.

Out in the street, Mary-Lee applies first aid-on-the-rocks. I can hear the unmistakable slushing sound of men collapsing in bushes.

"I hate jocks," says Mary-Lee.

"So do I."

"Where do we go next?"

"Retreat to Ivy."

"Retreat?"

"Yeah."

We pass through the iron gateway and follow the cobblestone path, skirting the minefield to the right. Ivy Club is ablaze with warm yellow light. Through the leaded windows we can see men in jackets and ties conversing in small groups. The steady rumble of the battle is now far away. As we pass through the ivy-shrouded portico, I feel Mary-Lee's fingernails dig into my arm. "It's beautiful," she whispers.

Inside, I scan the elegant furnishings of the foyer. There are maroon leather chairs drawn up around a backgammon set, and an old grandfather clock hunkers down in the corner. The ornate carving on the wood-paneled walls is interrupted by several gold plaques listing Ivy men who were killed in combat as far back as the Spanish-American War. To the left there is a reading room with an enormous fireplace, and in front of me a staircase winds up past a stained-glass window. To my right there is a portal through which I see old billiard and pool tables bathed in green light.

Jim Griffith, a fellow who lives near me in Little Hall, comes over with a big smile.

"So you're bickering at Ivy," he says.

"Yeah, Franz told me that I'd be mistaken for a servant but I thought I'd give it a try."

Griffith laughs. "Franz is just on the rag because he never got a bid here."

"Where do we start?" I ask.

"You look pretty tired," says Griffith. "They give you a hard time over at Cap and Cottage?"

"Nothing to write home about."

"What else did Franz tell you?" asks Griffith.

"That Ivy is full of snobs . . ."

"Snobs! That's a good one. Come on, I'll introduce you to a couple of snobs."

All quiet on the western front. In the course of the next few hours I speak with a dozen people, and stay long after bicker is officially over. These are the "snobs" I meet:

V. J. THANDANI: Born in India and plans to return there. Tall beanpole with a British accent. Extremely polite, almost painfully so. Enormous smile. Majoring in biology. We talk about slime molds and the British East India Company.

TAD ZIMMERMAN: Scruffy looks. Smokes Camels down to the bitter end. Solid physical build. Hard to talk to, but seems like a nice guy. Trying out for the U.S. equestrian team in the 1980 Olympics. Watches *Star Trek* every night.

PENDENTON KING: Southerner. Crew cut. Fair complexion. Charismatic smile. Terribly erect posture. Looks me straight in the eye the whole time. A real Southern gentleman. The kind who would become a Confederate officer in *Gone With the Wind*. Once I get used to his fluid drawl, I can't help but like him. A real straight shooter.

RICHARD PARKER (a.k.a. Parker Stevenson): Boyish good looks. Great big eyes. Looks familiar. Interested in acting. Even goes so far as to call himself an actor, but refuses to elaborate. Terribly modest. Later find out he had costarred in the movie *A Separate Peace*.

EBEN PRICE: A Texan. Talks faster than a D.J. on AM radio. Club joke is that when Eben was a baby, someone left a radio on next to his crib. Wears cowboy shirts and jeans. Very bowlegged— I'm not kidding. Runs the film society and entertains me with his self-mocking humor and encyclopedic knowledge of the inner workings of Hollywood.

PETE RICHARDS: Triangle technical director. Sharp eyes and a quick mind. His comments never fail to contain a double meaning or pun. Loves having fun at someone else's expense.

BERT OLDMAN: Another Southerner. But unlike the aristocratic Penn King, Bert is a good ole boy from backwoods Georgia. Grew up wrestling snapping turtles in the bayou. Short, plump, with an ear-wiggling smirk. His laugh is one part giggle, two parts squeal. Looks like the kind of person who as a kid was always having his feet tickled.

My final conversation of the evening is a "double bicker."

I am seated between Pete Richards and Bert Oldman. I detect from the sidelong glances and the half-empty bottle of Kentucky whiskey they exchange that the whole bicker process is one big joke for them. It becomes apparent that I am to be the source of their entertainment.

"If you could be any vegetable for one day," says Pete, "which one would you choose to be?"

They both look at me with straight faces. Trouble. At last, the "asshole" question Franz has warned me about. With an equally serious face, I reply: "I often fantasize about being an overcooked asparagus."

Bert squeals hysterically and the tension is gone. Pete hands me the whiskey bottle.

"You do have a sense of humor," he says. "I heard in the Triangle Club office that you accosted two of our bunnies the other day. I suppose you're big on practical jokes. You seem the type," Pete says.

"As a matter of fact, during my freshman year at Berkeley I learned a great deal about practical jokes," I tell him. "There was this senior. Ken House was his name, and he was a rhetoric major. He was a born speaker, and very popular, and it was my misfortune that no sooner had I moved into the dorm, but Ken selected me to bear the brunt of his jokes. He would pick the lunch hour, when all the residents of the dorm were gathered in the Commons, to stand up on a table and deliver a witty speech about John Aristotle Phillips' shortcomings. It was completely unprovoked, and I would just sit there wondering why this guy had chosen to torment me, and how long could this whole thing possibly go on. One night he went as far as accusing me of committing 'unnatural acts' with the Mascot of the Hall, a decrepit old dog named Iggy. Then he emptied my waterbed as a practical joke. I had taken all I could and started planning revenge."

"What'd you do?"

"During the night, I went down to House's room with a

feather pillow in one hand and a five-pound bucket of honey in the other. When I found his bed, I tore off the sheets, poured the honey on him, head to toe, and emptied the feather pillow over him. He was an instant shake-and-bake chicken. When he came down to breakfast the next morning, I shouted: 'Eggs for breakfast, hen?' and thereafter Ken House was known as Hen House."

Bert is off on one of his marathon giggles. Pete is on the floor. It seems I've wrestled a bid from Ivy Club.

# 8
# Marching to a Different Cowbell

College football games are a sociological phenomenon. They are one of the few places you can get smashed in public and still be in good taste. They are the mecca of exhibitionists and self-styled orators, who weekly deliver boozy tirades about the lack of talent on the field. They are the solace of over-worked students who wish to forget about the term paper that's due Monday morning, while directing the taunts of the crowd at the lady in row six who's wearing a big green hat. They satisfy the animal instincts of not only the players spending the afternoon smacking the pants off one another, but also the undergrads, who spend the afternoon trying to get into the pants of some other guy's date.

My first day at Princeton, when I was signing up for all those activities, an idea occurred to me. Although I had never been in a band before and couldn't play any instrument, I liked the idea of being on the field, marching around in formations at football game half times. The recruiting band members promised they would find me an instrument I could play, and when I showed up for the first rehearsal the only instrument left in the box was a cowbell. I was delighted to find something so simple to play, and soon became quite content to walk around the field hitting my cowbell and bumping into band members scurrying to make a formation. I never went to rehearsals, so I didn't have the slightest idea where I was supposed to stand in the ever-changing formations. During the Penn half time, a clarinet player who took the whole business very seriously saw me standing alone, hitting the cowbell way down on the twenty-yard line, and threatened to report me to the band leader if I blew it again.

The week before the Colgate game, I again have to skip band rehearsals to finish a particularly troublesome laboratory assignment. On Saturday, I grab my orange-and-black straw boater and my cowbell and head for the stadium. It is a crystal-clear fall day.

The Princeton Band's half-time programs are always in bad taste, much to the delight of the students and the disgust of the elderly alumni in the bleachers. Our band has a slap-dash, sophisticated-campy look with its sports coats, tennis shoes, and imperfect formations. The contrast with the precision-marching bands from other schools is acutely obvious during the Colgate game.

At half time, the Colgate Band marches onto the field in expert formation. They resemble a set of perfect, cavity-free teeth. They immediately launch into their traditional program saluting the Daughters of the American Revolution. Entirely unimaginative. Chants swell up from the Princeton side: "BORING! . . . BORING! . . . HIGH-SCHOOL! . . . HIGH-SCHOOL! . . ."

When the Princeton Band takes the field, I run behind the tubas so the band leader can't see me. I haven't the faintest notion about where to move next. All I know is that we're doing a formation which is supposed to look like Marie Antoinette getting it on the guillotine. The music starts and everyone begins moving. I'm happily whacking the cowbell thinking everything is going to work fine, when I realize I'm standing smack on the center of Marie Antoinette's neck.

A formation of charging band members representing the guillotine blade rushes forward, knocking me to the ground. I hear the crowd cheer. They probably think I'm supposed to look like a spurt of blood or something. I stagger off the field in a daze. When the program ends, the band leader comes over.

"Phillips, what the hell were you doing out there on the neck?"

"Nothing in particular. . . . Checking for signs of psoriasis. Why?"

"You fucked up the entire formation. That's why."

"I was only trying to play the cowbell."

"The cowbell! There isn't supposed to be a cowbell player in my band."

"Sorry."

"This is a serious band, Phillips. I've stuck out my neck for you long enough—"

I laugh at the unintended pun. He's not laughing. "Oh, sorry," I say.

"You are hereby officially fired."

The Yale game in November is the Big Game for Princeton. This year the Elis are tied for first place with Harvard. Princeton is in the cellar, but if we can beat Yale, we will knock them out of the championship race. Preparations are being made for a huge pregame bonfire behind Nassau Hall. According to Freddie Fox, Princetoniana expert, it is the first time since the midfifties that students have shown interest in building the traditional bonfire to burn bulldog effigies.

Cottage Club, which I haven't visited since the bicker skirmishes, will be hosting a casino with roulette, craps, and blackjack on Friday night. I like to gamble, and on Thursday night my mind is not on the thermodynamics exam I have the following morning. Sitting in the Ivy Club library, I idly flip through the pages of a probability textbook. I come across a short discussion entitled, "Games of Chance: Figuring the Probabilities." I devour the brief section about blackjack and want to know more.

I head out into the cold fall wind and jog over to Firestone Library, arriving just after closing time. The guard refuses to let me in. I tell him that I'm a graduate student in the Mid-East Studies Department. He looks skeptical. I explain that I've left an ancient Dead Sea scroll out on a desk on C floor and that if it sits all night in the open air, it will decompose. He gives me a curious look and then capitulates.

An hour later, I'm sitting on the floor between the stacks somewhere in the subterranean depths of Firestone. The silence is deadening. Scattered around me are a dozen books about blackjack odds. When a janitor discovers me at three-thirty in the morning, I've just finished committing the odds to memory. I walk back to 42 Little. Franz is still up, wrestling with some history paper about sports in America. He hasn't changed much since the first week, and although I basically like him, I am resigned that our friendship will probably remain on a superficial level, with competitive overtones.

"Do you have a date for tomorrow night?" asks Franz.

"No, I intend to make vast sums of money at the Cottage casino."

"Don't count on it. What happened to old Mary-Lay? Didja get the ax or what?"

"Nothing happened."

"I've got a great date," says Franz.

"Yeah, sure," I say, remembering the long string of moronic ladies which Franz regularly parades around on weekends.

"How's your work going?" he wants to know.

"Work? Oh, *shit* . . ." I suddenly remember the thermo exam at eight-thirty.

Five hours later, I'm sweating a waterfall in the exam. The material I'm supposed to know looks like the clues for a crossword puzzle and I detest crossword puzzles. In a situation like this, there's nothing to do but try to see the humor. I try. In response to the last question, I write: "To be brutally frank, I don't know a damn thing about fermi metals, but I can easily tell you how to bet on a hand of blackjack where you have aces back to back."

# 9

# Aces Back to Back

That night, I'm sitting at one of the blackjack tables on the second floor of Cottage Club. Smoke swirls. The room is jammed with guys in tuxedos and girls in evening dresses, all of them bunched around the game tables. The steady cadence of cards being dealt and chips changing hands is interrupted occasionally by the apologies of some idiot who has spilled a drink on a green felt table.

I've been playing for an hour and I'm already up twenty-five dollars. Eric Aaboe, a friend of mine from Yale, is winning at the same table. The dealer is one of those big-talk gamblers who claims to have beaten someone named Amarillo Slim in Las Vegas poker. He shuffles very efficiently. Snaps the cards when he deals. And talks. And talks.

He deals the next hand. I bet the maximum five dollars. The cards snap down in front of me.

I have the queen of spades showing and a ten in the hole. Aaboe shows the nine of diamonds.

"Phillips, do you want cards?" asks the dealer.

"No, I stand."

"Cards?" the dealer says to Aaboe.

"Hit me," says Aaboe.

Snap. The dealer drops the five of clubs on Aaboe's nine.

"Stick," says Aaboe.

The dealer goes around to the other players. Snap. Snap. Two guys go over twenty-one. The other stands on the jack of hearts.

The dealer's cards show fourteen. He deals himself the five of spades and stands on his total of nineteen. Being closer to twenty-one than the dealer, I win. The dealer doubles my five dollars. Aaboe shows twenty and wins. The dealer shuffles the cards quickly.

"I don't know what you're doing, Phillips," says the dealer, "but you're the only guy who's won five hands in a row tonight. You're a lucky sonuvabitch."

"Luck, my ass."

He deals the next hand. Snap. I win on a blackjack. I lose the next two hands and win the following three. On each hand, I calculate the odds and play accordingly. My midnight studies are paying off. There is something simple, almost inevitable about winning. The arrangement of the cards and the odds I've memorized are as symmetrical and pure as a physics equation.

The dealer takes off his tuxedo jacket and rolls up his sleeves. His Cottage Club bow tie is drooping. He looks around damply. I can tell he's worried about taking crap from his buddies about losing the club's money. He deals another hand. I win. Aaboe loses and bows out to the roulette table.

Aaboe's chair is taken by David Michaelis, a fellow I've met only briefly in French class. He buys thirty dollars in chips and lights a cigarette. He seems like an instinctive gambler. His movements are cool. Fluid. He sees my pile of winnings and winks at me. His eyes exude intelligence, warmth, and self-confidence.

Michaelis is sharp; maybe too sharp. There is something about him that makes him different from most people I've met at Princeton. Although he is only a freshman, he seems more sophisticated than some seniors I've met. Right away I can tell he has a definite sense of who he is and where he is going. The combination of an easygoing sense of humor and an aggressive personality makes him the kind of person whom people either like or dislike instantly. I can tell I'm going to like him. Even in the act of buying chips, Michaelis is tacitly challenging the dealer to take stock of a new situation at the table.

The dealer responds to Michaelis' first five-dollar bet by dealing him a natural blackjack. Michaelis shows almost no reaction to his own victory. But when I win on the next two hands he seems pleased. On the fourth hand, we both win. The dealer has run out of chips. The crowd around the table starts buzzing. Michaelis winks at me again. The look in his eyes seems to suggest that, together, we are going to take on the bank. The dealer leaves to get more chips. But apparently he is not deemed worthy by the Cottage president. A new dealer is sent in from the bullpen.

"So you guys have been winning some money . . ." says the new dealer, rolling up his sleeves. "Well, we're going to lift the five-dollar betting limit for the last half hour so we can win our dough back. Sky's the limit, suckers."

Most of the other players at the table have already dropped out. Michaelis looks at me. He smiles around his eyes. He is good-looking: light brown hair, strong chin. There is a friendly intensity about his face, yet he is also detached. I can almost sense him moving between an inner world of thoughts and ideas and the more superficial card game going on in front of us. I can tell there is a streak of arrogance in him, but I like that. He seems to be one part ego, two parts humanity, with a splash of amiable golden retriever thrown in for laughs.

I smile back at him. He acknowledges by raising his eyebrows and putting a cigarette between his grinning lips. There is a bond of conspiracy between us. We know we are going to win the game. And more important: We know we are going to be friends.

On the first hand, I bet ten dollars and beat the dealer. Michaelis loses. The dealer beats both of us on the second hand. He calls for three beers. Michaelis lights a cigarette and bets twenty bucks. He wins on a four-card twenty-one. A syncopated rhythm develops among the three of us with the merry-go-round of cards and the stacking and restacking of chips won and lost.

After twenty-five minutes, the dealer calls for more chips from the bank. He is beginning to look harried, but there is a touch of Hollywood in his voice when he announces that we will play only one more hand. Michaelis and I look at each other. We know this is it. We both bet thirty dollars. The dealer shuffles and deals.

Michaelis is showing the king of hearts.

"You want cards?" asks the dealer.

"Stand," says Michaelis.

"Cards, Phillips?"

I have the ace of clubs showing and the ace of spades in the hole. I decide to split aces, which means that I can now play two hands with two thirty-dollar bets. It also means that I can only draw one card to each ace.

"I'm splitting the pair."

"One card coming down on each," says the dealer.

He deals me two cards down. I pause, listening to the sudden hyphenated breathing of the crowd around the table. I turn the cards up, revealing the jack of spades and the jack of hearts: *double* blackjack. My stomach does a swan dive. The dealer pounds a fist on the table. Michaelis smiles. I wink at

61

him. The dealer quickly counts out one hundred twenty dollars and turns to his own hand. He has a sixteen count showing. He deals himself the eight of hearts, which busts his hand. Standing on a twenty count, Michaelis wins.

The dealer can't believe it. He's so tense that he looks like a huge white knuckle. He scans the stacks of chips in front of us and realizes that we've won over three hundred dollars between us. He yells for the Cottage president to come over and begins agitatedly picking his nose.

# 10
# "J. P.": A Nickname and a Friend

"If I were making a movie out of the dictionary, what word do you think I'd cast you as?" Michaelis asks me as we walk to the stadium for the Yale game the next morning.

"I don't know. Why don't we make a movie out of the Manhattan telephone directory. There's a whole page of Chinese people named Ng. It could be a disaster film about thousands of Ngs taking over the world."

"It wouldn't sell," says Michaelis. "Let's get back to the dictionary."

"Okay, which word?"

" 'Lucky,' " he says.

"I don't believe there is such a thing as luck."

Michaelis looks at me and smiles. "Yes." He says this nodding his head, as if he had known all along that I didn't believe in luck.

"And besides," I say, "I think I'd rather play an active verb."

"Don't be ridiculous. Adjectives always get top billing."

"I'm not even lucky in the conventional sense."

"I've never seen anyone split aces and come up with two natural blackjacks," he says. "You don't call that lucky?"

"No. If you're a smart gambler, you don't need luck. I was smart last night. You won too. We're both smart."

"Then what are we doing at Princeton?"

"You don't like it here?" I ask him.

"Let's just say it's different."

"Different from what?"

"Cambridge, Mass.—where I grew up."

"Why didn't you go to Harvard?"

"I didn't get in. They were crazy not to take me . . . but they wouldn't take me because they're crazy."

I can tell he has just thought of this collegiate Catch-22 because his face lights up.

"They didn't accept me either," I say. "But why is Princeton so different?"

"Mostly the people and their attitudes."

"Can you be specific, Herr Doctor Freud?"

"Okay. Let's start with your roommate."

Michaelis has a vaguely distasteful look on his face.

"What about him?" I ask.

"The first time I met him he insisted I use my goddamn class numerals when I introduced myself."

"Franz is all right once you get to know him. What else?" I ask.

"You don't think that's *strange*?" Michaelis looks at me, his eyebrows raised. I can tell he's trying to feel me out, to see how much of Franz's Princetoniana I have accepted.

"Sure it's strange. It'll grow on you."

"Yeah," says Michaelis. "Like a fungus."

"What else?"

"I saw him at a party the other night. I was with a girl, a friend of mine from Cambridge, and Franz comes up, gives me this very macho slap on the back and says, 'Is that your date, huh?' "

"Michaelis! What's wrong with that?"

"Two things. First of all, my friend was standing right there. It was as if Franz was saying, 'Is that your pet turtle, huh?' Secondly, this 'date' business has got to go. I've never heard anyone my age use the word 'date' before. It's archaic, for chrissake."

"You're exaggerating the whole thing."

"No, I'm not. That's what the sixties generation was trying to get away from: Archie asking Veronica for a goddamn date and Betty getting pissed off."

"Let's get philosophical about it," I say sarcastically. "It's only a word."

"At Princeton it's more than that. When a girl is referred to as someone's date, she is being seen in terms of the guy, not on her own terms."

"Okay, you have a point. In fact, I'll give you two points."

David smiles. He likes the way I throw my sarcasm into his seriousness. "No, really," he says. "That's the trouble with this whole place. People are seen in terms of the institution—like Franz and his goddamn Seventy-seven—and in terms of the eating club they join, never in terms of themselves as creative individuals."

"I've heard you're a writer."

"Who'd you hear that from?" He is curious, flattered.

"It gets around. They say you're pretty good."

"I try. I've a long way to go," he says matter-of-factly.

We walk on for a while without talking. The leaves are bright yellow against the blue sky. Finally David says: "What do you want to do? I mean with your life."

"I'm not exactly sure yet. Something important. Something that's going to change the world. But first, I want to write a Triangle musical comedy. I've been thinking about it—"

"So have I." We look at each other. "Do you want to do one together?" asks David.

"Sure. I already have some ideas."

"Can you write music?" he asks.

"No. Can you?"

"No. But I know someone who can. Is anyone else writing a show?"

"The competition's stiff. A couple of upperclassmen in Ivy are working on one."

"By the by," says David, "what made you join that place?"

"The food."

"The food. *Bull*shit."

"Eat it, Michaelis."

"Ah, J.P., you've already been Princetonianized," he says.

# 11

# A Cracker as Big as the Ritz

There are very few people who make me feel as if I've known them forever when I first meet them. Also there are very few people from whom I think I will really learn something important in the course of a friendship. And there are fewer still who have a terrific sense of humor. David is one of these rare people.

I have an intuitive feeling about him. In a short time, our friendship has developed that intangible quality where two people know instinctively what each other is thinking. If I begin a sentence, David will often know exactly what the ending is going to be. If David sees someone walking on Nassau

Street, I can tell just by looking at him what he thinks of that person. He is very perceptive about people. He observes and analyzes them closely, while I am more inclined to test people rather than interpret them.

Three weeks after we first talked about writing a musical comedy together, David and I sit down to plot the play. We chain-smoke cigarettes and make notes on a legal pad. The ideas come quickly. Characters begin to emerge. The story revolves around "The Ritz," a Mafia-run nightclub on Lincoln's head atop Mount Rushmore, where the lives of a con man named Loose-Shoe Baxter, a dozen strip-tease girls, the cast of a Triangle tour show, countless retired mafiosi in wheelchairs, a tribe of Indians, an Arab oil sheik named Oily-Baba-au-Rhum and his daughter, Esmerelda, become hopelessly intertwined. We decide to call the show *A Cracker as Big as the Ritz*, and after typing up an outline, we turn the sketches in to the Triangle director, Milton Lyon.

Milton is something of a legend around Princeton. He is a professional who has directed the last sixteen Triangle shows. Consequently, he is God. Whatever Milton says, goes. He is a feisty man who is lovable to some and anathema to others. Like any god, he is feared. Compared to Milton's temper, the wrath of Achilles is just so much cotton candy. After all we've heard about him, David and I are surprised when he actually says he likes our outline. The great and powerful Milton has spoken. He encourages us to continue.

My third roommate in 42 Little, Meadows, decides to drop out of school midway through December, leaving me with his crop of dope plants. David moves into the room, bringing with him a healthy distaste for Princeton to counterbalance Franz's fanaticism, a fine collection of jazz records, good books, and the unpredictable, flamboyant stuff that he is made of.

We begin to spend long hours writing the play on my typewriter, Capitalist Pig. We skip classes, drink too much, smoke too much, forget to shave, and compete to see who can stay at the typewriter longer. We argue about new turns in the plot and the way a character would say a line. Sometimes we act out sections of the play, David playing a Mafia godfather to my Loose-Shoe Baxter. Franz and Whitmore think we're crazy. The work goes well. Our schoolwork is ignored.

While we are working, things begin to go up on the walls. I discover that David has a passion for covering blank walls with all manner of bizarre Americana: an antique toilet kit "compliments of Hotel Commodore"; several half-filled packs of the old, green Lucky Strike; a fruit crate label, HIGH HAND, showing a man's hand holding four aces; a *New York Times* article about a backwoods storyteller who told the tall tale of the poisonest snake of all, the hairy hoop-snake; display sheets of tattoo designs; hundreds of photographs: dozens of girls he went to school with at Concord Academy, his dog, Peezner, the Flatiron Building on Fifth Avenue, his family, his grandparents, old tintypes of his great-grandparents on his mother's side—New Englanders all—steamships, the back beach in Provincetown, Massachusetts, the New York skyline during the blackout of 1965.

One day during the midst of writing Act Two, he brings back a wanted poster from the post office. The two photographs on the poster show a beefy, middle-aged escaped convict, named Patrick James Huston. He is wearing a white T-shirt, and, according to the poster, his body is "riddled with leathery bullet scars." But the detail that David points out to me is a tattoo on Huston's upper right arm. It reads: IN MEMORY OF MOM.

One afternoon, as David and I are trying to figure out how to work a scene where Loose-Shoe, the Indian chief, several drunken mafiosi, and the Triangle boys wearing grass skirts are all can-canning in the Italian nightclub, Mary-Lee calls. At one point in the conversation, David hears me say to her, "But, Mary-Lee, I *have* been thinking about you all the time." David's fingers stop typing. He looks over at me, his bloodshot eyes lighting up. "*That* is a hairy hoop-snake!" he yells, referring to the old liar-storyteller.

When the conversation is over, I walk back to the desk. David is drawing a chart titled: CHART OF DEADLY SINS. There is one column for each of us on the chart. Beneath the columns is a "hairy hoop-snake": a symbol for "telling an outrageous lie." The symbol is apparently worth two points against me. I already have one in my column. A hairy hoop-snake looks like this:

As I am protesting the first points against me, David is drawing two new symbols. They look like this:

"What's that mean?" I ask, pointing to the symbol on the left.

"That is a J'Accuse," explains David. "If you feel that you have been unfairly accused, you can put a J'Accuse in my column."

"Fair enough. What the hell is that?" I ask, referring to the things which look like pick-up sticks with a lobster claw.

"A joint snake," he says.

"A what?"

"You've never heard of a joint snake?" He is incredulous.

"No. What is it?"

"A joint snake exists in the Berkshires in Massachusetts and it has the ability to lie in separate parts under a pine tree so that it will be undetected. When some turkey like you walks along, the joint snake assembles in a flash, and leaps out at your crotch."

"You're kidding?"

"Uh-huh, that's the whole point."

"So what's it doing on the chart?"

"It's the symbol for telling an outrageous lie in order to get a woman into bed, you fool."

"A joint snake?" We both laugh hysterically. It takes hours before we get back to the musical. Fascinated by the myriad deadly sins, we invent new symbols (each with a point rating) intended to punish the other's individual proclivities.

After two weeks, we've finished most of the play. Dead tired, strung-out on No-Doz, we fiddle with the typewriter keys, stumped by the ending. Nothing seems to work. We are given to idly throwing darts, leafing through old copies of *Playboy*, thinking up new symbols for the chart, and making excuses to go out to buy a new pack of cigarettes when the old one isn't finished. But we remain optimistic. We know it's going to work, somehow. We take long walks on a golf course near the Graduate College in the thin winter sunlight.

One night, after I've gone to bed, David stays up to work on the show. It must be five in the morning when I feel him shaking me.

"Wha'th'hell," I mumble.

"I figured it out. I've got an ending," says David, still shaking me.

"Wha'timezit?"

"Never mind. Listen: it's all going to end in the nose."

". . . gonna get it in the nose if you don't lemme sleep," I tell him.

"No, listen, J.P. The last scene will take place in Lincoln's nose on Mount Rushmore."

"Why nose?"

"Because that's where the oil is, but the Indians don't tell anyone, because the old Indian legend says that if any white men tamper with it, the mountain will turn into a cracker."

"S'pose to be big as goddamn Ritz? . . . crazy . . . go to sleep . . ." I say, drifting back to my interrupted dreams.

"You haven't heard the rest of it. About Loose-Shoe and Esmerelda and everybody."

". . . Sounds like an Arctic Commissioner's discotheque . . ."

"What are you babbling about? . . . J.P.? . . . Ah, you're dreaming, you fool. There ought to be a chart symbol for that . . ."

We finish the play by the end of the week and take the script over to Milton Lyon. After we spend several days biting our nails, Milton calls and tells us to come over to his house. We tromp through the snow, discussing alternative titles and changes that need to be made. David wants to bring my dream character, the Arctic Commissioner, and his discotheque into the last act. I don't even know what an Arctic Commissioner is. David likes the idea of a discotheque in an igloo with all the Eskimos doing the Bump. When he suggests we have woolly hoop-snakes doing the Hustle, I begin to think we've been working on *A Cracker as Big as the Ritz* too long.

Milton is quite pleasant when we sit down in the living room of his small house. Photographs and mementos of past Triangle shows adorn the walls. I imagine a framed box of Ritz crackers going up next to the autographed Josh Logan photograph after our show is produced. Milton looks at us for a moment and clears his throat.

"I don't know what to say to you two. It's a *very* strange script."

"We have some new ideas for the last act," says David.

"Did you like it?" I ask.

"It's not a question of *liking* it," says Milton. "I don't think it would work. I can't *visualize* this—this comedy on stage."

"Oh."

"Can you give us some idea of what's wrong?" asks David. "The dialogue? Characters? Plot?"

"It's nothing specific. It just doesn't *do* anything for me."

"Oh."

Milton seems pained. He takes a deep breath. "I've been directing Triangle long enough to know what works and what doesn't. This *sim*ply won't work."

"I think we can improve it," I tell him.

"We have a whole new third act in the works with a scene inside a discotheque inside an igloo with woolly hoop-snakes doing the Bump," says David.

"*What?*" Milton's eyebrows arch like cats.

"Nothing," I say, quickly.

"Well, I don't like to say it, but I've read the script twice and I just can't *smell* the talent. It's not worth pursuing."

"Not even if we make changes?" asks David.

"No," says Milton.

"Oh."

"Damn."

# Interlude:
# The Fifty-ninth Street Bridge

New York. New Year's Day, 1976. The beginning of America's Bicentennial Year. David and I walk out on the pedestrian ramp of the Fifty-ninth Street Bridge. We are partially hung over from a half-dozen New Year's Eve parties. It is a fine, sunny day. When we get out to the middle, we dangle our arms over the railing. We watch the dark, changing currents of the river far below us. The windows of the city, like a thousand half-remembered dreams, wink in the sunlight off to the right.

I tap my foot on the bridge. The metal makes a nice sound. David picks up the beat. I back away from the railing and start into a drunken sailor's tap-dance step that I learned in a musical comedy troupe at Berkeley. David grins. He falls into step. *Ta-ta-tum—ta-ta-tee.* He hasn't quite picked it up yet. I show him how to change weight from toe to heel. He tries it. We link arms and fall into step together. *Ta-ta-tum —ta-ta-tee—rum-tata-tum-teetee.* We laugh, pleased with ourselves, and return to the railing.

We are silent for a long time. The beauty of the city is overwhelming. Finally David says, "Look at all the power out there."

"Yeah. It's fascinating."

"Yes."

"Walking through the city, don't you sometimes feel so alien?" I ask him. "And other times, you can be walking along feeling as if you have the whole city by the balls."

"Do you trust that feeling?" he asks.

"Yes. I think I need to feel that way sometimes. Don't you?"

"Sure. But why do *you* need that?"

"Well, it has something to do with being fascinated by power. I don't really understand power. I don't know if I want it."

"I think you do," he says. "You're a winner. Winners have power. Some people are losers, victims. They *want* to be victims. It's an easy way to go through life. They don't have to do anything but be victimized."

"What do you want to do in life?" I ask him.

"Have the power to change people with my writing. I want to create characters who are so alive, people will know them as their own brothers and sisters."

"You're fascinated by people, aren't you?"

"Yes," he says. "And you—you're fascinated by new experiences. Right?"

"I'm fascinated by what is unknown."

"Unknown." The word drifts out over the river. David takes out the little black notebook he always carries with him and writes something down. "Are you afraid of death?" he asks.

"No."

"Are you sure?"

"Yes," I tell him. "The closest I ever came to death was once when I was mountain climbing. I fell twenty-five feet before the rope caught me. But while I was falling, I was fascinated. I'm not kidding. I felt so *alive*. There was no fear, no —I can't explain it. I'm not like you. I don't feel the need to write these things down in a notebook. You can do something I'm not very good at. You observe and interpret and explain life."

"When are you most happy?" he asks.

"When I'm taking risks. Doing something that seems impossible . . . And you?"

"When I'm writing. Or sharing something special with somebody. I guess they're both the same thing."

We are quiet again. But smiling now.

"What do you think of Mary-Lee?" I ask him.

"I like her spunk. But I don't think she's up to you. But, then, that's *my* problem. I'm too critical of women."

"Why are you critical of *her*?"

"Because I don't like young women who *need* men. She needs you. She needs to marry you. She isn't strong enough by herself."

"So you admire women who are individuals. Strong women."

"Definitely."

"In some ways I agree with you. At this point in my life, I don't want a relationship based on need."

"Neither do I. But I'm also tired of relationships based on sexual need," he says. "They're damn fun, but they're so easy, so predictable."

"They don't have to be bad if both people know what they want."

"True. But isn't it better—less predictable—if the relationship is based on friendship?" he asks.

"Of course, but how many of those does one have in a lifetime? How many really work out?"

"Too few," he says, shaking his head.

We watch a helicopter sway out over the river, then dip and rise, angling toward the Pan Am Building downtown. The noise of traffic on the bridge grows louder.

"I have a feeling something is going to happen to us in this city," says David.

"Ah! The mystic speaks! What do you see in your crystal ball?"

"Shut up."

"What do you think is going to happen to us?"

"Nothing."

"What?" I press it because I can tell he is serious.

"Forget it."

"Come on, Professor Marvel."

"It's nothing, really."

I follow his gaze, leading down the river and out to the ocean.

# 12

## Old Nausea
## and the Screaming Rhubarbs

Gloom and slush. Princeton in winter: It doesn't snow. It doesn't rain. It slushes. The courtyards become a quagmire of mud, and the dormitories turn into steambaths or artificial penguin habitats. And every winter after New Year's Day, when I realize that the new year is not much different from the old, I become exceedingly morose.

This year is no different, and the rejection of our script does nothing to lift my spirits. When I discover that three Triangle veterans have had their show accepted after turning in only one scene, I start ranting. Depression sets in, and a whole series of events takes place which makes me seriously begin entertaining the conspiracy theory of life: *They are definitely out to get me.* Or as David would say, "The screaming rhubarbs have dropped in for a week-long ping-pong game with my balls."

The screaming rhubarbs are clever. They don't jump on you all at once. They creep up slowly, relishing your misery, and then, *smack, bang,* they're on you. And let me assure you, the screaming rhubarbs are tougher than a Bic pen: They're a bummer first time, every time. It all happens like this:

First I lose my wallet. My motorcycle gets ripped off. I begin putting on sweaters backwards, twice in a row. And then I start thinking about final exams. To my horror, I realize that I really should have gone to at least a couple of my mechanics lectures. I discover that no amount of pure and simple logic is going to deliver me an A, and as exam day approaches, I begin lowering my standards. At first I'm satis-

75

fied with a B, then a C, and then I'm just hoping that the professor will have mercy and pass me.

Like a desperate fool, I stay up two nights in a row before the mechanics exam, counting on nervous energy and gallons of coffee to pull me through. When I get to the examination room I'm manic. The screaming rhubarbs are leering at me. I can barely see, let alone hold the pencil. Somehow I doze off . . . my head is on the desk . . . I feel someone jabbing my shoulder and I see a huge pink blob in front of my eye. (What the hell is that?) Simultaneously, I realize that the pink blob is my pencil eraser and the jabbing is the professor telling me that the exam is over. He reminds me to sign the honor code pledge. I write, "I pledge on my honor that during this examination I was asleep. Consequently I never gave nor received assistance."

I hand in the empty exam booklet.

The rest of my exams are disaster areas.

Two weeks later, my grades come in the mail. Accompanying the merry list of D's and F's is a notice from the Dean of the College. It says that I am being placed on academic probation. This means that if I flunk another course, I'll be bounced out of the Big U. right on my ass.

I look out at the slush in the courtyard.

The screaming rhubarbs definitely have me by the balls.

# 13

## The War Room

As the new semester gets underway, the screaming rhubarbs abate somewhat. My courses begin to interest me. Three times a week, I walk through the whitewashed subterranean passageways of the Woodrow Wilson School of International Affairs. The old Defense Department maps and the stark black-and-white surfaces of the conference room where my seminar meets suggest a command center from which World War III might be launched. I've nicknamed this classroom the War Room because it reminds me of a scene from the movie *Dr. Strangelove*: An American bomber attack has been accidentally launched against the Soviet Union, and the president of the United States, an array of Pentagon brass, and the Soviet ambassador are collected in the supersecret War Room in the Pentagon. They are making a last-ditch effort to avert the third world war. Frantic deliberations are interrupted when General Turgidson and Ambassador Molotov begin wrestling over a wristwatch spy camera Molotov has smuggled in. The president intercedes, scolding them, "Gentlemen, please! You can't fight in here! This is the War Room!"

The course is Arms Control and Disarmament 452, in which three brilliant professors lead eight juniors and seniors through intense discussions of kill ratios, counterforce capabilities, and doomsday scenarios. The leader of the group is Hal Feiveson, the most popular professor in the Woodrow Wilson School. He is renowned for his sarcastic sense of humor and his strong command of the subject matter. Hal first studied physics and then got a Ph.D. in political science, going on to become one of the bright, young faces at the U.S. Arms Control and Disarmament Agency.

Assisting Hal is Marty Sherwin, also in his thirties, who is an undisputed authority in the field of cold war diplomacy. The third prong of this intellectual powerhouse is Freeman Dyson, one of the most eminent physicists in the world. In addition to his highly respected work in theoretical physics, he's been concerned with the problem of arms control for many years.

I have been impressed by Dyson's distinguished, almost ambassadorial appearance, and his crisp English accent. His thin features are complemented by a shock of thick black hair and large inquisitive eyes surrounded by gold-rimmed spectacles. He brings to class an enormous old valise, which is jammed with countless scraps of paper. Being a lowly physics student, I'm glad to see that a man of brilliance appears normal, and maybe even disorganized. But I don't understand how Dyson can look so refreshed at nine A.M. when the class meets.

I sip coffee and look around the conference table at my colleagues. They are an unusually sharp group of students, even for this time of the morning. Professor Feiveson yawns loudly.

"Good morning, everyone," he says. "Why is it that Freeman can look so good every morning, when the rest of us can barely drag ourselves out of bed? Freeman, out of consideration for the rest of us, don't you think you might yawn from time to time?"

Dyson fakes a yawn and Feiveson continues, "Today, we're going to be discussing the historical background of the atomic bomb and some of the early postwar maneuvering to establish an international authority to prevent proliferation. But before we go any further, I think it would help if Freeman would describe the more immediate effects of an atomic explosion so we get a feel for what we're dealing with."

"Of course," says Dyson, "although it's not something I relish thinking about. First, let me say that it is deceptive to think of an atomic bomb as simply a bigger bang. Describing the explosive force of the bomb in terms of the equivalent amount of TNT is helpful if you are Harry Truman trying to explain what we did to the Japanese, but it doesn't fully describe what happens.

"I don't suppose anyone here has witnessed the explosion of anything bigger than a firecracker. You really have to observe one of these things firsthand to comprehend what they're all about. You would really understand only if one were dropped on you.

"The fission bombs exploded over Hiroshima and Nagasaki were each twenty kilotons, which is to say, they yielded twenty thousand tons of TNT each. The fusion monsters which are the mainstay of our nuclear arsenal today are, on the average, one thousand times more powerful. A bomb the size of the Hiroshima model is needed simply to trigger one of the big bombs.

"Let me describe what occurs when a twenty-kiloton bomb is exploded: The first thing that happens is the sky becomes illuminated by a brilliant white light. Temperatures are so high around the point of explosion that the atmosphere is actually made incandescent. To an observer standing six miles away, the ball of fire, which begins to expand within the first few millionths of a second, will appear brighter than a hundred suns. The retina of a man's eye will be fused, and he will be permanently blinded as far away as three miles in daytime or four miles at night.

"As the fireball begins to rise upward to the upper air layers, where it will spread out into a mushroom-shaped cloud, temperatures will be extreme enough to spontaneously ignite all flammable materials for miles around. Wood-frame houses will catch fire. Clothing will burst into flame, and people will suffer intense third-degree flash burns over their exposed flesh. The very high temperatures will always produce a shock wave and a variety of nuclear radiations: gamma rays, neutrons, beta particles, and alpha particles. Neutrons and gamma rays will instantaneously penetrate all walls, including up to twenty inches of concrete. The shock wave will level everything in the vicinity of ground zero; hurricane-force winds will then rush into the vacuum left by the expanding shock wave and sweep up the rubble of ma-

sonry, glass, and steel, hurling it outward as lethal projectiles.
Persons as far as twenty-one hundred feet away will soon
vomit and undergo massive hemorrhaging by bleeding through
the skin. . . . I could go on, describing the firestorm and the
panic, and the horrible death that follows from radiation
poisoning, but that would be unnecessary at this point . . ."

Silence falls over the room. The titanic proportions of
the potential destruction begin to sink in. I decide to say
something.

"Listening to all this, I'm afraid I have to be a cynic.
Every American president since Truman has tried for nuclear
disarmament. But we still have the bombs. The Baruch Plan
put forth by the Truman administration posited that the manufacturing of atomic bombs would stop and that all existing
bombs would be destroyed. Then Eisenhower came into office
and he timed the first explosion of a hydrogen bomb to coin-
cide with a proposal to diminish the potential destructive
power of the world's atomic stockpiles. Kennedy proposed his
'Program for General and Complete Disarmament.' Johnson
signed the Nuclear Non-Proliferation Treaty. Kissinger now
has designs to 'cap' the arms race. There have been over six
thousand meetings and not one nuclear weapon has yet been
destroyed . . ."

Feiveson is nodding his head. He says, "Much of the
proliferation, as we will find out in the coming weeks, has
been made possible by the commercial export of nuclear technology by the U.S., France, and Germany. The implications
for the future of disarmament are even more bleak in this
respect, and before we break for the day, I'd like to propose
a scenario for you to ponder. It's a concept that has experts
worried: The F.B.I. released figures this week which showed
that there were two thousand seventy-one incidents of ter-
rorist-related nonnuclear bombings of one sort or another in
the United States last year. Remember, it takes only fifteen
pounds of plutonium to fabricate a crude atomic bomb. And

there is sufficient plutonium and uranium shipped around this country each year to fashion thousands of crude atomic bombs. Much of it is lost or unaccounted for, and it is said to be extremely vulnerable to theft or hijacking when it is being transported between nuclear facilities.

"Now, suppose a two-hundred-pound shipment disappears en route between a reprocessing facility and a nuclear reactor of the future. A massive search of the countryside by state and local police turns up only an empty truck and a dead driver. The plutonium has been stolen.

"Two weeks later, a crude fission bomb with a yield in the kiloton range is detonated in the Wall Street district of New York. Of the half-million people who crowd the area during the regular business day, one hundred thousand are killed outright. The destruction to the city is massive. In a communiqué to the president in Washington, a terrorist group claims responsibility for the bomb. They warn the president that if their extravagant political demands are not met, there will be another explosion within a week.

"Think about it. What can the president do?"

"That's impossible. It would never happen," a student objects.

"I don't think terrorists could build an atomic bomb, even if they stole the plutonium," says someone else.

"You have to be brilliant to design an A-bomb," adds a third.

"That's right, you'd need another Los Alamos project to pull that off."

"It's highly unlikely. Nearly impossible."

# 14
## The Roots of the Mushroom

Impossible?

Or is it?

The specter of terrorists incinerating an entire city with a homemade atom bomb begins to haunt me. My imagination runs wild. With the ingredients and the information widely available, why should nuclear blackmail be restricted to large, organized terrorist groups? When the bombs start exploding and concessions are extracted from paralyzed governments, criminal extortionists and just plain old lunatics will want to get into the act. I begin to daydream through most of my classes.

After lunch later that week, I shoot pool with Bert Oldman and Jim Griffith at Ivy. We are playing Screw Your Buddy, the object of which is to eliminate the other two players. Both Bert and Jim sense that I'm preoccupied with something and they use my weakness to eliminate me first. When I concentrate, I can be a good pool player, but at the moment, the atomic bomb issue has galvanized my thinking. Even the ricocheting pool balls bring to mind the fast fissioning of plutonium 239.

I line up the two ball for the corner, shoot, and miss. Bert giggles.

"Can the laughter, Southern boy," I say.

"Phillips, you haven't sunk a shot yet. What's bugging you?" Bert asks.

"I've been thinking."

"About what?"

"Do you think terrorists are going to be running around with A-bombs someday?"

"Aw come on, Yankee," says Bert. "Does a bullfrog have wings?"

I see an easy shot on the five ball in the side pocket. I shoot, miss completely, and scratch.

That evening, I have dinner with David, and my obsession with the bomb resurfaces. It's become almost absurd by now. Wherever I go, I wonder what would happen if an atomic bomb were exploded twenty, forty, sixty miles away. Who would survive? Why would it happen? At the dinner table, I silently observe the resemblance between David's buttered roll and a mushroom cloud.

"J.P., you seem preoccupied. You're not going home to Jerome are you?" asks David. "Home to Jerome" is an expression he uses which means going crazy. It's the next step after the screaming rhubarbs. Apparently, David knew someone in a mental institution in some town called Jerome, who referred to the nut house as "home."

"No, nothing like that," I say.

"What's the matter then? Did you flunk another course?"

"Very funny. One of the professors told my Arms Control and Disarmament seminar that terrorist groups will be going in for atomic bombs during the eighties. What do you think of that?"

"I just finished reading an excellent book about all that. One of the journalism professors here wrote it. Ever heard of John McPhee's *The Curve of Binding Energy*?"

"I've heard of McPhee, but I didn't know he teaches here. What's the book about?"

"A nuclear physicist named Ted Taylor, who postulated that a terrorist group could easily steal plutonium or uranium from a nuclear facility and then design a workable atomic bomb with information available to the general public."

"My god, that's exactly what Feiveson was talking about."

"It's pretty wild stuff. Published in 1973. Very well written. You should read it . . ." David looks at me pointedly. "What's the matter, J.P.? You look like you've got the screaming rhubarbs again."

"No, it's just that this whole nuclear thing has been plaguing me for the last few days."

"You *have* been looking kinda wild and woolly."

"Have you got a copy of McPhee's book in the room?"

"Sure, I'll find it after dinner," he says.

"No, let's go now. I've got to read it right away."

"Relax, J.P. The world's not going to explode before you read it."

"No, come on, let's go now."

"Okay, okay. Jesus, I've never seen you so hyped up about anything."

"This isn't just anything," I tell him.

Reading for me is not just a pleasure, it's a compulsion. Ever since I was very young, I've been reading everything in my immediate environment. Matchbook covers, cereal boxes, all twenty-three volumes of the encyclopedia, and the repair manual of the Singer sewing machine. When I was a kid, I hoarded the *Life* magazine when it came to our house, and I always woke up before my parents could get at the Sunday *New York Times*. I'll bet I'm the only seasoned air traveler who reads the directions on the motion-sickness bag every time I get on an airplane.

Anyway, when I finally settle down with McPhee's *The Curve of Binding Energy*, I don't read it, I devour it. Each page is a new revelation. Theodore Taylor is the nuclear physicist who quit his job designing atomic bombs at Los Alamos to pioneer the movement for stronger safeguards in the nuclear power industry. Because of his experience in the field, Taylor fears that a terrorist group or criminal organization may someday hijack, divert, or steal a shipment of plutonium from a relatively unprotected nuclear reactor. With possession of the fissionable materials, a determined individual with a limited background in physics, and access to unclassified documents such as those found in a good university library, might be able to build a crude but effective atomic bomb.

According to Taylor, construction of the bomb would be reasonably simple because all the ingredients—except plutonium—are legally available at hardware stores and chemical supply houses. The size of the blast would depend upon the ingenuity of the designer, but unless the federal government takes immediate steps to safeguard fissionable materials en route to the nuclear reactors around the country, Taylor and McPhee believe that we're likely to have the first instance of nuclear blackmail within the next decade.

The next day, when Arms Control and Disarmament 452 meets in the War Room, I sit through another barrage of my colleagues' statements about the improbability of a terrorist building a bomb.

"It's just not possible," says one.

"What about if someone like Ted Taylor were a terrorist?" asks another.

"But he's not one."

"Terrorists don't have the know-how to build a bomb."

"They don't have access to the knowledge."

"You'd have to be a genius with a million dollars."

"No way."

During all this, an idea suddenly comes to mind. It is at once ridiculous and brilliant. (I've found that these two things often go together.) Suppose an average—or below-average in my case—physics student at a university could design a workable atomic bomb on paper. That would prove the point dramatically and show the federal government that stronger safeguards have to be placed on the manufacturing and use of plutonium. In short, if I could design a bomb, almost any intelligent person could. The whole idea becomes even more preposterous when I realize that I would have to design it in less than two months to turn it in as my junior independent project. I'm required by the Physics Department to have an advisor, but who would be willing to sanction such a crazy undertaking?

By the end of the seminar, I've already planned to ask Freeman Dyson to be my advisor.

"Are you serious?" Dyson asks me.

"Perfectly serious, sir," I say.

"Come now, John, I'd be happy to serve as your advisor, but why don't you pick some other topic for your independent study?"

"I've thought about other topics."

"Well?"

"I really want to try the bomb."

"You seem to be stuck on it. Why?"

"Because if I succeed, I will have made a very strong case—in a dramatic way—about strengthening plutonium safeguards. This is very important to me at the moment."

"I see."

I can tell by the softening, distant look in Dyson's eyes that he's beginning to take me seriously. "You understand that my security clearance with the government will preclude me from giving you any more information than that which can be found in physics libraries," he says.

"Yes, sir."

"Stop calling me 'sir.' My name is Freeman."

"Okay, Freeman."

"And you understand that you will be completely on your own once I initially point you in the right direction? These are the ground rules. I'm very serious about sticking to them."

"Of course."

"And there's a law called the 'no comment rule' governing scientists such as myself who have clearance to atomic bomb secrets. It stipulates that if asked a question about the design of such a bomb, I can answer neither yes nor no. At best, I'll only be able to tell you when you're getting warm, and only when no classified information is involved."

"Of course."

"This won't be easy for you, John."

"I know."

"Your chances for success are minuscule."

"I understand that."

"Okay, then. We'll meet after lunch at the end of the week, and I'll have a list of textbooks outlining the general principles which you should know about."

"Thank you."

"I wish you luck."

"Thanks."

"Stop thanking me. It won't be easy."

"I know."

As we leave the Woodrow Wilson School, Dyson walks off, huge paper-stuffed valise in hand, oversized galoshes making squushing noises in the snow. I'd swear there's a bounce in his normally measured steps. Or it could be me bouncing. I'm tremendously excited, and I charge over to the Physics Department office to record the subject of my junior project. Under the close scrutiny of the departmental secretary's gaze, I can barely write down the title:

*John Aristotle Phillips*
*Dr. Freeman Dyson, Advisor*
*How To Build Your Own Atomic Bomb*

# 15
## Shuffle-Step, Kick

Evening. David and I walk through the snow-hushed courtyards on our way to a Triangle rehearsal in McCarter
Theater. Despite our script being rejected, we have both
auditioned and been cast in the big spring musical-comedy
production. Written by the three Triangle veterans (who, we
have discovered, are very buddy-buddy with the director,
Milton) the show is called *Mugs Money*. Set in Chicago during Prohibition, the plot revolves around a series of bizarre
gangland killings initiated by the kingpin mobster, Spats. At
the end of the first act, our mob, a bumbling collection of
misfits, is forced to dress up as dancing chorus girls in a
misguided effort to knock off Spats. Our plan is foiled, but
the traditional drag kickline with hairy legs and sequins never
fails to bring down the house.

We are standing up on stage with the other gangsters.
The arc lights are hot. Mobsters mill around. Big Maurice
is horsing around with Big Maxie. Fat Marvin, the gangster
who couldn't eat straight, is being chewed out by the stage
manager for coming in late. He bites into a banana and mutters his apologies. The tech crew smokes cigarettes, drinks
gallons of beer, and laughs at the cast.

"Okay. Enough! *Eee*nough!" shouts Milton. "Let's take
the kickline number."

"Kickline!" screams the stage manager.

"Kickline!" yells Big Gus Martin, the gangster leader.

"Kickline?" asks Fat Marvin.

The orchestra starts playing. We swing into action. Kick, one, two, three, kick, one, two, three. Shuffle-step, kick. Shuffle-step, kick. The music speeds up. Kick, onetwothree, kick, onetwo. I lose a beat somewhere along the way. We link arms and begin the can-can high kicks. I'm still off a beat. Everybody else is going kick, onetwothree, and I'm now stuck on onetwo-kick-three. The kicks are reaching the high point, our toes coming up over our heads—

"Cut! *Stop!* Orchestraaa *cut!*" bellows Milton.

Dead silence.

I can't see him out in the theater because of the stage lights, but I can feel him. He walks down to the stage very quickly, seething. Someone giggles and wishes he hadn't. Milton's glare. He is looking directly at me. Studying me. Analyzing me. Deciding whether to go for the jugular or simply make a nice, long incision on my head. He sneers:

"Phillips—for someone who *thinks* he's a dancer, you've got a lot of steps to learn."

# 16

# Pas de Deux

Who said I was a dancer? At the moment, I have to start thinking of myself as a serious atomic scientist because I *do* have a lot of steps to learn in that field. At the end of the week, I have my first meeting with Freeman Dyson.

I don't know if I'll ever meet a person who is as easy to get to know as Freeman. His large, sympathetic eyes perfectly express his personality: He is totally earnest, unbelievably brilliant, and remarkably patient. After lunch at Ivy, Freeman hands me a short list of books on nuclear reactor technology, general nuclear physics, and current atomic theory.

"That's all?" I ask incredulously, having expected a little more direction, at least in the beginning. I feel like a tenderfoot camper being sent off on a solo survival trip in the Himalayas with only three matches.

"There's plenty of material on the list to get you started. You're bright enough to take it from there."

"Doesn't the list seem rather short?" I ask.

"Remember, John," he says. "The object is for you to see how far you can get without the use of classified information."

"Isn't there anything else you can tell me?"

"No. You'll have to figure it out for yourself."

This would be the last time I would ask him for more information than he would volunteer.

At our subsequent meetings during the next three weeks, Freeman takes great patience to explain the basic principles of nuclear physics over and over again. He never tells me anything he's not supposed to, but I feel as if I'm making progress in the right direction. At our second meeting, after I describe a nuclear process that took me many hours to understand, Freeman says: "Very good, John. Now you're ready for the interesting part. There are two texts on high-temperature, high-pressure physics I want you to study . . ."

As the preliminary work for the bomb proceeds, Freeman's responses to my calculations grow ever more subtle and opaque. If I ask him for a comment on a particular design or figure, he will glance over what I've done and look up at me without saying anything. He will then smile and change the subject. At first, I think this is his way of telling me I am correct. To make sure of this at our third meeting, I hand him a figure which is intentionally wrong. He reads it, looks up at me, smiles, and changes the subject.

Damn.

## Pas de Deux

The whole process is becoming an intellectual pas de deux, with Freeman and me as the two dancers: one leading silently while the other follows the elaborately choreographed cat-and-mouse ballet as it skitters across the stage and into the wings.

# Part 2

$$\rightarrow C^2 F^2 \rightarrow$$

*"Just how few people could achieve the fabrication of an atomic bomb on their own is a question on which opinion divides, but there are physicists with experience in the weapons field who believe that the job could be done by one person, working alone, with nuclear material stolen from private industry."*

—John McPhee in *The Curve of Binding Energy*

# 17

## Admission to the Mushroom Club: $25

A few words about my generation:

College students in the sixties spent much of their time going to "love-ins," "be-ins," and antiwar demonstrations. They tried to be politically aware and socially hip. My generation is different. We have no war to protest against. We share no common passions. We share no common music. We share no common drugs. We are a fragmented group of individuals. There is no sense of common crisis among college students in the seventies. We have no collective itch, so we no longer scratch each other's backs.

My generation is not caught up in the drug mystique that was so important before. When joints were passed around by a group of kids during the sixties, a common bond was created. Dope set them apart from their elders because it embodied a state of mind that only kids could understand. The sixties generation created an entire new culture around dope. They perceived the world differently. Dope was mellow. Dope was anti-three-piece suits. You smoked it on the sly. You smoked it with kids your own age and they were your "brothers and sisters." People who didn't smoke dope weren't cool. It was you against them.

My generation does not share this spirit. When we go to parties, someone will always bring dope, but it is no longer the focus of the evening. There is no mystery about it. Beer and alcohol are my generation's equalizers: our Great Ice-Breaker. Drinking beer is not a political act the way smoking dope once was. Less commitment is required for a beer drunk than an acid high. Across the country each weekend, gallons of beer, rum, tequila, and vodka are being consumed by my generation. The Budweiser Mystique prevails on every college campus. And when the campuses empty out each spring vacation, thousands of us grab our bathing suits and our six-packs and make a pilgrimage to Fort Lauderdale or Daytona for a week-long party in the sun.

One of my roommates, Franz, wouldn't miss it for the world. I'd be going too, but my vacation is already cut out for me. David and I plan to go down to Washington, D.C., where I will search through government files at the Atomic Energy Commission for declassified records of the Los Alamos Project.

At the National Technical Information Service in Washington, I find a series of technical histories of the Los Alamos Project which describe in precise detail the problems encountered and overcome by the scientists who constructed the first atomic bombs. I also discover a copy of the lecture given to the new scientists who joined the Los Alamos Project in the spring of 1941. This text, *The Los Alamos Primer*, carefully outlines all the details of atomic fissioning known to the world's most advanced scientists in the early forties. These and other documents have been declassified between 1954 and 1961 as a result of Eisenhower's Atoms for Peace program. The whole batch costs me about twenty-five dollars.

I gather the leaflets and documents together and take them over to the matronly bureaucrat at the front desk. She looks at the titles and then looks up at me.

"Oh, you want to build a bomb too?" she asks matter-of-factly. She looks like a Cub Scout den mother.

"Yeah, ah, it's just a research paper. In school."

"Well, have fun," she says, as if I were going off to earn my merit badge in bomb building. I pay her and leave.

I can't believe it. Do people go in there for bomb-building information every day? The more I think about it, the more it hits me: Joining the atomic mushroom club might be as easy as joining the Cub Scouts. With a little know-how, fifteen pounds of plutonium, and the right circumstances, I might just become part of some absurd worldwide nuclear jamboree.

On the bus, I look at one of the documents: *Manhattan District History, Project Y, The Los Alamos Project.* On the inside front cover I read the legal notice:

> *Neither the United States, nor the Commission, nor any person acting on behalf of the commission assumes any liabilities with respect to the use of, or for damages resulting from the use of any information, apparatus, method or process disclosed in this report.*

# 18
# Resigning from the Ifida Club

When I return to Princeton, I have a short meeting with Freeman Dyson. He asks about my progress. I show him the documents I've brought back from Washington. He takes them from me very casually, the way an oblivious parent might ask a child, "What did you find when you were playing in the woods, dear?" and then suddenly realize he has a live snake in his hands.

"Good Lord," says Freeman. "Where did you get these?"

"At the National Technical Information Service."

He inspects them very closely. His face is a study in disbelief. "I was sure this kind of information was still classified."

"It only cost me twenty-five bucks."

"Good Lord," he says again.

I tell him about the den mother lady at the desk and what she said. He shakes his head, takes off his spectacles, and wipes them clean. "Well, all I can say is you've done some pretty good detective work, John. From now on you'll be on your own." He pauses for a moment and pats the documents. "These will help you far more than I can. I'll be expecting your design in five weeks."

"Do you think I have a good chance?"

"Let's just say I'll be expecting your design. Good luck."

When Freeman leaves he is visibly shaken. He has this distant, glazed look in his eyes, somewhere between shock and fright.

His reaction to the documents can only mean one thing: With them in hand, he must figure that I actually stand a chance of coming up with a workable design. The preposterous assumption that a college student could design an atomic bomb might well be plausible.

The whole project is no longer a game. Up to now, my work has just been the mechanical exercise of digging up declassified information and grasping the general principles of nuclear physics. From here on in, I'll be designing an atomic bomb that will fit into a car trunk and have the potential to wipe out a quarter of Manhattan.

I believe that there are very special moments in everyone's life. Call them turning points, golden opportunities, or watersheds. They come without warning when you least expect them. When one comes along, you have to recognize it and seize the opportunity as if it were your last chance on Earth. Because if you let it slip by, the next one may be years away.

There are thousands of people who belong to the Ifida Club. The older they get, the more you hear them say, "If I'd a done this, and if only I'd a done that . . ." It does them no good to say so; it only makes them more frustrated with themselves. The point is not to regret what you haven't done, but to do it when you have the chance.

Having witnessed the look in Freeman's eyes, I know I'm going to do it. The only question is: how?

# 19
# Joining the Mushroom Club

When the average layman—let's say an usher in Radio City Music Hall—contemplates an atomic bomb, he probably thinks about a complicated scientific process created by a "genius." If this usher were to see a movie showing the explosion of the Hiroshima bomb, he might well stand in awe of the incredible power of the bomb, but he would probably not relate the enormous mushroom cloud on the screen to his own life or his own understanding. It probably would seem too distant, too inaccessible. Like so many others, this usher wouldn't appreciate how relatively simple the concept of an atomic bomb really is.

The material necessary to explode my bomb is plutonium 239, a man-made substance. It is the same element that was used in the bomb which destroyed Nagasaki in World War II. The reason why I must use plutonium—as opposed to, say, lead—is because plutonium is a heavy and *unstable* element: Its atomic structure is constantly changing. The best way to understand the instability of plutonium is to imagine a cliff by the side of a highway where the rocks are crumbling and occasionally falling, thereby dislodging other rocks. The constant decay of the cliff in time haphazardly breaks the rock formations apart, causing the cliff to be unstable. If a runaway avalanche were induced on the cliff by the use of explosives, the energy of the rocks falling would represent the action of plutonium atoms being split apart in the runaway chain reaction of an atomic bomb.

Visualize an atomic bomb as a marble inside a grapefruit inside a basketball inside a beachball. At the center of the bomb is the initiator, a marble-sized piece of metal. Around the initiator is a grapefruit-sized ball of plutonium 239. Wrapped around the plutonium is a three-inch reflector shield made of beryllium. High explosives shaped as breastlike lenses are placed in a symmetrical order around the beryllium shield. Wires are attached to each lens and each wire runs to an electrical source. By the time the lenses and wires have been installed, the bomb is about the size of a beachball.

When the electrical current runs through the wires to the lenses, an explosion is triggered. Because of the symmetrical nature of the placement of the explosives, a spherically imploding shock wave is set off, instantly squeezing the beryllium, plutonium, and initiator. The beryllium shield is pushed inward by the explosion, compressing the grapefruit-sized ball of plutonium to the size of a plum. The plutonium has now gone from a subcritical to a supercritical density, and the initiator at the center has been similarly squeezed. At this moment, the process of atoms fissioning—or splitting apart— begins.

Neutrons released from the initiator strike the plutonium atoms at an extremely fast rate. Each time a neutron hits a plutonium atom, the atom splits, creating two more neutrons, which in turn hit two more atoms, which split into four neutrons, which find four new atoms, thus splitting into eight neutrons, sixteen, thirty-two, sixty-four, one hundred and twenty-eight, two hundred and fifty-six, and so on. This tremendously fast splitting process is called a runaway chain reaction. If this does not occur with precise timing, the bomb will not explode with superior force. Each time an atom is split, a terrific amount of energy is released along with a variety of lethal atomic particles. The sum total of all atoms splitting in the chain reaction creates the atomic fireball which rises into the sky as a great mushroom-cloud energy release. This energy is comprised of heat waves, shock waves, and lethal atomic particles that are exploded outward across the countryside.

There are many subtleties involved in the explosion of an atomic bomb. Most of them center around the actual detonation of the explosives surrounding the beryllium shield. Normally, only a very small fraction of the plutonium has a chance to fission before the bomb assembly is blown apart by the energy released from the atoms already split. For this reason, the size of the final mushroom cloud explosion depends upon how long the chain reaction of splitting atoms can be sustained. The timing and efficiency of the chain reaction is in turn determined by the specific arrangement of the explosives surrounding the plutonium.

The grouping of these explosives around the plutonium is one of the most highly classified aspects of the atomic bomb, and the area around which the most intense postwar espionage was centered. (Julius and Ethel Rosenberg were executed in 1953 allegedly for passing this secret to the Russians.) In the bombs exploded over Hiroshima and Nagasaki, TNT was the explosive used to set off the chain reaction. But since that time, the U.S. Army has designed more sophisticated and efficient explosives to do the job. How to arrange the explosives and which explosives to use pose the biggest problems for me as I begin to design my bomb. The correct arrangement around the plutonium is the critical factor without which my design will be worthless.

My base of operations is a small room on the second floor of Ivy Club. The large conference table in the center of the room is covered with my books, calculators, design paper, notes, and the ever-cranky Capitalist Pig. My sleeping bag is rolled out on the floor. The ashtrays are full. As the next three weeks go by, I stop going to classes altogether. I work all day and all night in the room. My progress is slow at first. I pretend not to listen to the noise coming from the other rooms in the club. Sometimes I find myself in a trance, staring out at the first buds on the magnolia trees beyond the leaded windows. I drink coffee from a thermos, and when I feel drowsy I go downstairs to the kitchen to refill the thermos. I stop eating at regular meals, taking only a bologna sandwich when I'm hungry. The other members at Ivy begin referring to me as the Hobo because of my unshaven face and disheveled appearance. I develop a terrible case of bloodshot eyes.

Sleep comes rarely.

I devise several mind-sets that help me solve some of the problems I come up against. In my work (and even in my dreams now), I place myself in the position of a terrorist. I approach every problem from a terrorist's point of view. The bomb must be inexpensive to construct, simple in design, and small enough to sit unnoticed in the trunk of a car or abandoned U-Haul trailer.

At other times, I put myself in the shoes of the Los Alamos scientists working on the first bombs. By closely following the technical accounts of their progress which I bought in Washington, I design the bomb as they did, working on each component separately, one at a time. But the one terrific advantage I share with the nations which developed the bomb after the United States is that I know it can be done. The scientists at Los Alamos were not sure that such a bomb would be successful until after the first Alamogordo test. Furthermore, according to *The Curve of Binding Energy*, every bomb that has been designed and built since 1945 has worked on the first try.

\* \* \*

As the days and nights flow by, linked together by the cups of coffee, I learn how to scan the government documents looking for gaps and omissions which indicate an area of knowledge that is still classified. Essentially what I am doing is putting together a huge jigsaw puzzle that has already been completed before. But pieces are still missing. The edge pieces are in place and various areas of the puzzle are slowly getting filled in. Whenever the outline of a missing piece shows up, I fill my coffee thermos and sit down to devise the solution that will fill the gap.

With only two weeks left, the puzzle is nearly complete. There are only two missing pieces: which explosives to use, and how to arrange them around the plutonium. The proper functioning of this aspect of the design continues to elude me. I begin to wonder if I'll be able to finish in time. I sleep less, drink more coffee, and leave the room only when I have a Triangle rehearsal. My eyes begin to feel like bowling balls.

# 20
## Stepping Out

The opening of the Triangle show and the day my project is due will ironically fall on the same date. Rehearsals are becoming more intense. The tech crew is rushing to finish the sets in the basement of McCarter, and the professional costumer is putting the finishing touches on our outlandish kickline costumes. Most of the cast has given up going to classes. Between numbers they slouch in chairs and sleep in the aisles of the theater. Camaraderie prevails around stale doughnuts and shared cans of soda.

# MUSHROOM

Because of my erratic work schedule, I arrive late at every rehearsal and consequently suffer the wrath of not only the stage manager but also Milton, who is maintaining a hawk-eyed lookout for any error I might make. And I continue to pull the most outrageous bloopers on stage. During one song-and-dance number called "Spats" I will often begin thinking about some problem I'm having with the bomb and then won't realize until it's too late that I was supposed to be off stage six beats ago. I keep telling myself to concentrate on the number, but it doesn't work. Trying to figure out how the Los Alamos scientists created a perfectly symmetrical imploding shock wave is more important than "Spats" at this point. The whole cast, except David, who knows about the bomb, thinks that I'm permanently out to lunch. I am dubbed the cast "airhead."

On the night when we are supposed to do the first rehearsal run-through of the entire show, I almost forget about going to the theater. I get so involved with my work on the bomb that I don't look at my watch. When I discover that I'm over an hour late, I run like a madman across campus to McCarter, dashing in through the stage door. A musical number in the second act is just starting up. I recognize a familiar cue and follow a group of people out on stage.

I am blinded by the sudden change going from darkness into light. Everyone begins singing, and I suddenly realize that I'm not supposed to be in this number. Surrounded by two groups of dancers moving in opposite circles to my right and left, I start easing off stage. Everyone is looking at me with a bemused expression as if to say, "The poor airhead, he's fouling up again." I see David soft-shoeing his way over to me. He grins and whispers, "If it isn't Oscar Wilde making a total fool of himself . . ."

David has begun calling me Oscar Wilde in honor of Dr. Ernest Lawrence, one of the scientists at Los Alamos, who was assigned the code name Oscar Wilde.

When the run-through is over, the cast gathers on stage

for notes. Milton hurries down the aisle with his clipboard. He does not look pleased. I can see his chest heaving beneath his fishnet T-shirt. Milton silences the cast with a karate chop to the air. He taps his clipboard with a pencil over and over again, tum-ta-ta, tum-ta-ta, looking at all of us on stage. He doesn't say a word until he finally sees me.

"Well?" he says, arching his eyebrows. He seems to expect me to say something.

"What?" I ask.

"I'd like to find out *exactly* what motivated you to join the election march in the second act."

"Nothing. I'm sorry. I wasn't thinking."

"You weren't thinking," he says in a minty voice. "Wrong, Phillips. You were *late*." His eyes spit sparks. There's no getting off the hook this time. "Can you tell me why you were late?" he continues.

"I was working. I'm sorry."

"Sorry? *We* have a show to put on. Everyone else has work to do, but everyone else managed to get here on time."

For a second I'm tempted to say, "Yeah, but no one else is designing an atomic bomb." But I keep quiet. Finally Milton goes on to someone else. David leans over and imitates Milton's voice, "*Every*one else managed to hand in their little bombs on time. Where's *yours*, Oscar?"

# 21

# The Fashion of My Topic Boat

The atomic bomb was the biggest surprise of World War II because it was "America's best-kept secret." The Counter-Intelligence Corps of the Manhattan District, which saw to it that the secret was kept, left evidence of their precautions in the documents I brought back from Washington. Code names for the various parts of the bomb include: "top" for atom, "topic" for atomic, "boat" for bomb, "fashion" for fission, "topic boat" for atomic bomb. Hence, if a scientist at Los Alamos were looking at my unfinished design and had to send a coded message regarding my progress, he would SAY: "TOPIC BOAT OF OSCAR WILDE NOT YET FOUND SUCCESS IN HIGH FASHION."

This would tell the recipient that I hadn't yet devised a method for imploding the plutonium to create a fast-fissioning chain reaction to set off the explosion. During the middle of the week, I read in one of the documents that a high-explosive blanket around the beryllium shield might work. But after spending an entire night calculating, I conclude that wrapping the bomb in an explosive blanket is not enough to guarantee a successful implosion wave. The yield would probably be sub-kiloton, which would be sufficient, but I would like to improve on it. The early morning light is harsh in the room. I decide to put aside the problem of arranging the explosives for a while. The question of which goddamn explosives to use begins nagging me. The growing light goads me. I feel my topic boat sinking slowly. Coffee, more coffee.

I come down with a mild case of the screaming rhubarbs.

I have virtually given up eating and sleeping. With seven days before the design is due, I'm still deadlocked on the implosion problem. I've gone through every document from Washington at least a dozen times. No clues. I spend hours in the engineering library poring over sheet after sheet of microfiche. A headache turns me cold in the afternoon. I begin guessing wildly. Nothing seems to work.

Even if I come up with the answer at this point, I am skeptical whether I can finish in time. Before I hand in the paper, I will have to draw the design on countless pages of graph paper, showing each component of the bomb from several angles. I also realize that more is at stake than just an atomic bomb design. With my month-long absence from my lectures and classes, I fully expect a repeat performance of my first semester report. Except now I'm on academic probation. If I flunk any courses, and if I don't get an A on my bomb project, I'll be leaving Princeton forever in June.

The alarm clock falls off the table and breaks. I take this as a sign to do something drastic. For a moment, I hesitate, but then I know it is the only thing to do. I start all over again at the beginning. Once again I try to piece it together step-by-step so I can view the problem from a different angle. Nothing new comes up right away. Occasionally I find errors in my old calculations and correct them. I don't sleep. Whenever I burp, I hear a long, hollow clanging in my ear.

I lose sense of time.

David appears in the room one afternoon sometime during the week. He looks different; more alive than usual. But then, I guess that he probably looks just the same as always, because my altered state of mind makes me perceive everyone as more alive than myself. I can barely talk, I'm so exhausted. He seems to sense that I want to stay quiet and save my energy.

He says, "Oscar, I brought you something."

"What is it?"

"Rhubarb pie. To remind you not to miss the show."

"You're a prince," I say as he slips back out the door. I feel too sick to eat the pie. Grouchy stomach. The bomb, *the bomb.*

# 22
## Satori in the Kickline

Triangle dress rehearsal. The line of hairy-legged chorus "girls," arms interlocked, sways first to the right, then to the left. Shuffle-step, *kick* . . . right foot, left foot . . . one, two, three, *kick* . . . right *kick*, left *kick* . . . So far so good. Even the red glitter high heels aren't bothering me too much. This is the first time we've done the kickline in full drag, and the rest of the cast is standing in the wings having a jolly old time laughing at us.

We are dressed in blue sequin bathing suits with enormous false tits, silver lamé tights, and tall headdresses made from red crepe which are supposed to resemble roses in bloom. When I was coming on stage before the number, I knew I was late, and in my rush I partially dislodged my headdress in the door frame. At the moment, it's falling over my right eye, bouncing up and down to the heady beat of the can-can music. I look at David, three rose headdresses and six foam rubber boobs over. He knits his eyebrows and smirks at me, as if to say, "Oscar, you better put your rose on right before Uncle Miltie catches you . . ."

Milton is standing somewhere out in the theater. I can feel his eyes on me. I try to pay attention to the sequence of steps, but my mind keeps returning to the implosion wave, the symmetry that has eluded me for so long. Step, *kick*, step, *kick*. Something in the lower periphery of my vision catches my eye. Damn! One of my rubber boobs has worked its way out of my bathing suit. It begins waving wildly across my chest, hanging on by an elastic cord. The hell with it. Can't stop the kickline for one haywire tit.

## Satori in the Kickline

Right-step, *kick* . . . left-step, *kick* . . . The high kicks are beginning. We surge toward the front of the stage, arms linked. The music builds and the line is finally kicking in unison. A dozen hairy, lamé right legs arch up into the brilliant light. The rest of the cast is shouting and clapping. The left legs follow upwards, each kick timed precisely, hitting the apex at the same moment. Wait a minute. The implosion wave. Might work. Could it? Yes! Have to try it. Step-*kick*, step. Yes, yes, the wave, *yes*!

When notes are over after rehearsal, I dash back to Ivy to test my new idea about the implosion wave. I run through a series of calculations, mathematically figuring the arrangement of the explosives around the plutonium. If my equations are correct, the implosion wave of my bomb might be just as effective in triggering a runaway chain-reaction fissioning as the bombs dropped on Hiroshima and Nagasaki. But I can't be sure until I know the exact nature of the explosives I will use. I plan to call the Du Pont Corporation chemical explosives division first thing in the morning. It's a gamble, but I may be able to get them to hint at which explosives would work best. If they give me even the smallest lead, I'll be able to figure out the rest by myself.

It is just after midnight by now. The project is due at the Physics Department by five o'clock in the afternoon. Seventeen hours. I'll have to stay up all night again to finish the final drawings and text. With a little luck and a cooperative Capitalist Pig, I might be able to finish by midafternoon, incorporating the new equations into the design. I hope like hell that the people at Du Pont will give me some minor shred of information to go on. Otherwise I'm finished.

I slide forward into the night. Mesmerized by Capitalist Pig's electric purr, I begin typing the text. The puzzle pieces fall into place. There is still some guesswork involved, but I'm on my way.

\* \* \*

By ten o'clock in the morning, I've progressed far enough in the final draft to know that if my new implosion wave equation is correct, and if Du Pont gives me some information, I will have a respectable atomic bomb design by five P.M. The bomb will be about the size of a beachball; small enough to fit in the trunk of a car. By my calculations, it could yield a nine-and-one-half-kiloton explosion. (The Hiroshima bomb, Little Boy, was thirteen kilotons.) In other words, my bomb could level the entire financial district of Manhattan . . . Wall Street! Incredible! In the past three weeks, I've become so immersed in the technical aspects of the bomb that I've neglected the human side. I've forgotten that what I'm designing is capable of killing hundreds of thousands of people.

An atomic bomb. A goddamn *A-bomb*.

# 23

# Oscar Wilde
# Makes a Phone Call

The moment of truth. This telephone call determines success or failure. Sitting in the pay phone at Ivy, I call a Mr. S. F. Graves, head of the chemical explosives division at Du Pont in Delaware. A secretary answers and puts me on hold. Then a voice: "Graves speaking."

"Hello, Mr. Graves. My name is John Phillips. I'm a student at Princeton University, doing work on an independent project in physics. I'd like to get some advice if that's possible."

"What can I do for you?" Graves sounds authoritative,

but willing to help. I imagine a lean man in his fifties, probably a family man, wearing a white laboratory coat with a small black pocket calculator slung from his hip.

"Well . . ." I stammer for a second, knowing that if I say right out that I'm designing an atomic bomb, I'll never find out what I need to know. "I'm doing some research on the shaping of explosive products which create a very high density in a spherically shaped metal."

"I see," he says.

"Can you suggest a Du Pont product that would fit in this category?" God, how obvious. Why don't you just say you want to implode Pu 239?

"Of course," he says, in a helpful manner, as if there were no question that Du Pont had such a product. "Let me see . . ." I don't get the feeling he suspects. But just to make sure, I decide to try a bluff, "One of my professors told me that a simple explosive blanket would work in the high-density situation."

"No, no. Your professor is quite wrong. Explosive blankets went out with the Stone Age. We do some of the chemical work for the U.S. Army nuclear division. We sell them ———— to do the job in their atomic bombs, which have a similar density problem to the one you're talking about."

"Oh really?" I do my best to sound sincerely naïve.

"Yes, that explosive has certain burning characteristics which are ideally suited to creating a spherically imploding shock wave. Perhaps that will help you, Mr. Phillips."

"Yes, yes it will. Thank you very much, sir."

"You're welcome."

I hang up the phone and let out a whoop. I haven't felt this good in weeks. I don't believe it. Mr. S. F. Graves of the Du Pont Corporation has just given me what I suspect is classified information. Does he divulge the ingredients of the United States Army's atomic bombs to everyone who calls on the phone? Incredible.

I go back upstairs to the typewriter. It looks as if my calculations are correct with respect to the new information. Now
all I have to do is type up the rest of the paper by five.

# 24
## My Topic Boat Sets Sail

Five minutes to five. I race over to the physics complex and
bound up the stairs three at a time. Inside the Physics Department office, a group of juniors are standing around congratulating one another on finishing their projects. When I come in,
everybody stops talking and stares at me. At first I don't get it,
but then I realize: I haven't shaved in over a week and I must
look pretty scuzzy.

"Phillips, what are you doing here?" says an old lab partner of mine. "Old Man Henderson told me you flunked his
course last semester. We thought for sure you'd been bounced
out of the department."

"Are you still in school?" asks another guy.

"What does it look like?" I say.

"Is your razor broken, young man?" asks Mrs. Herring,
the departmental secretary. She is the classic, starchy, hatchet-
faced, old woman of an Ivy league institution.

"I came to hand in my project. I didn't have time to shave.
Sorry."

"Is that so?" She gives me her glacial look.

"I wanted to get here right on time."

"Yes," she says, giving me another icy look.

I walk over to her desk where the box for junior papers
is sitting. I glance over the fastidiously bound discourses of the
other students, which analyze such fascinating and contro-

versial subjects as "The Behavior of Cooled Helium" and "A Better Way of Proving Coulomb's Law." I put my thirty-four-page report, now titled, "An Assessment of the Problems and Possibilities Confronting a Terrorist Group or Non-Nuclear Nation Attempting to Design a Crude $Pu^{239}$ Fission Bomb," at the bottom of the pile, hoping to obscure the title from the other students.

All of a sudden, I feel extraordinarily lightheaded. The pressure that has built up in me because of the bomb snaps loose, and suddenly everything strikes me as wacky. *And* the secretary, who is looking at me the way a nurse might look at a very sick patient. Wild! I bow very deeply in front of her and with a crisp British accent, I say, "The Knight of the Prickly Chin bids Lady Starched Bottom adieu . . ."

I don't know where that came from, but it just about kills the other juniors who are standing around gawking at me. Lady Starched Bottom doesn't know what the hell is going on, and for that matter, neither do I. It's just one of those times when the impulsive side of me takes over. As I'm heading for the door, I hear one of the juniors say something about "Phillips flipping out." (One thing about human nature: When people expect you to act crazy, you do.) I execute a pirouette and then tap-dance out the door. The juniors start cackling away. Someone lets out a hoot. My own laughter propels me down the stairs on a short circuit of hysteria.

That night is the opening of the Triangle show. The giddy mood of the afternoon stays with me all the way over to the theater. But inside the atmosphere is grim. Walking to the dressing room I share with David on the second floor, I say hello to several jittery-looking cast members. Some people nervously shuffle through a routine. Others smear on makeup. Milton is nowhere to be seen.

Waiting in the wings for the kickline cue during the first act is excruciating. Dressed in our costumes, David and I sit on a piece of scenery backstage, sharing a beer. We can hear the laughter and applause of the audience. The sequins dig into my skin. I tell David all the details of handing in the paper to Lady Starched Bottom and about the guys in the department who thought I'd flunked out, and we have a rollicking laugh about that.

"Sometimes you slay me, Oscar," says David. "I know exactly who Lady Starched Bottom is. I met her my first day when I was signing up for beginning physics."

"*You* took physics?"

"No, but that's beside the point. Do you think it's really going to work?"

"What?"

"The bomb. Could it really explode?"

"I don't know. I'll find out soon enough."

"And if it doesn't?"

"I guess I'll flunk out of here."

"You can't."

"Why not?"

"Because we're going into business next year. We're going to become millionaires by starting a pizza delivery service," he says.

"You're crazy."

"So are you. That's why we're going to do it."

"David, sometimes *you* slay me."

We hear the cue for the kickline. All twelve of us crouch together behind a small curtain upstage. We each hold a small rose to throw out to the audience. In our crouch positions, with our headdresses pointing out, all the audience will see when the small curtain opens is a quivering bouquet of red crepe roses. The music builds. The curtain opens. A small murmur goes up when they see the bouquet.

We are led downstage like girls in a beauty contest, mincing and smiling ghoulishly. Whenever the Triangle kickline starts, half the audience, being Princeton students or alumni,

114

knows what's going on. This half starts laughing right away, and when the other half sees that we're men in drag, a tremendous howl goes up. I see my mother in the fourth row and throw her my rose. Bessie catches it. We launch into the routine.

By the middle of the number, the audience is really rocking. Whistles and catcalls hit the stage. I hear a few guys from Ivy yell something about my legs. The kickline is much more fun to do in performance than in rehearsal because even the smallest mincing twitch brings on storms of laughter. But it's the shock on people's faces that is so interesting to watch. When we link arms and start into the high kicks the noise in the theater is tremendous. The music rocks on.

Da-da-da-dadada-boom-*kick*. Doo-doo-doo-dee-dee-da-da-boom-*kick*. The applause builds and crashes. My adrenaline is running triple speed, and I'm kicking higher than I ever did in rehearsal. So high in fact, that near the end of the number, one of my red glitter shoes sails off into the audience, shimmering briefly under the lights. This brings down the house. The audience begins stomping for more shoes, so I kick off the other, and then a full-blown high heel shoe epidemic sets in. One by one, each of our shoes wings out into the house in time to the music. Finally, the first act curtain falls.

Behind the curtain, we're all laughing and yelling congratulations and pounding each other on the back. I look over and see David rolling on the stage floor, convulsed with laughter. The kickline was funny, but David looks like he's ready to go home to Jerome.

"What's the scoop?" I ask him.

He can hardly breathe, but he manages to say, "You mean you didn't see her?"

"Who? My mother?"

This strikes him as even funnier and he's off again. "No, no," he shrieks. Pulling himself together, he stands up. "Come here, quick," he says, leading me over to the edge of the curtain at stage right. He opens it a crack. The intermission lights are on in the theater. David pushes my head up to the curtain. "Look in the eighth row on the left . . . four seats in." Most of the audience has gone up the aisles. I look to the left, and there she is! I start laughing uncontrollably. Lady Starched Bottom is sitting very primly in her seat, holding onto her pocketbook, looking as if she's just seen an atomic mushroom cloud.

The show rocks on.

# 25
## Coming About

A week later, I return to the Physics Department to pick up my project. Only this time I'm not racing up the stairs. Tired and hung over from five performances of Triangle and the endless after-show parties, not to mention the weeks of work on the bomb, my brain feels like melted butter. My body feels like an unmade bed. Also, one thought persists in my mind: If I didn't guess correctly about the implosion wave, or if I made a mistake somewhere in the graphs, I'll be royally screwed.

When I get to the departmental office, Lady Starched Bottom isn't there. Another secretary points to the box where the graded papers are. I flip through the stack quickly, occasionally sneaking a look at the grade on someone else's paper. Somehow, I must have skipped mine. This time, I pick through the pile more cautiously, looking at each paper one by one. My insides do a roller-coaster dip when I get to the bottom of the box and I still can't find my paper. I go through them once again. It is a fact. My paper is not there.

Trying to remain calm, I ask the secretary if all the papers have been graded.

"Yes, of course," she says. "They were returned to the office yesterday morning at nine o'clock." She has one of those irritating telephone operator voices, saying "nine" as if it were "ny-un."

"I see. You're sure there aren't any missing?"

"They are all there in the box."

"Oh."

"Would you like to make an appointment with the chairman of the department? Perhaps he can tell you what happened."

"I guess I'm going to have to."

Slowly, because there is no hurry anymore, I make my way back to 42 Little. The absence of my paper can only mean that I blew it somewhere. Dyson is probably holding on to it so that he can spare me the embarrassment of finding an F on it in the departmental secretary's office. It's all over. Flunked out of the Big U. Damn, damn, damn. And I was even beginning to look forward to coming back to Old Nausea next fall to start up the pizza business with David. It'll be the first time two friends have said good-bye to each other because one of them couldn't build an atomic bomb.

I can already see the look on my mother's face. Old Bessie is going to hit the roof. I should have known all along that any attempt by a twenty-year-old to design an A-bomb would be doomed to failure. After all, it took the most brilliant minds in the world to design one at Los Alamos.

The closer to 42 Little I walk, the gloomier I become. I'm too depressed even to have a case of the screaming rhubarbs. The party is over.

# 26
## Praise from Allah

Ever since I bought my motorcycle, I've used it under many circumstances. I've made a three-thousand-mile cross-country trip on it from Berkeley to Princeton and have driven it in all kinds of weather. When it was stolen in January, the Princeton police found it with a slashed tire behind a dry-cleaning store in town. After owning it for two years, I've discovered that the best time to ride is when I'm depressed, angry, or frustrated. Which just about sums up my mood at the moment. I spend the next couple of days roaring around the back roads of Princeton on the Honda.

I burn rubber marks on the road. I race through long fields of brown grass, leaving parabolic curves imprinted on the soil. I ride without a helmet or shirt, letting the soft spring air pummel my body. There are times when I surprise myself with a burst of giggles. The speed intoxicates me. I shift the gears, gunning the engine, pushing the bike faster, faster, higher, and higher until the passing countryside is just a light green whirl. The engine sings. I never stop, never slow down. The danger and the speed let me forget.

In the middle of the week, I go to the Physics Department office, hoping to catch the chairman for a few minutes. It's just possible that I can convince him to write a recommendation for me to use when applying to another university which will explain that I at least tried to design a bomb. F for performance, A for effort. That sort of thing.

I step from the hallway into the office and see Lady Starched Bottom crouched over a file cabinet in the rear of the office. I clear my throat and prepare for the inevitable tirade, what with the tap-dancing out the door and all. She looks up quickly, returns to her file, and then freezes. Slowly, her head turns back in my direction. The look she gives me is neither friendly or angry. She is incredulous. She gets up from the file cabinet and looks around furtively, as if someone were about to come into the office any second. Then she stares at me. Her mouth opens, but no words come out.

"Aren't you John Aristotle Phillips?" she asks in a very soft, almost meek voice that doesn't sound like her own.

"Yes, I wondered if the chairman is around. I'd like to speak with him for a minute."

Lady Starched Bottom seems incapable of uttering another sound. I begin to feel sorry for her. If I'd known that tap-dancing in her office would cause such a catatonic state, I wouldn't have done it. Finally, I break the silence, "Listen, I'm sorry about the other day. The work kind of got to me." She doesn't respond. "But I was wondering if I could get my paper back. It wasn't here the last time I came in. It's the one about the bomb."

"Aren't you the boy who designed the atomic bomb?" she asks, as if she hasn't heard a word of what I've just said.

"Yes, and my paper wasn't here . . ." She is looking at me very sternly. I figure she wants some kind of explanation about my performance in my other physics classes. "I know about flunking," I explain, "but I just didn't have time for everything."

The stern look turns into a funny, cockeyed, suspicious glare. Something is going on, but apparently I'm not supposed to get it. "You are John Phillips, are you not?" she asks.

"Yes. I don't understand."

She takes a deep breath. "The question has been raised by the department whether your paper should be classified by the United States government."

"What? Who's being classified?"

# MUSHROOM

Lady Starched Bottom smiles for the first time. For a second she looks almost relieved. "Yes, it's quite a surprise to all of us. I'm sorry I didn't tell you just now, when you first came in, but I wanted to be sure it was really you."

"You mean I passed? I didn't flunk?"

"Yes, of course. Didn't you know? Oh my!" She pauses, wringing her hands. "Hasn't anyone told you?"

"No, what? *What?*"

"You got the only A in the department."

"Oh my god."

Lady Starched Bottom comes out from behind the desk now and takes my limp hand, shaking it vigorously. "Congratulations," she says, all smiles. "Congratulations. Isn't it funny that you didn't know?"

"Yes, isn't it?" Now *I* can barely speak.

"Dr. Wigner wants to see you right away. He says it's a fine piece of work." Then she whispers, "And that's like praise from Allah, you know."

"Praise from Allah?" I mutter, remembering that Dr. Wigner is an eminent Nobel Prize-winning physicist.

"Yes," she says, really having a time of it now. "And Dr. Dyson has been looking for you everywhere. Your roommates didn't know where you were."

"I was out riding my motorcycle."

"That's very dangerous, isn't it?" She sounds playful. "We wouldn't want the star of our Physics Department getting hurt, would we?"

Star? Getting hurt? The whole conversation is beginning to take on an unreal quality. Crazy!

"There's going to be a reception in the Physics Department this afternoon and we're hoping you can come."

For a second I don't say anything. I'm trying to figure out if there's something I've missed in the conversation. I put it on rewind: Classified? A? Star of the department? Incredible. All at once the irony of the whole situation hits me. A small air bubble of giddiness rises in my throat. Here I was on my way to flunking out, ready to snivel up a good excuse so the chairman would write me a recommendation, and then suddenly I'm the star of the department. Lady Starched Bottom has gone back behind the desk and is looking for something hidden in a file drawer. She pulls out a pack of Salem 100s and offers me one.

"I think a little celebration is in order," she says.

She winks, and then I know I'm finally going home to Jerome with the screaming rhubarbs in tow.

# 27

# Heading Downwind

When school is over in June, I fly out to Mountain View, California. Dr. Gerard K. O'Neill, a physics professor at Princeton who is not Allah but a mighty deity nonetheless, has invited me to participate in the NASA Space Colonies Summer Study at the NASA Research Center. Dr. O'Neill is a visionary thinker with a fantastic dream of seeing tens of thousands of people living, eating, sleeping, and working in colonies in outer space. Whether or not such a thing ever transpires in my lifetime, I will never forget the genius of Dr. O'Neill and the dream to which he has dedicated his life.

On Friday evenings throughout the summer, O'Neill has a barbeque-swim party at his house. The guests can usually be grouped into two categories. There are the older men: NASA personnel, engineering types, family men with wives and children. They remember the excitement of working on the Apollo program as young men during the sixties. Now they look to

Dr. O'Neill and his space colonization dream as a means of rekindling that excitement.

Then there are the half-dozen students such as myself who were handpicked by Dr. O'Neill during his lecture tour around the country. We consider ourselves the Fortunate Few. Our first assignment is to design the cooling system for a lunar habitat projected for use in 2020. We work like ants in the laboratory, slowly solving the problems of the habitat. There is some competition among the ants, but for the most part, it is good-natured and productive.

The only bone I have to pick with my fellow ants relates to a matter on which I stand virtually alone. This may not be a very popular thing to say, but I hate *Star Trek*. I loathe it, detest it. I abhor Captain Kirk, and Spock makes me nervous. Worst of all though are the "Trekkies," as the fans of the show like to be known. I'm told that they number in the thousands and hold annual Trekkie conventions where everybody shows up wearing plastic replicas of those pointy little Spock ears. But the only real gripe I have is about the time when *Star Trek* is aired every day. For three years, I've been doing fierce battle with Trekkies in TV rooms from Berkeley fraternities to Princeton eating clubs, trying to get the channel switched to my beloved *CBS Evening News* with Walter Cronkite. It's a losing battle. The Trekkies always outnumber the Cronkkies.

I've watched Walter for years—through the Kennedy assassinations, the Vietnam War, the Apollo launchings, the Nixon nightmare—and whenever Walter reports an event, he makes it *real*. For me, Walter is the voice of reality. If he told me that Gerald Ford was holding a Trekkie convention at the White House, I'd believe him. I really would.

The one person at the summer study who understands my dislike of Trekkies is Frank Chilton. Physically, intellectually, and emotionally, Frank Chilton is a big man. He stands six and a half feet tall. He must weigh close to three hundred pounds. Yet there is not an ounce of fat on his body because he plays soccer incessantly. When Frank was a student at the University of Chicago, he was known around the physics department as a wonder boy. His professors were so impressed by his genius and independence that they granted him his graduate degree before he completed the usual course of study. Frank has been at various times an inventor, a soccer coach, a nuclear explosions expert for the Navy, a pioneer in the field of advanced interurban mass transit technology, a gastronome, a father, and a husband. I get to know Frank and his wife, Janet, a psychiatric social worker, quite well.

On one Friday night, after a particularly intense week working on the lunar habitat, I go to the barbeque in Gerry O'Neill's backyard. I have just completed the circuit past the food table and my plate is stacked with burgers and Coors beer. As I make my way around the edge of the pool, I scan the available clusters of lawn chairs. I'm looking for a seat where I won't have to listen to another interminable *Star Trek* trivia discussion. I spot Frank and Janet at a picnic table in the corner of the yard. Frank waves.

"We were saving a seat for you," says Frank, making a place for me.

"No *Star Trek* people allowed at this table," Janet adds, smiling.

"I guess that explains why we're sitting by ourselves," I remark, sitting down.

I ask Janet to pass me the ketchup and we start eating. Frank looks at me over his burger.

"Gerry O'Neill told me today that you designed an atomic bomb at Princeton this past spring."

"Yeah."

"Why didn't you tell me?" he asks.

"Well, I haven't thought about it much lately. You're the first person who's brought it up since I left Princeton."

Actually, I've almost forgotten about it. The combination of becoming immersed in the space colonies project and getting away from Princeton with the daily references to Oscar Wilde by David has made the bomb seem distant. Frank's interest surprises me.

"Why did you do it?" asks Janet.

"I don't know. Just seemed like the thing to do, I guess."

"No, come on," she says. "Tell us the truth."

"Well, I guess it was to prove that if an average undergraduate could do it, so could an average terrorist group."

"That's a good point," says Janet.

"Where's your paper now?" asks Frank. He is very serious and businesslike all of a sudden.

"The Physics Department at Princeton said the government was going to classify certain sections of it."

"No kidding?" says Janet,

There is a long pause in the conversation. They both seem to be thinking about something.

"You've worked with atomic bombs, haven't you, Frank?" I ask.

"Yes. Yes, I have. I was a nuclear explosions consultant to the Navy for several years." Frank stops, thinks. "Do you know if your bomb would work?"

"No, but my professors were pretty impressed. And the government—"

"Can you tell me what sort of material you used to create the imploding shock wave?"

"I don't think I'm supposed to tell anyone, but I guess if you have security clearance, you already know."

"Of course I know," he says. "I was wondering if you knew."

"I do."

"How did you find out what it was?"

"I made an educated guess at the most obvious material and its design arrangement, and then, well, you're not going to believe this, but I gave the chemical explosives division at Du Pont a call, and a man there told me the specific product name that Du Pont sells to the U.S. Army for their atom bombs."

"Wow," says Janet.

"That's amazing," says Frank. "What did they tell you they use?"

"Come on, Frank." Janet chides him, elbowing his ribs. "He told you he's not supposed to say."

Frank looks her in the eye and smiles. Janet returns the smile, fakes a sigh, and goes over to the barbeque.

"Can you tell me?" says Frank when she is gone.

"How about if you hint at it, and I answer yes or no?" I ask.

"Fair enough," he says and then makes an oblique reference to something the man at Du Pont told me.

"Yes, absolutely."

Frank looks down at the paper plate and shakes his head. He looks spooked. "Amazing," he says again. "Just amazing. How could they tell you that over the telephone?"

"I don't know. I just called them up and asked."

"Amazing."

I'm beginning to feel almost guilty for knowing. "Do you think my bomb would have a fair chance of exploding if I built it?"

"I can't say for sure without seeing the entire design, but let's just say that with what you know, it would have a very good chance of working."

"Awesome."

"Awesome is right," he says, leaning back on the bench and looking up into the twilight summer sky, as if searching to see the ghost of a towering mushroom cloud.

# Part 3

GC + Pimp → Personality =  Whoopee

*"Toto, I have the feeling we're not in Kansas anymore . . ."*
—**Dorothy**

# 28

## Going Back to Nausea Hall

Going back—going back,
Go-ing-back-to-Nas-sau-Hall,
Going back—going back
To-the-best-damn-place-of-all.
Going back—going back,
From-all-this-earth-ly-ball,
We'll-clear-the-track-as-we-go-back,
Go-ing-back-to-Nas-sau-Hall.

I can already hear the song coming from a courtyard as I drive down University Place in the September afternoon sunlight. One thing about Princeton: They won't let you forget what you're coming back to. Not for one second. I am in town for two minutes and it is already rah! rah! and all that jazz. I see groups of returning students parading up and down University Place, looking relaxed and full of themselves, singing and clapping each other on the back, and drinking beer from the ubiquitous orange-and-black mugs. Freshmen are clearly recognizable because they are trying too hard to look confident. Individually, or in small clusters, they wander aimlessly about, clutching sheaves of papers intended to orient them to the campus. They would soon learn that all you do during your first week at Princeton is orient yourself to the inside of a beer mug.

I park in front of my new dormitory right across from McCarter Theater where the Triangle show had been put on the spring before. Opening night seems like yesterday. As I'm unpacking the car, I look up and see David sauntering down the street. David has spent the summer living in New York, writing pieces for *The Paris Review*, a literary quarterly edited by George Plimpton. In August, we stayed for a week at David's summer house in Provincetown on Cape Cod. We'd had a fine time fishing, eating huge lobster dinners, and playing poker.

David and I had long talks at the Café Blasé in town. We were getting closer then, finding out more about one another. During our first year at Princeton, our friendship had existed on an easygoing humorous level. We loved bouncing one-liners off each other. But behind the one-liners there was a growing understanding, an unspoken trust that managed to get us through the ups and downs of that year.

It is good to see David walking down University Place. He always adds another dimension to Princeton. But I'm not anxious for the round of jokes to begin. You see, I had made a weak attempt at growing a beard in California, and then shaved it off after taking verbal abuse from David every day in Provincetown. I have salvaged the mustache though. For some reason, I couldn't part with it.

David makes elaborate trumpeting sounds and beckons to me like some medieval courtier, "Ah, good fellows rally round! Oscar Wilde, the Knight of the Prickly Chin, has returned for yet another year of revelry and mirth!"

"I beseech you, good sire, helpeth me to take all this crapeth to my lodgings yonder."

"No problem," says David. "What's up?"

"Not much. Just pulled in."

"A-a-aah," says David, grinning. "I detect a rather malnourished spider growing above your upper lip."

"Oh shut up."

"Such a spindly little spider. Seems to be missing a few legs."

"Give me a break."

"Why, no—wait—can it be? Yes!" says David, looking at my mustache closely. "I do believe that spider of yours is wearing an orange-and-black sport coat and—wait—yes! He's got a little nameplate. It says: HAIRY FURBISH, PRINCETON SEVENTY-SEVEN. . . . Give 'em hell, Hairy."

Henceforth my mustache is known as Hairy Furbish '77.

We unload the car. My room is on the fourth floor of the ultramodern Spelman Hall, the most popular dorm on campus. Each suite contains four single rooms, a kitchen, private bathroom, living room, and balcony. Only seniors have the opportunity to live in Spelman; consequently David and I won't be rooming together this year. I have three new roommates: Ralph Taylor, Worth D. MacMurray, both members of Ivy, and Peter Goundie, who belongs to Cottage. When picking a roommate, I look for two mandatory qualifications: a sense of humor, and courtesy. If these requirements are met, I would accept an orangutan as my roommate.

I know Ralph Taylor best of the three. He is at least as courteous as any primate I've met, and his wit has evolved well beyond the neanderthal stage. I got to know Ralph from countless pool games at Ivy, and our friendship is based on an amiable rivalry. I would wager bottles of wine from the Ivy wine cellar against his promise to introduce me to the prettiest girl on campus. Although I financed his alcoholic indulgences, I never got the promised introduction to Debbie Oliver, an attractive brunette in the Architecture School. But Ralph and I get along famously. We can't be together more than two minutes without finding something to laugh about. He enjoys life and always wears a big smile. After David, I feel closest to Ralph.

Mac, Worth, Worthless, or the more formal Worth D. MacMurray is an entirely different kind of person. Serious, bright, career-minded, Mac is intent on getting accepted by the best law schools. His unrelenting dedication to his goals leads him to be, by turns, charming and stubborn. You can't argue with Mac. You can cajole him, beseech him, yell at him, and insult him, but it won't do you any good. He is a born lawyer. I consider Mac a friend, but his guard, which he never lets down, prohibits me from getting very close to him.

Peter Goundie is entirely different. He is big, handsome, strong; the quintessential Cottage man who lifts weights in the bathroom, grunting and groaning until the veins pop out. Unlike Mac, Peter is unpolished. Although he is boisterous and jovial at all hours, he goes overboard to be considerate and polite. He is a "Princeton Man" and proud of it. But unlike Franz, he builds on the fact that he goes to Princeton rather than relies on it. Peter is an ardent capitalist who will someday become a captain of industry. But he is full of contradictions. He will stoutly defend the capitalist system while devouring a pizza delivered by my pizza delivery agency, and then refuse to pay because he says I am a greedy capitalist.

Actually, I shouldn't say "my" pizza agency. It was David's idea, and as the fall semester gets underway, we become join partners in the enterprise known around campus as Aristotle's Pizza Delivery Agency. But before I go any further, let me say a word about student agencies at Princeton.

They work like this: Say you have an idea for a product or service needed by students on campus. Let's use bubble-gum balls as an example. (There was, in fact, a student bubble-gum ball agency.) If you think there is sufficient demand for your product, you rush over to the Student Agencies office in West College and tell Bob Cunningham, Ralph DeMarco, or Mrs. Poole about your idea. As directors, their job is to insure that once you start selling bubble-gum balls, no other student on campus is allowed to compete with you. No matter how outrageously priced your balls are, there can be no competition from other students. This is Princeton's way of giving the future business leaders of America a working knowledge of the economic system. Once an agency is established, vendors from the town are likewise prohibited from selling that particular commodity on campus. There are about forty such monopolies at Princeton, selling everything from bagels to beer mugs.

When David and I go to see Bob Cunningham about a student pizza delivery agency, he shakes his head and says, "You can give it a try, but I honestly don't think there's any money in it. Some kids tried a couple of years ago and they lost their shirts."

"It's an impractical idea," says Ralph DeMarco, the leisure-suited assistant director, who spends most of his time seconding Bob Cunningham's expert opinions on the workings of a successful capitalist enterprise. The only person who likes the idea is Mrs. Poole, the secretary of the office, who confides that she herself loves pizza. David and I immediately dub her the Pizza Princess.

Despite repeated warnings that it is a stupid idea, David and I decide to make a go of it. We begin talking to a Greek named Stavros, who runs a joint on Nassau Street called the Parthenon. After a series of marathon negotiating sessions, we settle on an agreement. Stavros, his wife, Athena, his brother, Joe, and his assistant, Butch Brownell, will take students' telephone orders from nine P.M. to two A.M., make the pizzas, and sell them to us at a discount. We will hire drivers from the student employment office, who will deliver the pizzas to students' rooms on campus during alternating shifts.

We have no idea whether the operation is going to be successful because the logistics of timing vis-à-vis cooking, delivering, and selling are so precarious. There are a hundred details to check on. We set up a tight delivery schedule which Stavros ignores, saying he has a better system. It is painful to do business with Stavros because he always has "a better way." He is always sure that his is the right way. Also, he continually reiterates that he is doing us a big favor by selling us pizzas, completely ignoring the fact that the volume of his business will increase by fifty to a hundred pies a night. It is just his way of maintaining the upper hand.

Stavros' assistant, Butch, is our ally. He is aware of Stavros' sly tricks and becomes sympathetic to our cause. Butch is an aggressive young entrepreneur in his late twenties. He is sharp, and when we first meet him, we think he is trying to hustle us all the time. He has the eyes of a con man: fierce and friendly at the same moment. We like Butch because, despite his entrepreneurial obsessions, he is a warm person.

David and I devise a carefully plotted publicity campaign announcing the opening night of the pizza agency in the *Daily Princetonian*. Instead of hiring drivers for the first night, we decide to operate the delivery vans ourselves to see if our system will work. Mrs. Poole, the Pizza Princess, promises to buy a pepperoni-and-mushroom pie. Good for you, Mrs. Poole.

At nine P.M. sharp, the phone in the Parthenon begins ringing off the hook.

# 29
## The Mushroom with Extra Cheese

Breathless in bedlam. The phone never stops ringing. There are more telephone orders for pizzas to be delivered in the first hour of operation than we can possibly take care of in an entire evening. Stavros the Greek panics. He runs helter-skelter around the Parthenon shouting orders at everyone. There is no possible way to keep up with the volume of demand, but Stavros keeps taking new orders before the old ones have left the Parthenon. He smells money. There is no way to convince him that it would be better to sell fewer pizzas which would arrive hot and on time than hundreds of cold pies delivered two hours late.

The Greek rages. He screams at Butch to make pizzas faster. (He pronounces Butch as "Boots.") Cries of "Boots! Boots! Hurry!" fly across the counters, now littered with sausage coins and shards of cheese. The Greek's wife, Athena, is at the phone, but her understanding of the English language is limited. An order for a mushroom pizza turns into an order for sausages with extra mushrooms, and the address of delivery is invariably translated into Athena's own special language.

David and I are delivering the pizzas. We rush into the Parthenon, hot and sweaty, hours behind schedule. Thirty pizzas are waiting in cardboard boxes on top of the ovens. Each box is tagged with a receipt, identifying the pizza and where it is going. We look at the addresses before running back out to the van. I read one receipt that says, "1 saus, ex-ch, qk ck, 23 Leedle."

"What does this mean?" I ask Athena, showing her the check.

"Oh, seemple," she says. "One sausage pie wit ayxtra chiz and a quark of Coke."

"But what's the address?" I can feel the sweat drizzling down into my shirt.

"I dunno. Somewheres called Leedle Hall."

I look over at David, who is balancing fifteen pizzas and three quarts of Coke in his arms. "What do you s'pose Leedle Hall translates to?" I ask him.

"*Little* Hall, you fool." His voice is muffled by the boxes. "Come on, let's get out of here with these pies."

We grab the boxes and hurry out the door. Butch yells after us, "Don't forget the sodas!"

We charge out into the night. We've discovered that de-

135

livering thirty pies to all the different locations takes about an hour and a half. But on this run, all the receipts on the pizzas get mixed up in the back of the van. Customers who wanted pepperoni get mushrooms, and customers who wanted mushrooms get nothing.

"Where is that goddamn large mushroom with extra cheese?" I shout at David. We are both rummaging through the stack of pizza boxes.

"Hell if I know," says David. "I'm trying to find a medium anchovy and peppers."

"Some rugby player in Blair Tower was screaming at me about his mushroom pie. He said he was going to tear us apart if he doesn't get it within the hour."

"So give him a sausage instead."

"But he's big."

"So give him a big sausage."

"Very funny."

And so it goes on through the night. By twelve I'm ready to have a nice, quiet nervous breakdown. David has stayed at the Parthenon to make sure Stavros doesn't continue taking orders. I've just finished making a delivery to Witherspoon Hall (or as Athena has written on the receipt, "Widderspun Hill.") I check the pizza boxes to find out where my next delivery is. Five pies are missing. Someone must have stolen them when I was in Witherspoon. The bastards. I hope they choke on them. I turn the ignition key in the van: *sputter*, clunk. I turn it again: nothing. The gas gauge is merrily pointing at E. Jesus! I call the Parthenon to have David bring me some gas.

"David, you're never going to believe this."

"What? What?" he shouts. I can hear screaming and pizza pans clattering on his end of the connection.

"I ran out of gas."

"J.P., are you high? What do you mean you ran out of

gas? The Pizza Princess promised us that Student Agencies would fill it up."

"Never mind what they promised us, goddamnit. I tell you I'm out of gas."

"What? I can't hear you. There's too much noise in here."

"I said, we're screwed. There are twenty pizzas in the back of the truck getting cold and I'm already an hour behind schedule."

"Make that three hours behind," says David. "People are calling here every minute to ask where the bloody pizza they ordered two hours ago is."

"Well? Where is it?"

"Where is what?" shouts David.

"Their goddamn pizza."

"Sitting here on top of the oven. There are thirty-seven pizzas waiting to be delivered. Get your ass back here and pick them up."

"I ran out of gas, you idiot."

"That's right, I forgot. There're too many things going on in here."

"What're we going to do?" I ask him.

"I don't know. Cry?"

"What's going on at the Parthenon?"

"The Greek is screaming at Butch and Butch is screaming at me. Athena went home to take care of her baby, but Stavros keeps taking orders and promising them for a half-hour delivery. It's very simple, Oscar. It's all over."

"Whose idea was this goddamn agency anyway?"

"Don't blame me. You wanted your name on it," he says.

"I think I'm going to cry."

On that first night, we ended up giving away more pizzas than we sold. But by the end of the week we got the whole system straightened out. We had five students working for us every night, three as drivers and two to answer the phone. David was in charge of hiring and firing, and I ran the books. The Greek screamed a lot and Butch was the only one who did any work. We would sell seventy-five pizzas on a good night. As time went on, David and I made fewer and fewer visits to the Parthenon. It was the great capitalist system at work: We went to classes, wrote our papers, did our work, and the money just rolled in by itself.

From time to time I was reminded that there actually was an Aristotle's Pizza Delivery Agency out there making money for us. Late at night, when I was falling asleep, I would often hear the curses of an employee and the jingle of his coin changer as he jogged by my window, delivering a pizza somewhere in the darkness.

# 30
## The Tiger on the Unicycle

During the sixties, people joined mass movements to improve the world. In the seventies, we are joining mass movements to improve ourselves. Transcendental meditation, yoga, Erhard Seminars Training, and kung fu have replaced love-ins and antiwar demonstrations. Self-improvement is the kick. Or, as they say these days: "Getting your shit together is a mellow trip."

Over the summer, while I was working at NASA, I discovered that people in northern California get their shit together for a living. Having been curiously infected by this state of mind, I decided to improve myself also. I went out

## The Tiger on the Unicycle

and bought a unicycle. I'd never ridden a unicycle before, but I quickly learned how to maneuver it. By the end of the summer, I could hop on my unicycle, boogie over to the grocery store, buy my dinner, and then ride back with two bags of groceries in my arms. The northern Californians would stop their cars and honk their horns, as if they were approving the fact that I'd gotten my shit together. Maybe they just thought I was crazy.

You have to be a little crazy to ride a unicycle. After all, there's only one goddamn wheel that persists in shooting out from under you at every turn. Whenever I rode the unicycle around the Princeton campus that fall, I got into a crazy mood. I would ride it to and from all my classes. I rode circles around people walking on the paths. I raced dogs. The unicycle gave me this wacky, slapstick frame of mind. People who were already beginning to point me out as the Aristotle of Aristotle's Pizza Delivery laughed when they saw me riding around. When students began expecting me to be wacky because I was on a unicycle, I began acting even more that way. I became a completely different person when I was riding the unicycle. The world turned into my circus. Anything was possible.

One day, I get out of my aerospace systems design course and hop onto the unicycle. I am cruising down a path when I pass a sign that says: "ATTENTION: CHEERLEADER/ TIGER MASCOT TRYOUTS THIS AFTERNOON! DON'T MISS OUT!!!!" I ride on, and then stop short, almost falling off the cycle. I think about the sign for a moment. Why not? I might as well check it out. I'm not planning on becoming a cheerleader. I detest cheerleaders. Especially male cheerleaders. But the Tiger mascot is another matter altogether. I've always wondered who the little guy was inside the tiger suit, running around the football field goosing the cheerleaders. He always seemed to have a wild time. The possibilities are infinite because your identity is concealed by a leering tiger face, so you can do all manner of outrageous things in front of thousands of people.

When I get over to Dillon Gym, where the tryouts are being held, I see two dozen bouncy freshman girls and this lecherous senior male cheerleader, who can't take his eyes off their bodies as they do somersaults and handstands. I walk over to him.

"Excuse me, how do I try out for the Tiger mascot?" No answer. "I brought my unicycle down in case you want to see me ride it."

He gives me this very annoyed looking over and then says something that sounds like "you got it" in a husky voice.

"What's that?" I ask.

The cheerleader looks at me again, this time with a half smile on his face. "I said, you got it. You're the only one who showed up. You got the Tiger." He turns his attention to the freshman girls, then swivels his head back to me. "Hey, aren't you that John Aristotle Phillips guy with the, you know, the pizza business?"

"That's me," I say, beginning to wonder why no one else tried out for the Tiger. Definitely a bad sign.

"Listen, I ordered a pizza from you guys the other night. It came two hours late and it was colder than a box of penguin turds."

"Don't blame me. I just own the agency. I have nothing to do with the pizzas. Talk to the Greek at the Parthenon. He makes the pies for us. Blame him." I'm beginning to get defensive because I get into one of these hassles at least five times a day now. "Tell you what," I say. "The next pizza you order is on me. How's that?"

"Great, thanks a lot," he says. "We'll see you at the Columbia game Saturday. You pick up the tiger suit and head from the trainer in the locker room a half hour before game time."

## The Tiger on the Unicycle

\* \* \*

"You're the *what?*" asks David, slamming his beer bottle down on the coffee table. It's three in the morning and we've been discussing the pizza business in my room.

"I'm the Tiger mascot at the football games. You know, the guy who dresses up in that tiger suit and horses around the field at half time."

"Are you high, J.P.? This orange-and-black stuff has finally gotten to you. Ivy Club, pizzas, Tiger mascot, what's next? Oscar is becoming a goddamn renaissance man."

"So are you, ya goddamn capitalist. Did you fire anybody today?"

"I had to fire that new guy, the engineer. What's his name, Peabody, Beanbody, Stringbody, something like that. He ran into another gatepost while cutting across a courtyard. The campus police were on his ass."

Just then, the phone rings. "Who the hell would be calling at three in the goddamn morning." I pick up the receiver: "Hello?"

"Is John Phillips there?"

"You're speaking to him. Who's this?"

"Look, I'm sorry to be calling this late. My name is Alex Wolff. I'm a junior and—"

I cap my hand over the receiver and ask David if we have an Alex Wolff working for the agency.

"I don't know," says David. "Maybe he crashed the van or something."

"Do you work for the agency?" I ask Wolff.

"No, I'm a stringer for the *Trenton Times* newspaper."

"The what?"

"The *Trenton Times.* I heard from a friend that you designed an atomic bomb last year for a physics project, and my paper is interested in running a story on it. Is there any time tomorrow when we can talk about it? I'm sort of under a deadline."

"I'm not sure if I'm supposed to talk to reporters about the project. Certain parts of it are sensitive."

"Have any other reporters called you about this?"

"No, but you're going to have to talk to Professor Theodore Taylor to get his permission before I'll say anything. My advisor, Dr. Dyson, is out of town this week."

"Okay, I'll get back to you tomorrow. I'd like to ask you not to talk to the campus stringers for the other papers until I contact Taylor. It's sort of a competitive thing where I don't want to get scooped."

"Okay, I'll talk to you tomorrow."

"Thanks, John. Goodnight."

I hang up the phone.

"Who was that?" asks David.

"Some student reporter who wants to write a story about my bomb for the *Trenton Times*."

"Sounds cool," says David, yawning. "Just put in a plug for the pizza agency."

# 31
## The Whoopee Begins

"Phillips, telephone for you. Somebody named Barron."

"Whaaaa? . . ." I mutter, turning over in bed, hoping to fall back asleep. But the sunlight is already beginning to marinate my eyeballs. "Don't know any dukes or barons . . . tell 'em to call me back later."

I can feel Ralph Taylor's grinning face inches from my head. He knows how much I like being awakened before ten. "Barron says it's important. And besides, if you don't get up now, we'll miss breakfast. So move your ass, Phillips!"

I stagger out of bed and down the hallway to the phone.

"Hello, John? This is James Barron calling. I'm a senior and I work for *The New York Times* as a stringer. My editor wants a story about your A-bomb. Professor Taylor gave me your name. I'd like to do the story. When can we meet today for an hour?"

"I don't believe it. The *Times* wants the story?" I ask, wondering in my sleepy state if this guy has the right person. I figure that it must be David playing a joke. I decide to play along: "All right, Red Baron, you've got me . . ." (I make sounds of a plane falling and crashing.) "You can do the story if I can put in a plug for the pizza agency," I say, waiting for David to start laughing any second.

"What pizza agency?" he asks. "Is this John Phillips?"

I notice that the voice doesn't really sound like David's. "Who is this?" I ask, a little confused by now.

"I told you. James Barron. I work for the *Times*. The *Times*!"

"This isn't David?"

"No. What paper does David work for?" Barron asks urgently. He sounds worried.

"The *Sleepy Hollow Sentinel* for chrissake. Now could you please tell me what's going on?"

"Have other papers been calling you for a story?"

"A kid named Wolff from the *Trenton Times*."

"Take my advice, Phillips. Forget about Wolff. Wouldn't you rather have your name in *The New York Times* than in the *Trenton Times*?"

"Frankly, Barron, at eight in the morning, I don't really care. And I really don't know what you're going to write. I can't tell you too much about the design."

"No problem," he says.

"All right. I've got classes all day, but I'll meet you and Wolff over at Ivy Club at eight tonight."

143

# MUSHROOM

"Both of us?" he asks, pained. And then: "All right, all right, but don't tell anybody else about it, okay?"

"Sure. See you at eight."

This whole cub reporter business has put me in a contemplative mood. Ralph has already left for breakfast without me. I get dressed, grab my unicycle, and head out into the clear fall morning.

*The New York Times.* I'll believe it when I see it. The prospect is too bizarre to dwell on. For the first time since I sat down to design the bomb, the many implications have come to the fore. At first it was the impossibility of the task and the challenge that kept me going. Then it was the beauty of the physics and the thrill of the detective work. When I had finished, the implications stayed in the background. Sure—so I designed an atomic bomb, startled my professors, and got myself off academic probation. Do I now have some kind of responsibility to do something about it? And if I speak to the press in hopes of dramatizing the need for stronger safeguards on plutonium, might I be planting the idea in terrorists' minds. Questions, questions, never answers.

"And that's the way it is, Wednesday, October sixth, 1976," intones Grandad Cronkite at seven-thirty. I shoot pool with Ralph for the next half hour. As usual, I lose a bottle of wine. At eight P.M. the stringers arrive. The interview is conducted in the very same room where I designed the bomb just months ago. Only now the sleeping bag is gone, Capitalist Pig is gone, the stacks of books have long since been returned to the library, and there is no trace of the countless scraps of paper that once littered the floor.

Alex Wolff and James Barron walk through the door first. Within minutes, six more student stringers for local newspapers have arrived. Each one clutches a notepad to his or her chest like a poker player trying to conceal cards. Alex Wolff is wringing his hands, looking at me with a helpless expression as if to ask how all the other reporters knew to come. I shrug my shoulders. I honestly don't know. As I'm getting coffee for everyone, the reporters banter among themselves:

"Who's the guy who built the bomb?"

"Right there, with the coffee cups."

"That's *him*? He doesn't look like a grind."

"My editor wants to see the secret plans before he'll run the story."

"Fat chance, Jack."

"I'm just doing this story for practice. My editor laughed when I told him I had a story about a student who built an A-bomb."

Wolff and Barron are silent through all this. Both have carefully selected the seats to my right and left. The interview begins. I answer all the questions slowly, one at a time. I explain right away that I never built an actual prototype of the bomb. Rather, I designed it, to point out the need for stronger safeguards on fissionable materials. But one kid isn't listening and five minutes later, he asks me where I keep the bomb stashed. I don't realize it at the time, but this is the beginning of the Great Where-Do-You-Keep-Your-Bomb? Hassle.

The interview continues. Someone asks about the nuclear energy controversy. No, I'm not opposed to the nuclear power industry on principle. We simply need stricter controls on the plutonium and uranium in reactors. Yes, it would be possible for a terrorist group to steal plutonium and fabricate a crude bomb using my design. Excluding the plutonium, it would conceivably cost several thousand dollars for the materials. Could I make it in my basement? Maybe yes, maybe no. I have no way of knowing unless I try to construct it.

Many architects are capable of designing plans for sky-scrapers, but it takes a team of engineers and construction workers to actually build the structure.

What about the presidential race? I'm going to vote for Carter. Is that because of Carter's campaign position on stronger nuclear safeguards? Yes, in part. What kind of student am I? About average . . . maybe a little below average.

As the interview rambles on, I begin to feel more re-laxed. At first, I find it very strange to be going through this press conference charade with kids my own age. You might think it's fun being interviewed by a bunch of reporters. But it's not what it's cranked up to be. As I'm sitting there in Ivy, I find a certain ambivalence about the situation. On the one hand, I enjoy the attention—who wouldn't? But there is also the pressure: Here is my one and only opportunity to make the point about plutonium safeguards. Suddenly I have a forum for all my ideas and opinions and I don't want to sound like an uninformed charlatan. I don't want to blow it. As the interview is coming to a close, I discover something interest-ing: By virtue of having designed an atomic bomb, it seems that I am expected to have an opinion on every issue, from capital punishment to the outcome of the World Series.

The next morning, I am again awakened by the tele-phone. This time at eight-thirty. It is Nancy Nappo, the stringer from the New York *Daily News* whom I saw at Ivy last night.

"John, David Abromowitz and Alex Wolff asked me to call. We've got some photographers who want to take your picture sometime this afternoon."

"They want my picture? Are you serious?"

"Of course. The Trenton papers are going with the story tomorrow and the *Times* and the *News* are running it on Saturday."

"My picture?"

"Is it okay for the photographer to come this afternoon?"

"Sure. I guess. I have a class at one-thirty, so can you have them meet me at Ivy at one."

"Will do," she says.

"What should I wear? I can't believe this."

"It doesn't matter. Just look like a student. Bye."

Look like a student. I imagine a scrawny Latin Quarter type with a long scarf and suspenders, puffing lackadaisically on a cigarette.

At one-twenty, ten minutes before my class is to begin, a big, hulking photographer from one of the Trenton papers huffs and puffs his way through the front door of the club. He puts down his camera bag and says he is looking for "the kid."

"I'm the kid," I tell him.

"Nice place you got here, kid. This your fraternity or something?"

"Something like that. Listen, I've got a one-thirty class. I can't be late. Can we possibly speed it up?"

"Sure, kid, sure. They told me you built an A-bomb. That true?"

"I didn't build one. I *designed* one. On paper."

"So I can't shoot you standing next to your bomb?" He sounds massively disappointed. I imagine the picture he had all planned: me wearing a crew neck sweater or something collegiate-looking with my arm draped casually around the shoulder of my bomb. Very Boy Scouty.

"No, there is no bomb."

"You got some books here I can photograph you next to?"

"Sure. Let's do it in the library," I suggest, starting up the stairs.

"Are there books up there?"

"What do you think?"

"I dunno. I never seen a liberry in a frat house before. Just lots of beer."

"Listen, I've got five more minutes. Let's hurry."

"I'm moving as fast as I can, kid." With a grunt, he lifts his camera bag to his shoulder. "I been in this business for twenty years, but I never done a story on a kid who built a bomb." He stops on the stairway and gives me a strange look. "You some kinda genius or sumpin?"

Up in the library, he decides that he likes the big oak reading table. He has me slouched in a chair reading two textbooks at once. I have to smile. Maybe he thinks that a "genius" can read two books at the same time. He starts clicking away. I become acutely self-conscious about Hairy Furbish, my mustache. Whenever I try to shield it from the camera with a finger or a pencil, he tells me to get my hand away from my face. I'm also beginning to regret my choice of clothes for the occasion. Originally, I'd decided to wear the usual blue jeans and T-shirt. But out of deference to Mom, Dad, and posterity, I threw on the old jacket and tie at the last minute. In short, I look like a real turkey.

Twenty minutes later, I'm late for class, and the photographer has been saying, "Just a couple more, kid" for the last ten minutes.

"Look, man. I've gotta get to class."

"Okay, kid, one more minute." He continues moving around me, taking shots from every angle. He must have enough to fill up the whole newspaper by now. He stops and looks at me very gravely. "Listen, kid, I know you're hiding it for the country and all, but you sure we can't do one of you standing next to the bomb?"

He is really hooked on that Boy Scout pose. "How many times do I have to tell you? I never built the damn thing. *There is no bomb.*"

"Okay, okay. I was only asking ya. Don't get mad or nothing."

"Listen, I've really got to be going."

"Come on, kid, you should enjoy this. Tomorrow's gonna be your big day. Your name's gonna be in the paper and all, and the next day everyone'll forget who you was. Take it from me. This is my business. I know what I'm talking about. Enjoy it while it lasts."

"Great. Do you want to explain that to my professor?"

"Hey, there's an idea," he says. "How 'bout a coupla classroom shots?"

On Friday morning, since I'm not awakened by any reporters, I forget all about the papers. I rise at my customary ten o'clock, sing a few off-key bars of "Give My Regards to Broadway" in the shower, get screamed at by MacMurray, who's trying to sleep, get dressed, and then stroll over to Ivy for a leisurely breakfast. I love Fridays. It's a fine morning, and I cut through Prospect Garden, enjoying the crisp, clean air and the sound of crunching gravel beneath my feet. The football game at Columbia is tomorrow, but I've decided not to go as the Tiger. Rain is predicted, and I have better things to do than slog around a wet field in a sweaty tiger outfit. If I really liked any of the cheerleaders, it might be a different story. I've already promised Josh Rafner, a budding politico who lives in my dormitory, that he can be the Tiger on Saturday. I didn't tell him it was supposed to rain.

When I get to Ivy, I walk past the newspaper table and into the dining room. I notice a congregation of guys crowded around the table. Bert Oldman turns around and sees me. He grins beatifically.

"Phillips, you're such a turkey," he says.

"Thanks Bert. I'll remember that."

Some of the other guys turn around now.

"Nice picture, Phillips. What's that growth on your upper lip?"

"Looks like he's trying to hide something."

# MUSHROOM

Suddenly I realize what they're talking about. I elbow my way through the crowd to the table. I don't believe it. On the front page of the *Daily Trentonian* there are three big stories: GOV. BYRNE WANTS DEATH PENALTY BILL, Edgar Smith Charged/Kidnapping, Attempted Murder, and PRINCETON STUDENT DESIGNS A-BOMB.

> Princeton—It took John Aristotle Phillips only four months last spring to prove to himself that he could design an atomic bomb. Ignoring his undergraduate course work to concentrate on the project, the Princeton University physics major spent last semester researching and writing a 34-page report which outlines how a terroristic group might design a crude atomic bomb using information available to the public. . . .

Someone thrusts the *Trenton Times* at me. On the front page, I see the picture that was taken yesterday. No words can describe how ridiculous I look attempting to conceal the ever-scrawny Hairy Furbish with a number-two pencil. The banner headline reads: "THE UNTHINKABLE IS REALITY/ PRINCETON SENIOR CREATES PLAN FOR A-BOMB."

> Princeton—A young Princeton University student proved something nuclear experts have feared for years—a layman with a relatively basic understanding of nuclear physics can design, and perhaps build, a crude but effective atomic bomb. . . . The experts say it would work. . . .

The *Trenton Star-Ledger* has more of the same, except just below the story about me is the headline FRANCE TO PROCEED ON A-SALE. This refers to the controversial sale of nuclear reactor technology to Pakistan, which would give Pakistan the fissionable material necessary for an atomic bomb.

My reaction to seeing all the stories and photographs is

a mixture of shock and excitement. I'm beginning to feel like Dorothy when she lands in Oz. The world suddenly seems different. There I am in the public consciousness right next to the France-Pakistan sale. When I'd spoken with Professor Theodore Taylor about whether to talk to reporters in the first place, he told me that I had every right to my privacy but that the nuclear safeguards issue would be furthered if I disclosed what I'd done. If I decided to go public, he urged me just to tell the truth, not disclose the bomb design itself, and reiterate my reasons for undertaking the project. He also warned me that the ensuing publicity would very likely be a tremendous pain in the ass. "It's a decision you yourself will have to make," he had said. "It wouldn't be fair if I were to force you one way or the other. Think about it."

I'd thought about it. At least I thought I'd thought about it. I was glad to do my bit for the nuclear safeguards issue. But I had no idea it would involve the whole range of little annoyances from the early morning phone calls to the cover-up, albeit funny, of Hairy Furbish. Yesterday I was delivering pizzas and minding my own business. Today I'm the "unthinkable reality": an undergraduate atomic bomb designer. And tomorrow, according to yesterday's photographer, I'll be forgotten.

The next day, when I wake up, it is pouring rain as I'd expected. Thank God I let Rafner be the Tiger up at Columbia. Right now, he's probably on the team bus somewhere in the New Jersey wastelands, looking out at the downpour and swearing that he's going to fix my ass. I turn over and decide to get another hour of sleep. I hear the phone ringing. I pray that someone else will get it. The phone stops. MacMurray is yelling in an aggrieved voice: "No, goddamnit, he's asleep. . . . What? . . . Listen, buddy, he ain't gonna call you. . . . No, I'm his roommate. . . . No, you call him. . . ." I hear Mac slam the phone down. I wonder who that was.

# MUSHROOM

In answer to my question, Mac bursts into my room and starts screaming that the phone has been ringing all morning. Reporters want to talk to me and photographers are coming down to Princeton. I try to get him to slow down, but he's yelling a mile a minute. Ordinarily the reserved lawyer, Mac-Murray is showing new stripes. At that moment, Taylor pirouettes into the room with an armful of newspapers. He throws *The New York Times*, the *Daily News*, and the *Philadelphia Inquirer* onto my bed.

"What's going on?" I ask.

"You tell us," says Taylor. "The next time you design an A-bomb, give us some warning."

Just as I'm opening the *Times*, Goundie runs in out of breath and claps my face between the palms of his hands. "Phillips, you're a star! My roommate is a star. You made *The New York Times*!"

"What does it say?" growls MacMurray.

I read aloud: " 'Princeton, October eighth—After listening to his professors describe the future of atomic weapons in doomsday terms, a Princeton University physics student designed an atomic bomb to prove that nearly anyone with information now publicly available could do the same thing . . .' It goes on, blah, blah. Wait, listen to this, ' "Any other physics major could do this better," Mr. Phillips asserted. "It was just luck that I got on the right track. I'm really one of the poorest students in the physics department." ' "

I read the last line again and wince. I never said that.

"Poor Mr. Phillips," says Ralph, laughing.

What has me a little worried is the headline in the *Times*: STUDENT DESIGNS $2,000 ATOM BOMB. I had said that it could conceivably cost *several* thousand, and now the *Times*, our "newspaper of record," is stating the two-thousand-dollar figure as if it were an indisputable fact. Maybe I'm just dreaming. Maybe I did say two thousand dollars. No, not possible.

Just then the phone rings. I decide that if this is all a dream, the quickest way to reality is to answer the goddamn phone myself —although I'm not yet sure if it's a good dream or a bad one. (The same way Dorothy wasn't sure upon her arrival in Munchkin Land whether Glinda was a good witch or a bad witch.) I run down the hall and pick up the phone.

It's my mother and father. Her tone is somewhere between laughter and tears. My father is on another phone in the house chuckling. My mother says, "Johnny, why did you tell *The New York Times* you were the dumbest student in the department?"

"Oh, now, Bessie," says my father, cutting in. "Johnny, congratulations. We're both very proud of you."

"Why didn't you warn us you were going to be in the *Times*?" asks Bessie. "Daddy was reading the paper at breakfast and he spilled coffee all over his new suit when he saw your name—"

"And Mommy burned the eggs," says Aris, giggling. His Greek accent is more pronounced than usual. "We're both very proud of you."

"How *are* you?" Bessie asks. "What's going on down there?"

"I'm sure he's all right, Bessie," says my father.

"What about those vitamins I sent down? Did you get them?" she asks.

I don't believe it. "Yes, I got them. Thanks. Listen, can I call you back? I can tell it's going to be one of those red-letter days with the telephone calls."

"Okay, please let us know what's going on," says Bessie. "Take good care of yourself."

"Right. Thanks. Good-bye, Mom, Dad."

I hang up the phone. Right away, it starts ringing again. "Hello?"

"Is this John Aristotle Phillips?"

"Who's this?"

"My name is Rich Rein. I'm a reporter for *People* magazine in New York. Is this John?"

"Yes."

"Howya doin', John?"

"I'm fine, Rich. Howya doin'?"

"My editors read the story about you in the *Times*. They want one for *People*. "

"*People* magazine. You've got to be kidding."

"No, not at all. I'd like to do a personal profile. How does that sound?"

"Do you want my honest opinion?"

"Of course."

"Ridiculous."

"It won't be that bad. I read in one of the papers that you dress up as the Tiger mascot for the football games. John Simpson, the photographer for the story, wants to get some shots of you as the Tiger at the Columbia football game today. Could you swing that?"

"I don't know. It's complicated."

"What's complicated?"

"Look, call me back in twenty minutes. I want to think about this in the shower."

"All right, John. We'll talk to you later. *Ciao*."

I put down the phone and stand up. Immediately it starts ringing again. I stare at it, willing it to stop. But it continues to ring. I decide that before I speak with any more reporters, I'm going to have to have a good long think about all this. I take the phone off the hook and slowly walk toward the shower.

# 32
## The Peephole Magazine Mentality

In the shower, I decide to do the *People* interview. There are a number of reasons. I figure that an article in *People* will reach hundreds of thousands of people across the country, driving home the message about safeguards on fissionable materials. I also realize that I will have an impact on people because I'm young. After all, the idea that anyone with a strong physics background could design a workable atomic bomb with declassified documents is not a new concept. John McPhee's book *The Curve of Binding Energy* has proved this notion beyond the shadow of a doubt. But the larger public hasn't really taken notice.

Rich Rein calls back and says he will pick me up in Princeton and take me up to the Columbia game. An hour later, a green Toyota pulls up in front of my dorm. A young man in his late twenties jumps out. Wearing a brown leather pilot's jacket and Levi's, he fiddles with a broken umbrella as he dodges puddles on the pathway. Instead of waiting, I bound out of the entryway and meet him halfway up the walk.

"Are you the person from *People*?" I ask somewhat stupidly.

"John? Pleased to meet you. I'm Rich Rein. John Simpson, the photographer, is in the car. Let's go."

We pile into the car. John Simpson introduces himself, and we're off for New York City. By the time we swing into the traffic of the New Jersey Turnpike, the windows have fogged up with our conversation and laughter. I'm beginning to think this could actually be fun.

Rein is fiddling with a compact, efficient-looking tape re-corder. "Okay, it's working," he says. "I'd like to start the interview now, if that's okay, John. This way we can concentrate on shooting you when we get up to the game. Mind if I tape-record this?"

"No, I guess not." I'm hesitant because I don't really know if I mind or not.

"Look, just relax. I can tell this is all new to you. Just remember that you can say whatever you like. Afterwards if there is anything you don't want in there, just let me know. I won't make you look bad. I don't do that." He presses the record button. "Okay, John. Just talk."

Silence. The sound of the windshield wipers.

"What do you mean, just talk? What do you want me to say?"

"Tell me about school. About being the Tiger. About the bomb."

I start laughing. "What's so funny?" he asks.

"I forgot to tell you guys. A friend of mine is wearing the tiger suit up at the game. I didn't want to go because of the rain."

"Don't worry, we'll find him. Now, what about the bomb?"

"Right. Well, I guess the reason I agreed to do this interview is the same reason why I decided to design the bomb in the first place. I wanted to dramatically demonstrate that it would be easy for a terrorist group to design an atomic bomb from declassified, publicly available information. The point is, if we're going to stop some kooks from building a bomb, we've got to put stricter safeguards on the manufacture and transport of plutonium between nuclear facilities. Plutonium is a man-made substance—and we can eliminate the risk if we don't use it for nuclear power-plant fuel in the future. Some of my professors at Princeton have proposed so-called proliferation-resistant fuel-cycles, but they have yet to be proven workable."

"How would these kooks get the plutonium from the reactors?" Rein asks.

"There are a lot of possibilities. A terrorist group might get an employee on the inside of a plutonium reprocessing facility to divert a little bit of plutonium every day. The quantities would be too small to be detected, and at the end of a month or two, he would have enough for a bomb."

"That's incredible," says Simpson.

"Why doesn't someone do something about it?" asks Rein.

"A lot of it has to do with the push for nuclear energy that came out of Eisenhower's Atoms for Peace program. Also, there are so many large corporations now which have heavy investments in the nuclear power industry that it's getting harder and harder to pull out."

"Are you saying that you're against nuclear energy?" Rein asks.

"No, I'm not. We're running out of uranium, which is the fuel used in reactors today, but corporations with the investments in the nuclear power industry are putting pressure on the government to switch over to a plutonium fuel-cycle for the reactors of the future. It's much easier to build a bomb with plutonium than uranium. My bomb was designed to work with plutonium. If the construction of new nuclear power plants isn't stopped now, tons of plutonium will have to be shipped around the world in the future, presenting a nearly hopeless international safeguards problem."

"That's really something," says Rein. Silence descends as the implications of my remarks sink in. We listen to the mad, spastic action of the windshield wipers.

"I'm going to turn on the radio to see if we can get a weather report for the game," says Simpson.

". . . In the top of the news this Saturday morning . . .

# MUSHROOM

President Ford, under increasing pressure from candidate Jimmy Carter, again apologized to Polish Americans in a speech last night for his remarks during the last debate in which he . . ." Simpson turns it down until it is just barely audible. The interview continues.

"Why did you decide to become the Tiger, John?"

"I don't know. It seemed like another adventure. I'm a little wacky sometimes."

"What sort of things do you do during the games?"

"Entertain the little kids. I love children. They get a bang out of being with the Tiger. Whenever I walk up into the stands, students offer me a joint and the old alumni insist that I have a drink with them. It's all a big game: Get The Tiger Tipsy."

"What do your parents think about the bomb?"

"They were pretty amazed when I first finished the design."

"What kind of people are they?"

"Terrific people. My parents have a great philosophy about raising kids. Don't have children unless you're going to bring them up right. And to do that, you have to love them more than anything else in the world. I owe everything to them."

"What do they do for a living?"

"My father is a professor of engineering at Yale, and my mother got her master's degree in educational psychology, but now she's a consumer advocate."

"What about your brother?"

"Dean is a freshman at MIT this year. He's also a lot smarter than I."

"Speaking of smarts, what's this I read in *The New York Times*?"

"You mean about being the dumbest student in the department. I never—"

Suddenly Simpson turns the radio way up. "Listen, listen," he says.

"And a story out of Princeton, New Jersey, this morning. . . . A twenty-one-year-old Princeton University undergraduate has designed a homemade atomic bomb as a part of his coursework. He did it to point out the need for more restrictive safeguards on nuclear materials. John Aristotle Phillips could not be reached for comment this morning, but this station has learned from one of Phillips' college roommates that he will be making an appearance this afternoon as the Princeton mascot at the Columbia football game at Baker Field. . . . It promises to be an *explosive* game. . . ."

The announcer thinks he's a real comedian when he pauses one beat and hits "explosive." Simpson turns the radio off and whistles.

"Trouble," says Rein. "You're going to be mobbed when we arrive."

"Mobbed?" I ask. In my mind's eye, I see a large black-and-white mob of girls chasing the Beatles down an alley in London. That couldn't happen to me.

"Just remember you belong to us for the day," says Rein.

"I don't believe all this," I mutter.

"We'll be there in a couple of minutes," announces Simpson. "When we pull in, John, I'd like you to stay as close to me as possible. We want to find the guy with the tiger outfit and get you suited up."

"At least it stopped raining for a little while," says Rein.

"I still can't believe it," I continue to mutter.

Rein begins to laugh as Simpson negotiates the car into the stadium parking lot.

"I think I know how you feel, John," says Rein. "Just remember to enjoy it, and don't let it go to your head. Not many people get to be famous at the age of twenty-one. Even fewer earn it as you did. So enjoy this while it lasts. After all, the publicity will be gone in two weeks and you'll be just an ordinary undergraduate again."

159

# 33

## Paper Tiger

The game hasn't begun yet. Simpson, Rein, and I are standing near the field laughing hysterically. There on the forty-yard line is Josh Rafner, dressed in the tiger suit, running around in circles. He is being pursued by a half-dozen photographers and a couple of autograph seekers. He keeps shaking the big papier-mâché tiger's head as if he is trying to explain something. The photographers take his picture. Pads of paper and pens are thrust into his tiger paws for autographs. Someone grabs his tail and yanks him back. Backward and forward, Rafner is pulled herky-jerk through the small crowd. But suddenly he is loose. He runs down the field. I yell at him, but he can't hear. The stadium crowd is cheering him on as he runs. It's crazy, totally crazy, and I decide that the only thing to do is enjoy myself. I take off after him, shouting back to Rein and Simpson that I'll meet them on the field in ten minutes.

On the twenty-yard line, with the photographers behind me and Rafner in the end zone, I yell, "Rafner! Rafner! What the hell are you doing?"

He hears me, turns, and runs back in my direction. Just as he gets near me, he sees the photographers coming at him. He veers off, cutting sharply to the right. He waves a paw at me, indicating to follow him up the field. Rafner is fast. I sprint after him and catch up as we cross the fifty. I see his face through the mouth of the tiger head, all hot and sweaty.

"Phillips! What the fuck is going on here? Why are they trying to get me?" screams Rafner. He can be very high-strung at times.

"Relax, man, relax," I shout over to him.

160

"How can I relax? There's going to be nothing left of this tiger suit in a minute."

"Just keep running. We'll duck into the locker room. The entrance is over there."

"Did you know this was going to happen?" he yells. "I'm going to kill you."

We cut to the right and dash into the Columbia locker room. The football players are getting ready to go on the field. Rafner pulls off the tiger head and looks around wildly.

"All right, Phillips. Now what the hell is going on?"

"I'll fill you in later. Haven't got time now. There are some guys from *People* magazine out there. They want some pictures of me in the tiger outfit. Let me get suited up for just a couple of minutes and then it's all yours."

"First tell me what this is all about. Did you rob a bank or something?"

"No, I designed an atomic bomb," I say, putting on the tiger head.

"That's what I thought those guys were saying. I thought I was just drunk or something. They kept asking me where I was keeping my A-bomb. Why the hell did you build a goddamn atomic bomb? Are you crazy or something?"

"I didn't build it. I designed one on paper. Give me the other tiger foot."

"Oh. Some kid ripped it off on the field. It's gone for good."

"This is wild! Have you got anything to drink?" I ask. "Like a quart of rum maybe?"

"Would I let you down?" Rafner produces a flask with a flourish. Rafner is famous for coming to the rescue at times like this.

"Here's to the tiger's foot," I say, giving a toast and taking a chug from the flask.

"You're a madman, Phillips. Did anyone ever tell you that?"

161

"Oh, shut up. You want a drink?"

"A goddamn A-bomb, huh? No, you finish it. You're going to need it."

"Please. Don't remind me." I hear a huge cheer go up in the stadium.

"The game's starting. You better get out there. See you at half time." From inside the tiger head, I look out at Rafner through the hole in the mouth. He is smirking. "Enjoy!" he says.

The minute I'm out on the field, the photographers see me. It's hard running in the tiger suit. I make a quick dash for the Princeton bench, but the photographers make a wedge, blocking me. Their motor drives fire away. The game has already begun, but no one is paying much attention to the action on the field. New Yorkers in the stands are climbing over one another trying to see what's going on around me. Simpson appears out of the phalanx of photographers. He swings into action. Gaining ground on the Associated Press and United Press International photographers, Simpson directs me to raise a paw here, swing a tail there.

The people in the stands have given up trying to understand what's going on, so they've taken to throwing things. Scraps of food and a few empty beer cans land near us. Neither team is making much progress on the field. During a Princeton huddle, an announcement comes crackling over the public address system: "And Princeton might just have a dynamite secret weapon today. . . . Hiding inside their Tiger mascot is an undergraduate atomic bomb designer . . . young John Phillips. . . . Not since the days of Hobie Baker has Princeton posed a serious threat, but Phillips' A-bomb will surely upset the balance of power in the Ivy League . . ."

# 34
## Reductio ad Absurdum

Rein and Simpson return me to Princeton early Saturday night. We drive down Nassau Street in the twilight. The changing colors of the trees are reflected in the stillness of the rain puddles along the street. There is already a sharp coolness in the air. Instead of having Rein take me to my room, I arrange to be dropped off at the Parthenon. I've already missed dinner at Ivy, and I'm so exhausted that I just want to grab a 'za and have one of our vans drop me off at my dorm on the next run.

But it may not be that easy. I'll probably have to go through the requisite hassle about money with Stavros. I've explained to him a thousand times that we pay him for the delivery pizzas at the end of every two-week period. But every time I show up at the Parthenon, he demands his money immediately. At the moment, I don't have the patience to listen to his threats: Whenever he wants to talk about money, he takes his long pizza knife from the counter and sharpens it in front of my face.

I walk into the Parthenon and say hello to everyone in Greek. (My parents tried to teach my brother and me the language of our ancestors when we were kids.) The tomato-and-grease smell of the pizza ovens makes me gag. I ask Butch if he can fix 'za with 'shrooms to go.

"Got one in the oven now, chief," Butch calls back from the ovens.

"Yassoo, Yanni!" Stavros hails me from the back of the store. He strides toward me grinning broadly. "You got any A-bombs for sale to me? I'm needing a few for that Turk down the street." He starts laughing loudly at his joke. I attempt a laugh and look nervously to Butch for my pizza. "What's your hurry?" asks Stavros. "Sidown. *Sidown.* Athena! Get our celebrity a Coke. You wanna Coke, Yanni?"

"Ah, sure. But I've got to get back to my room. Butch is fixing a pie for me now. Put it on my tab. How was our business last night?"

"Wunnerful. We delivered seventy-nine pizzas. Why you no tell me you design atom bombs? We're all very proud of you, Yanni. You see, over there . . ." Stavros gestures to the wall where the *Trenton Times* article is pasted up. "You're a Greek national hero, Yanni," he says, smiling with his mouth, but scrutinizing me with his eyes as he always does.

"Pizza's ready," says Butch.

Stavros gets up, takes the pizza from Butch, and picks up his long knife. For a moment I consider leaving right away. Butch gives me a "watch-out!" expression with his eyebrows. Stavros brings the pie over to me. He smiles. The corners of his eyes wrinkle.

"That'll be one thousand, three hundred dollar," he says. He wipes the knife blade on his apron.

"How many times do I have to tell you? We pay at the end of every two weeks. That means the next payment comes Friday."

"Whaddya mean, Friday? You owe me money. You pay me. I got bills too, ya know."

That's the funny part about Stavros. One minute you're his national hero, and the next second, he's ready to slice your head off for money.

"Give me a break," I say. I take my pizza and start backing up toward the door. "We agreed when we started this thing that you get money every two weeks. If you don't like the deal, we'll take our delivery service to the Turk."

"Hookay, hookay. I'll get it next week. But it bedder all be there."

"It will be."

164

## Reductio ad Absurdum

"You want that I should have Dimitri give you a ride somewhere, Yanni?"

"No thanks. One of our guys just pulled up outside. See you later."

"Yassoo."


When I get back to the room, I find David lying on the couch in the living room. My roommates have cleared out for the evening. David is manning the telephone. The receiver is cradled between his shoulder and his ear. He glances up at me and smiles sardonically. I put the pizza down on the coffee table. He makes a face feigning revulsion. He continues talking on the phone, making notes on a legal pad in his lap.

"Right . . . *Los Angeles Times* . . . No, I'm sorry, but Oscar is not in right now. . . . What's that? . . . Yes, his nickname is Oscar. . . . He'll want you to call him that. . . ." I give David an annoyed look. "Okay, try again in an hour. . . . No, that's all I can say. . . . I don't even know what an implosion wave *smells* like. . . . I told you, I don't know where he is. Probably out designing an H-bomb somewhere. . . . Okay, pal, later."

David hangs up the phone and looks at me. He has a wry, crooked look on his face. He takes a long dramatic pause.

"Nice weather we're having, isn't it?" he says, deadpan.

"Certainly is. Bit on the wet side, what?"

"The phone's been just a tad busy," says David, mimicking a secretary. "WCBS has been calling all day. That was the *L.A. Times*. They want a quote from you. And before that it was the *Atlanta Constitution*, the *Nashville Tennessean*, the *Boston Globe*, *Newsweek*, *Time*, and the *New Brunswick Home-Geriatric*. Here. I made a fastidious little list." He gives me the pad with two pages of names and telephone numbers. "Oh, and your mother called. She wants to know what's going on." David pauses as he grabs a slice of pizza. "By the by, Oscar, what *is* going on?"

"Hell if I know. The whole world went berserk today. You should have seen the people in the stands up at the game. You'd have thought I was Charles Lindbergh or somebody."

"Didn't you know?" says David. "Atom bomb designers are the latest thing."

"*Très chic*," I agree.

We eat the pizza and talk some more. After the insanity of the day, it feels good to be back in my room. Far from the madding crowd. And I'm glad David is here. I feel as if I'm on the verge of some crazy new life. And I'm not sure if I like it yet. David's perennial joking and role-playing shtick reminds me of who I really am and where I've come from. You see, that was a different me out there on the field today. The me that is being whoopeed is contrary to the me that designed an atomic bomb. There is a side of me that finds the whoopee fascinating: the wacky half that wants another adventure. And there's also the side of me that sees it as superficial nonsense.

David senses what I'm thinking about. "You don't look any different. A little tired maybe. How do you feel?"

"Strange."

"How so?"

"I don't really understand what's going on. I can't believe this is happening to me. Do you?"

"No. Not in a million years," he says.

"What am I going to do about it?"

"I don't know. You don't have to do anything. Although it's a great chance to get your point across. But you've got to watch out, J.P. You've got to beware."

David is very serious all of a sudden. He is looking at me pointedly.

"Of what?" I ask.

"Yourself. You know as well as I do that you love this stuff. You thrive on it. You're a demagogue at heart, but you're still just J.P. to me."

"Thanks."

"I mean it."

"I hear you. And I thank you. It's important. Your job is to prevent me from going off the deep end."

David smiles. "Have you ever heard about how the American Indians felt about photographers?" I shake my head. "Think about what a photographer does: He *takes* your picture. When the early photographers began taking pictures of the Indians on their reservations, the Indians were suspicious of them. They were scared as hell. They believed that part of their soul was caught each time their picture was taken."

"It's true, I guess. Every picture does take away something."

"They called the photographers 'shadow catchers.' "

The phone rings. David takes the receiver off the hook and buries it under a couch cushion. Muffled sounds can be heard. We look at one another, smile, and simultaneously say, "It's a shadow catcher!" David hangs up the phone. A moment later it rings again. This time I pick it up.

It's my mother. "Johnny! Johnny, what's going on?"

"Hi, Mom. Oh, you know, just the usual."

Just then my father also comes on the line. "Johnny, hello?"

"Hi, Dad. How are things?"

"Don't be silly," says Bessie. "What's going on down there? Your phone has been busy all day."

"Sorry. I was up at the Columbia football game having my soul taken away by a shadow catcher from *People* magazine." David winks at me.

"*People* magazine!" says Bessie. "Oh come on now . . ." She pauses, waiting for me to say I was just kidding. She is apprehensive.

"There were a couple of other photographers also."

"What did you wear?" she asks, concerned. "You had a tie at least," she says, half statement, half question.

"Mom. A tie with a tiger suit?"

My father cuts in, "We've been getting all sorts of calls here as well," he says.

"Yes," says Bessie, "the *New Haven Register* wants to do a front-page profile on you. We told them it was up to you."

"Thanks. Who else called?"

"We got one sort of suspicious call. A man named Roberts said he was from the Associated Press, then he changed —said he was from U.P.I. He wanted to know where you were staying and if you had a bodyguard. Daddy didn't like the sound of his voice."

"That does sound suspicious. What else did he want to know?"

"That's all. Just where you live on campus and if you have a bodyguard. Daddy finally hung up on him. We're worried for your safety, Johnny," she says.

"Now don't get melodramatic, Mom. I'll be all right. It was probably just some kook. The guys from *People* suggested I talk with campus security tomorrow first thing—" David whispers to me that the campus police chief called while I was out. "David says the chief has everything under control."

"But be careful," says Bessie.

"I will."

"Don't go anywhere alone."

"Mom! What do you want me to do? Buy a bulletproof vest? Please don't be worried."

"Tell us what's going on this week," says Bessie.

"I will, don't worry. I'll fill you in when I know more."

"Take care of yourself."

"Don't worry. Bye, Mom. Bye, Dad."

I hang up the phone. David raises his eyebrows. "Have you been taking your vitamins?" he asks, scarfing down an entire piece of pizza.

"Vitamin pills. I need some antipublicity pills. My parents think I'm going to be kidnapped. Can you recommend anything, Herr good doctor?"

## Reductio ad Absurdum

"A small mozzarella, light on the mushrooms, heavy on the rhubarbs?"

"Do you think they're coming back, doctor?"

"The screaming rhubarbs? Are you kidding? They never left. You've got a terminal case, J.P."

The next day, I feel silly going over to the campus police chief's office. It seems like a big deal, but I promised my parents, and they'd never forgive me for not talking to the chief if I got kidnapped. *Kidnapped?* I can't even think about it seriously. It's just another one of these new absurdities that I'm supposed to be dealing with. In a way, the idea intrigues me. There is something romantic about it: like the Orient Express and stolen Ferraris and attaché cases with stacks of crisp new bills in them.

The chief of campus police is a big crew-cut type. He tells me that my parents called him at home last night. As a normal precaution, he is going to place extra security patrols around my dormitory entryway.

"Does that mean I'm going to have a bodyguard?" I ask. I'm beginning to wonder how much I like the idea of having a lurch type following me around everywhere.

"Not in the absence of any more specific threat you don't get one. We'll have a man keeping an eye on your entryway twenty-four hours a day. Don't go anywhere alone, and if you have to leave the campus for any reason, please notify us. If you notice any suspicious behavior, be sure to tell us."

"Don't worry, Chief. You'll be the first to know."

"The problem with your dormitory is that it's located right on the street. If someone were trying to kidnap you, they could just pull a car up in back. For that reason, we've wired the fire alarm in your room to a special emergency system which alerts local and state police. The fire alarm is located just inside your door, so if someone tries to kidnap you, just pull the alarm on your way out."

169

# MUSHROOM

Obviously the chief is a regular comedian. What does he mean "just pull the alarm on your way out"? I can already see the kidnapping: "Ah, excuse me, fellas, but you're going to have to untie me for a minute so I can pull the fire alarm. . . . No, honest, it's just a normal fire alarm. . . . Why don't you just wait in the getaway car while I give a little pull. . . . I'll just be a minute, honest, guys. . . ."

During the next couple of weeks, I hardly ever think about being kidnapped. What I am beginning to wonder about is what Rich Rein said about becoming an ordinary undergraduate again. I'm getting five requests for interviews every day now. I can spend an entire afternoon just coming back to the room and answering all the phone messages. I can always tell if it's been a particularly hectic day with the phone when Ralph and MacMurray aren't speaking to me. I can't really blame them. When David and I were living with Franz last year, he was always getting calls from sensuous-sounding girls in the middle of the night, and we would have to stumble around in the darkness looking for a pencil to take a message like: "Suzie wants Franz to call her very, very badly. She's got a little *surprise* for him. She says he'll know what she means."

But Peter Goundie is the one who really amazes me. A-plus for Goundie. Not once has he gotten pissed off about the phone ringing. He always takes the message, dutifully letting me know right away who called. Actually, I think he's secretly getting off on the whole thing more than I am. One day, I apologize to him for the phone ringing so much. He tells me to shut up. You can't argue with that. The guy is a prince.

After a while, I begin to enjoy the interviews with reporters. I learn quickly about the fast-food journalism mentality. I become adept at manipulating the reporter. Journalism is a strange business. It is like juggling, because it requires both the journalist and his subject to possess the will to keep numerous objects moving under all circumstances. I discover that the interview, like many other things in life, is a mutual use: I am using the journalist to get across my message about proliferation. He in turn is using me to make a living. I learn that most journalists are flattered if they think I'm enjoying their company. On the other hand, I find that a journalist's respect for me increases if I let him know at the start that it's a tremendous inconvenience for me to be meeting with him at all. And yet, I will often skip a class to do an interview with a reporter who sounds particularly intriguing over the phone.

One day, a very sexy-sounding Frenchwoman from *Paris-Match* calls me at Ivy. I set aside an entire afternoon and a chilled bottle of champagne for the occasion. Unfortunately she brings along two male photographers who decide they want to shoot me in a classroom scene. We wander around the McCosh lecture halls looking for a class. We find an old professor giving a lecture to about sixty students on *The Education of Henry Adams*. I take a seat in the back. The photographer tells me to "look involved." He begins snapping pictures. A few students look around, trying to figure out what's going on. I find it hard to look involved. I compromise and look interested. The photographer tells me to raise my hand as if I were asking a question. Without thinking about it, I raise my hand.

The professor stops speaking. The only sound in the room is the camera shutter opening and closing. The professor takes off his glasses. He looks at me with an inquisitive, wry expression. Obviously he is not used to being interrupted. Sixty heads turn in my direction, giving me a collective, curious stare. The photographers are also looking at me in a funny way, as if realizing what they made me do. The professor taps his glasses on the lectern, "For students who wish to ask me questions, I will be glad to cover material during my office hours. Thank you." He gives me an irritated, starchy glance over the top of his spectacles, and continues with the lecture. Someone near me giggles.

I get two interview requests which strike me as rather strange. A photographer from "Sygma" calls and assures me that Sygma is the second largest photojournalism agency in Europe. Later, a photographer from "Gamma" calls and assures me that Gamma is the second largest photojournalism agency in Europe. Somebody is lying. The only way to resolve the issue is to have both photographers come down to Princeton at the same time. I schedule them both for a Wednesday morning. David tells me I'm making a mistake. He says when I start treating the press like idiots, I'm taking the first step toward the deep end. When the two shadow catchers finally show up, they almost come to fists as they elbow and shove each other. One yells in French, and the other hurls insults in German as they follow me around campus between my morning classes.

One "journalist" who makes an uninvited appearance does not work for either Sygma or Gamma. In fact, I'm skeptical whether he works for any newspaper or magazine. One afternoon in late October, I return to my room after classes. I fix myself a sandwich in the kitchen and take it into my bedroom. My stomach takes a high dive. I see a dark-haired man in his early thirties sitting at my desk. He wears stylish European clothing. He is nervously fiddling with a small camera hanging around his neck. He jumps up when he sees me. I wonder for a second how he got in.

"What are you doing here?" I ask him. My voice sounds more calm than I would have expected. "Who are you?"

"Mr. Phillips? My name is Giuseppe Verdini," he says, a bit too shakily. "I am an Italian journalist."

## Reductio ad Absurdum

"How did you get in my room?"

He ignores my question. "I have read much about you, Mr. Phillips. I would like very much to do a story about you."

"For what publication?"

He rattles off the name of some Italian magazine. There is something about him that makes me feel uneasy. His eyes are opened quite wide, and they never stay in one place for more than a second. His eyebrows remain permanently raised in the classic spook-house expression. He looks as if he's expecting someone to come screaming into the room any second to put the shackles on him. I consider going out to the living room to pull the fire alarm.

"I'm sorry, but I'm not giving out any more interviews," I tell him. He looks bewildered. "No more interviews," I enunciate slowly. "I'll show you to the door."

"Please, Mr. Phillips," he says. "I am a young man like yourself. Please understand. I need a scoopa for my magazine."

"I told you. I'm not doing interviews anymore."

"Then, please, if I might have a copy of your design report, I—" (He says this as if he were asking for a cigarette.)

"I'm afraid that's not possible. Now, if you'd just—"

"Please be sympathetic, Mr. Phillips. I need the design for a scoopa."

"You've got to be kidding. First you let yourself in my room and then you won't leave. Now, get out, goddamnit, or I'll call the campus police."

This seems to make some impression on him. He moves toward the door. "If you have a change of mind, Mr. Phillips, I will be—"

"I won't. Now leave."

He looks at me sharply. Now, I'm really tempted to pull the old fire alarm. Just before he takes the door handle in his hand, he grabs his little camera and snaps a picture of the

173

room. He lunges for the door and passes out into the hall. I hear him running down the stairwell and out the door.

Immediately I call the campus police.

The chief tells me he'll "look into it."

# 35

# The Hunchback of Whoopee

Reading *People* magazine is like masturbating. Everybody does it, but no one wants to admit it. When the article that Rich Rein wrote about me comes out, I discover a great number of closet *People* fans on the Princeton campus. Even the most austere professors seem to avail themselves of a clandestine *People*-reading session. Whenever I'm walking around campus between classes, the people I see on the walkways inform me that I'm in the current issue.

Each time this happens, I begin to feel more and more distant from the other students on campus. I can tell by people's expressions that they feel differently about me now. A peculiar look is written all over their faces, as if to say, "I read about this guy in *People*. He's famous. I wonder if all this publicity has gone to his head?" Sometimes I think I'm exaggerating the whole thing. Maybe it's just my lurking paranoia. But I've begun to have a curious feeling of isolation. For some reason, people now expect me to be different from them. They want to set me apart. I think I'm the same John Phillips I was before, but in the eyes of my acquaintances on campus, I'm supposed to be different. I begin to rely on my close friends, like David, to keep me in touch with my former self.

On Friday, I walk over to David's room in Little Hall.

I find him sitting on his bed rereading his all-time favorite book, *Stop-Time* by Frank Conroy, for the fourth time. He doesn't look up when I come in.

"Been kidnapped lately?" he asks, with his eyes still in the book. "You're looking paranoid, J.P."

"That's what I like about you, David. You're perceptive without even looking at me."

"What's up?" He gives me a cocky grin.

"I've got to get out of here for the weekend. I'm so sick of hearing about Peephole magazine that I'm going to start breaking things. How long do you think this whole publicity thing is going to go on?" I ask him.

"As long as you want it to. Why?"

"No reason. I just wondered."

"It's starting to bug you, isn't it?" David looks over at me.

"In a way. I don't know yet."

I stop talking for a minute. I'm trying to figure out why I suddenly feel vaguely dissatisfied. It's not the old rhubarbs; it's a deeper funk. That's the strange part about life after whoopee: The highs are higher, and the lows are lower. David starts whistling taps.

"You look bereft," he says.

"I feel bereft. Ever since the publicity started, eighty percent of my life has been governed by superficial conversations about the bomb with people I don't really know, or want to know for that matter."

"What about the other twenty percent?"

"I'm not sure. Probably just more phony conversations with people who pay attention to me for the wrong reasons. . . . What do you mean the publicity is going to go on as long as I want it to?" I ask him.

"Look, J.P., all you have to do is stop giving interviews to reporters. It's that simple. After a while, everyone will forget about you. The media always need new personalities to hype. Once they've finished with you, they'll go on to someone else."

"That's simplistic, and you know it."

"Simplistic hell; it's true," he says.

"I don't know. I have this awful feeling of being deformed. As if I'm going to walk around for the rest of my life as the goddamn A-Bomb Kid. Like a hunchback who's always trying to hide his hump."

"Don't give me that hunchback crap. You've been enjoying the attention and you know it. It's irresistible."

"Maybe I have. I don't know. It's a love-hate relationship."

"I'm okay, you're okay," say David, beginning to smirk. We both sense another round of one of our favorite games coming on. It's called The Be-Relevant Game, and it starts whenever one of us inadvertently slips into the cliché-ridden vernacular of the seventies. The object is to out-relevant the other guy:

"Be your own best friend," I say.

"Earth shoes and crunchy granola," David counters.

"Brown rice and est."

"Far out and be mellow," he shouts.

"Our bodies, ourselves."

"'Take charge of your erogenous zones."

"Naugahyde and polyester," I say. David does a double take. He winces.

"Highly unrelevant," he says. "You lose."

The point is not contested. We look out the windows for a while, our relevancy spent. David lights a cigarette.

"I still feel like a hunchback," I tell him.

When I get back to my room that afternoon, my roommates aren't speaking to me. There is a long list of messages on my bed. But I'm too tired to make any phone calls. I throw together a sandwich and fall asleep before I finish half of it.

Hours later, I wake up. The phone is ringing. I am lying on my bed, still dressed. I look at my digital alarm clock: three-thirty-three A.M. I get up and shamble down the hall, tripping over Goundie's rugby ball. I pick up the phone.

" 'Lo?"

"Hello, John Phillips? Hello?" The voice has a vague English accent. If it's David playing a joke, I'll kill him.

"Whoozis?"

"John Phillips?" The connection is bad. Sounds like the voice is on the moon.

"Yes?"

"Mr. Phillips. This is the Australian Broadcasting Company in Sydney. . . . You're on the air!"

# 36
## Shove It Up Uranium

Toward the end of the fall, the whoopee begins to die down. I've been quoted and profiled, wrapped and packaged: one more Big Mac eaten and digested in the fast-food whoopee chain. But I am still contacted by the stragglers of the international press corps, who must honestly believe that there are people back in the mother country who are dying to hear more about the kid who designed the bomb. Once a week, they find their way down to Princeton to interview me or take my picture. I try to oblige them partly because I suspect that David may be right. The whoopee is going to be over soon, so I may as well enjoy the attention while it lasts. I also know that I will probably never read any of the articles published abroad. However, one Italian reporter, with whom I've spent the better part of an afternoon sampling Italian wines, sends me a copy of the article he wrote for *Gente*.

As I'm flipping through the magazine, I pass by a picture of an Italian sex-symbol type who looks vaguely like me. I study the photograph for a second and realize that it *is* me. I've designed the bomb to demonstrate the need for stronger safeguards, and the Italians—God bless them—take my picture, touch up the photograph, and turn me into a stud. Even Hairy Furbish has joined the ranks of neo-Roman virility. I haven't shaved him off yet, and in the picture his legs are at once jet-black and very becoming. My complexion has been made flawless. My eyes are deep set and very seductive, and my hair is curly and godlike. But essentially I look like a turkey: sort of like those jerks on the Winston cigarette billboards who state their preference for "The Box." I laugh. While the rest of the world has been racing to get the bomb, the Italians have perfected plastic surgery with an airbrush.

About this time, the Japanese counterpart to *Playboy* sends a woman journalist and a photographer down to Princeton. While the photographer is hopping around with eight different kinds of cameras, I realize that the Japanese woman is more interested in getting juicy tidbits about my sex life than in reporting the more serious implications of my bomb. We are sitting in the library at Ivy Club. She is writing down every word I say in miniature print inside a tiny notebook.

"Do you have any girlfriends?" she asks me.

"Yes."

"How many?"

"I'm not sure. I don't count them."

"What kinds of girls do you like?"

"All kinds. Mostly blond ones."

"Do you have any oriental girlfriends?"

"No, not at the moment," I say.

She seems disappointed. "Thank you very much then. That's all I need to know.' '

Some weeks later, David drops by my room on his way back from New York City. He has been assigned by *New York* magazine to write a profile about me.

"How's my favorite Personality?" he asks.

"Terrific. What's new in the Big City?"

"Not much. This and that." He fiddles with a bundle of newspapers and magazines he's carrying. He finds the one he's looking for. "Well, J.P., they finally got you."

He tosses me a magazine. It is the new issue of the Japanese counterpart to *Playboy*. "Honolable J.P. is on page ereven," he says, mimicking a Japanese bow.

I open it to page eleven. I see several columns in Japanese, a picture of an atomic bomb explosion, and a Japanese guy sitting in a chair with a ridiculous grin on his face. I look up at David, waiting for him to let me in on the joke.

"Why J.P. rook conflused? Rook at honolable magazine again. Old Japanese haiku say: 'Whooping crane/ Have slanted eyes/ With help of airblush.' "

And by God he's right. There I am sitting in the chair at Ivy, with my eyes and face looking distinctly oriental. But the really eerie part is the way they've exaggerated my smile. With the photo of the nuclear explosion only a half column away from my picture, it appears as if I'm smiling *because* of the explosion. I seem to be taking great pleasure in contemplating the massive destruction caused by what a hurried page-flipper might assume to be *my* bomb. I hate to think what the readers in Hiroshima and Nagasaki will feel when they see this horror show. Luckily I don't read Japanese. If they doctored the photographs, the text of the article must be loaded with all the atomic bomb-related sex scandals in my life.

"Where did you find this?"

"At an international newsstand in the city. They're selling like hot cakes."

"How can they get away with this kind of plastic surgery?"

"Easily. What I want to know is *why* they do it," he says.

"I can't believe that's me there."

"Don't worry about it. Look on the bright side. Some film producer is probably going to want you to star in the remake of *The Seven Samurai*."

"Great. That's all I need now."

In early December, a German television station calls to say they want to do a video-taped interview with me in New York. The German who is organizing everything is very courteous and considerate, putting me up the night before the interview in the kind of very expensive hotel where people stroll around the lobby as if it were the deck of their private yacht.

The next day, he and his crew set up their cameras right near the zoo in Central Park. While we're waiting for the technicians to get ready, a group of onlookers assembles around us. In New York, whenever people see movie cameras and a cluster of professional cameramen, they gather around them like moths on a summer night. The group of onlookers grows. A bunch of very tough, streetwise black kids presses in around us. The German technicians look visibly nervous. I'm sure they think we're all going to get mugged. They begin to say things to each other in rapid German.

"We're going to try and speed this up," the producer explains to me. He shuffles some papers around on his clipboard and signals to one of the cameramen. All this time, I've been feeling as if I'm in one of those Jack Lemmon comedies about New York, such as *The Out-of-Towners*. Maybe it's just one of those days when everyone you see seems to fit some cinema stereotype. The Germans, the black kids, and the crowd of onlookers all seem to have been sent over by Central Casting. Even their dialogue seems to have been written in Hollywood: "Hey, man. Like what's comin' down here?" says one of the black kids to a German technician. The technicians looks confused and irritated. He shrugs his shoulders and goes back to his light meter. The black kid persists. "Like who's this dude who's getting his picture taken anyway?"

The German nearly kills me when he responds with the classic, "Vas is dis 'dude,' Fritz?" The other German cameraman looks equally puzzled.

"Who's the dude?" the black kid asks again.

"Him? Das is John Aristotle Phillips."

"What's he?"

"He make hay-bomb," says the German a little too nervously.

"What's that, man?"

"Hay-bomb. Hay-bomb."

"Oh . . ." A wave of recognition passes over the black kid's face. He looks at me with real curiosity for the first time. "I can dig it. You mean *A*-bomb." The technician nods his head. The black kid turns to the crowd and shouts at the top of his lungs (just to be sure that the people down on Wall Street don't miss it); "Hey, this dude makes atomic bombs!"

The producer starts yelling at the technicians in German. The crowd stares at me. One of the black kids wants my autograph. Something catches my eye near the sea lions' pool in the middle of the zoo. I see a very sad-faced young man wearing a rugby shirt. He is holding an umbrella over his head. I watch as, in one cinematic instant, he throws the umbrella, spearlike, at the sea lions in the pool.

That afternoon I go down to Penn Station to catch a

train back to Princeton. I'm ten minutes early, so I settle down at the hot dog stand that seems least likely to give me food poisoning. I order a hot dog with sauerkraut. The waitress is one of those people who always take great pleasure in irritating others with their slowness. She has this phlegmy cough, and when she brings my hot dog over, it seems as if she's about to fire a huge hockle right onto the counter. The hot dog tastes like it was made by the Firestone Company. I'm in a really bitchy mood.

Just after I've taken my first bite, I notice that someone has sat down beside me. I glance over to my left and then look back at the dog. It strikes me that I know the person who's sat down. I look at him again. It is Giuseppe Verdini, the Italian "journalist" who wanted my bomb design for a "scoopa." All at once, I wonder what the hell he wants and how he knew I'd be in Penn Station this afternoon. He must have been following me around.

"So we meet again, Mr. Phillips," he says with a cool half smile. Wild! He actually says, "So we meet again." I figure he's been watching too many James Bond movies. When he puts down a pen in front of me, I *know* he's seen too many spy flicks. He takes a clean napkin from the counter and places it next to the pen. Then, for emphasis, he pushes the pen and napkin in front of me. I feel a little uneasy when he puts his right arm around the back of my chair.

"What the hell do you want?" I ask him point-blank.

The look in his eye is deadly serious. I begin to feel as if Verdini's Bond film is closing in around me. In fact, I'm beginning to wonder if this entire day is secretly being filmed by someone.

"You know what I want," he says, nudging the pen closer to me. "Now draw the high-explosive configuration."

Who wrote this guy's dialogue? "Are you crazy?" I say, much too loudly. Heads turn in the hot dog stand. Verdini looks panicked. Suddenly I feel more in control of the situation. "Who are you anyway?" I say more loudly than usual. I want everyone in the hot dog stand to think that Verdini is about to kill me.

"I told you before. I am a journalist."

"Right, and I'm Enrico Fermi. Don't hand me bullshit."

He looks at me squarely. He seems a bit surprised that I can be sarcastic at a time like this. "Just draw it," he whispers.

He's blocking my way to the exit. I figure that if I can move quickly enough, I can get around him before he has a chance to grab me. I don't want to fool around though. Judging by the strange, panicky look on his face, anything could happen. Especially with this cloak-and-dagger cinema specter hanging over me.

"Mr. Phillips," he begins to say. I realize that I'm suddenly fed up with Verdini. I grab my water glass and my bag in the same instant. He swivels around in his chair, trying to block me. I throw the water in his face and dart around him. My adrenaline pushes me out into the station concourse. I don't look back. I dash diagonally across the flow of people.

I run to the nearest escalator going down to the train platforms. My train is waiting. I jump on and spend an agonizing half minute before the train doors finally close. I hurry back into a coach and look out on the platform to see if he's gotten on. No sign of him. Then, a second later, I see him running alongside the train, stooping to look in the windows. I slouch down in the seat and cover my face with my jacket. The train begins to move, slowly at first, then lurching out into the smoky bowels of the tunnel.

Five minutes later, the conductor comes up the aisle taking tickets.

"One way to Princeton," I say to him.

"I'm afraid this train doesn't go to Princeton."

"What do you mean? It's got to go to Princeton."

"I told you. This train doesn't go to Princeton. This is the four o'clock *Montrealer Express*. You're on the wrong train, kid . . ."

# 37
## Good-Bye Mr. Zai

After that day, I don't hear from Verdini again. And I never discover whom he really works for. He is another one of the question marks in this whole story. (For example, I never find out if anything happened to S. F. Graves at the Du Pont Corporation after it was reported in the newspapers that he had given me classified information.)

Christmas comes and goes and the New Year is upon me. For a change I feel good about the New Year. I sense that it will be wilder, wackier, and even more extraordinary than the one that's just passed. I feel strong and happy and self-confident. No trumpets or cymbals. I'm just going forward on an even keel, steady and aggressive.

Toward the end of January, I have resigned myself to the fact that the whoopee is all over. I'm washed up in the newsmaker department, a has-been in the out box of Whoopeedom. Apparently, I'm not the only one who thinks so. Some of the kids at Princeton who suddenly became my friends when I was whoopeed are already beginning to show less interest when we pass on the walkways around campus. This doesn't exactly break my heart. Nor am I unhappy that people no longer ask me about the bomb. At last, my life is becoming normal again.

I decide to turn over a new leaf. To signify the "new me," I shave off Hairy Furbish once and for all. I resign my post as the Tiger mascot so that I won't be reminded of my "A-Bomb Kid" legacy by the fans at basketball games. And I decide to really apply myself to final exams, which are coming up in two weeks. After finals, I plan to head south to Florida with Ralph Taylor for a week in the sun before cracking the books for spring semester.

A week later, during the middle of exam period, I get a phone call just as I'm on my way out to play squash.

"John, this is Dean Ayala's secretary calling."

Right away, I jump to the conclusion that they're putting me on academic probation again. But then I realize that they can't. I haven't even finished all my exams yet. "What can I do for you?" I ask.

"Well, there is a gentleman who has called our office several times in the past few days. He requested a copy of your atomic bomb design, and each time he called, I told him that the paper was unavailable, but he insisted that I send him a copy as a personal favor."

"You're kidding. Who is this guy? When did he call?"

"At first he wouldn't tell me who he was. I thought maybe it was a student playing a practical joke. But he finally identified himself as an assistant to the ambassador at the Pakistani Embassy. And he requested your phone number, but I didn't give it to him. Maybe if you—"

"Wait a second. He's a Pakistani?"

"That's what he said."

I start thinking. In the last three months, I've gotten many requests for the bomb design from crackpots, but none from official government representatives. If this guy is really a Pakistani, it could be an important matter. I remember reading recently in the *Times* that the Pakistanis are attempting to purchase a nuclear facility, including a plutonium reprocessing plant, from France, against the objections of the United States. The Pakistanis say they have no intention of developing nuclear weapons, but the U.S. suspects otherwise. The last report I read stated that the French are going through with the deal.

"But he wouldn't give me his name or anything," the secretary is saying. "The last thing he said was, 'Let's keep this between you and me, just try and get me Mr. Phillips' phone number.' Do you want me to have him call you? The Dean thought you should stay out of it."

I think for a moment. I'd like to ask him about Pakistan's "peaceful" nuclear power program in light of his desire to obtain plans for an atomic bomb. "Sure," I tell her. "Give him my number."

"Are you sure? The Dean said—"

"I don't care. Give him my number. I'll take care of it."

I grab my squash racket and bound down the stairs. I'm already a half hour late for my game with Josh Rafner, the "paper tiger" of the Columbia football game. The pathway to the gym is covered with slush. I start jogging, my sneakers slowly filling up with muck. As I round the corner of Spelman, I run straight into a friend of mine named Phil Gould, knocking a handful of his papers into the slush.

"Omigod," says Gould, rushing to pick up the papers. "My invention . . ."

"Jesus, Phil, I'm sorry." We both gather the papers. Gould is a senior who hopes to make millions off his inventions after graduation. He is an aspiring hustler, and over the last several months he's been after me to go in on one invention or another with him. For some reason, he thinks that if the A-Bomb Kid endorses his inventions, people will buy them.

"I was just coming over to talk to you about this idea I had," he says, smiling.

"I hope it's better than the last one."

## Good-Bye, Mr. Zai

"Now, Phillips, listen. It's a great idea. Gonna make us a million bucks each."

"Sounds terrific. I'd love to talk about it some other time. I'm late for a squash game with Rafner. Call me later in the week, okay?"

"Phillips, this is the invention of the decade. You've seen Richard Nixon watches, right?" He is beginning to walk along beside me, holding up his sketches. "Well, this is even better . . ." He trumpets his voice for a second and waves the diagrams in the air before saying in basso profundo: "Introducing . . . the Gary Gilmore Yo-yo!" He pauses for effect. "Well, what do you think?"

"Really poor taste. I think you're crazy."

"That's beside the point. We'll make a million each."

I start trotting toward the gym. "Why don't you make two million by yourself?" I shout back over my shoulder.

"Phillips," he yells, "you're missing the opportunity of a lifetime!"

When I get to the squash courts, Rafner is warming up.

"Sorry I'm late, Josh. I got tied up on the phone."

"Playgirl magazine, I'll bet."

"Not exactly. The secretary in Ayala's office says a Pakistani has been trying to get my bomb design."

Rafner freezes in mid-serve. "Are you serious?"

"Why would I make up something like that?"

"Who is he? Has he called you yet?"

"He'll probably call tomorrow."

"What are you going to tell him?" Rafner looks immensely interested. As a leading politics major in the Woodrow Wilson School, he makes it his business to get involved in international intrigue of any sort.

"I'll probably tell him to go hang it in his ear." I start hitting the ball against the backboard.

"Phillips, do you realize the implications of this? Would

187

you please stop hitting the ball for a minute. Did you know that the Pakistanis have been trying to buy a nuclear power plant and a plutonium recycling facility from the French?"

"Yes, I've read about it."

"Well, Christ, don't you see? Pakistan wants the nuclear facilities so that they can develop a bomb to maintain the balance of power with India. As a matter of fact, I remember reading five years ago when India detonated its first nuclear explosion, Ali Bhutto, the Prime Minister of Pakistan, declared: 'We will get the bomb, too. Even if our people have to eat grass.' "

"So why are the French going to sell them the nuclear facilities?"

"Because the French are political shits," says Rafner. "They're doing it for money and they defend themselves by saying that no one has yet been able to prove that the Pakistanis are trying to develop the bomb."

"So if this guy is really from Pakistan, we've got proof that they *do* want to build a bomb."

"Exactly," says Rafner.

"Well, what do we do?"

"I don't know. Play squash until I get an idea."

"That's what I like about you, Rafner. You've got such a sense of priorities." I serve the ball.

"What do you suggest we do? You're the guy who designed the bomb in the first place," he says, slamming a return. We trade forehands.

"Well, you're the goddamn international relations wizard. You tell me what to do, Dr. Kissinger." I slam a killer shot in the corner.

"Good shot. Look, I've got an idea," he says. "I worked for Senator Proxmire in Washington last summer. Why don't we give him a call. He's extremely interested in nuclear proliferation and he'll know what to do."

\*   \*   \*

188

Five minutes later, we are sitting in my room. Rafner produces a card from his wallet with several Washington phone numbers on the back.

"It's the third number," he says.

"What the hell do I tell him? I'm the kid who designed the bomb, maybe you've heard of me?"

"Sure. Something like that. He's a really nice guy."

I dial the number. A secretary answers. "Hello, this is John Aristotle Phillips calling. I'm a student at Princeton University. I designed an atomic bomb last year, and I'd like to speak with the Senator about a matter that's just come— what? . . . Oh, sorry . . . Good-bye . . . No, never mind . . . Good-bye."

"What's the matter?" asks Rafner.

"Wrong number, jerk. That was the Capitol Hill News Service."

"Sorry, try the second number."

The next phone call gets me through to Proxmire's administrative assistant, a man named Ron Tammen. I explain who I am and why I'm calling. Tammen sounds uninterested, but he asks for my phone number, and then says good-bye.

"What'd he say?" Rafner wants to know.

"When I told him about the bomb and the Pakistani, he said that was nice and then gave me the old don't-call-us-we'll-call-you routine."

Seconds later, the phone rings.

"Mr. Phillips, this is Ron Tammen calling. Sorry to have been so abrupt. We just wanted to make sure this wasn't a hoax. We are extremely interested in this inquiry you've had. The Senator is on another call right now, but as soon as he's finished, I'm going to tell him about this."

"Good. I was beginning to wonder about you guys."

"Well, you'd be surprised at some of the crank calls we get. Now, I'd like you to give me all the details. Can we begin with the phone call from the Dean's office?"

# MUSHROOM

As I'm describing what happened, David comes into the room and takes a seat. Rafner fills him in on what's going on. David lights a cigarette. He looks intrigued. I finish telling Tammen about the Pakistani and he says he will get back to me. I hang up the phone and look over at David.

"Oscar meets the Pakistanis," says David. "For a publicity hound, you sure have an imagination. What did Rafner's buddy, the Senator, have to say?"

"Not a helluva lot yet."

"Why don't you call my father?" suggests David. "He was an assistant science advisor to J.F.K. and he's done consulting work for the Atomic Energy Commission. He'd know what to do." I ponder the idea momentarily, and then decide to give it a try. I like Mr. Michaelis. He's easygoing and he always knows what he's talking about. I call him at his office in Washington.

"Yes, John. How are you?" he asks. Mr. Michaelis has one of those up-beat voices that practically beam across the phone at you.

"Fine, thanks. David suggested that I give you a call. This morning I was told by the Dean of Students that an assistant to the ambassador at the Pakistani Embassy is trying to get a copy of my bomb design. I've just spoken with Senator Proxmire's office and they were interested and said they would get back to me. Do you think there's anything serious here?"

"There could be. Particularly in light of the French deal that's about to go through. As a matter of fact, this could be very, very important. Let me see . . . I know a man named Gilbert Hill who used to work for the C.I.A. specifically on the disarmament and proliferation problem. He'd know what to do next. Why don't I put him in touch with you?"

"The C.I.A.?" I ask. Rafner's eyebrows begin to arch. David sits up.

"Yes, I'll talk to him about it and have him give you a call if he thinks it's necessary," says Mr. Michaelis.

"Okay. Thanks, Mr. Michaelis."

"Anytime, John. Oh, and tell David to call me. He's been bouncing his checks again."

"Will do. Good-bye."

I hang up.

"What'd he say?" asks David.

"He says you've been bouncing checks."

"What did he say about the C.I.A.?" asks Rafner.

"He's calling an ex-C.I.A. man about it. He thinks it could be serious."

Rafner whistles. "Hot damn. First the Pakistanis, now the C.I.A."

"Calm down," says David. "We don't even know who this guy *really* is."

"That's true," says Rafner, looking at me very seriously. "Phillips, how *do* you know that this man is a Pakistani?"

For a moment, I begin to wonder about this whole episode. It does seem absolutely preposterous: the Pakistanis, the C.I.A., and me. But then I think about all the unbelievable events of the past several months—from Giuseppe Verdini to the international plastic surgery in that Japanese magazine—and I realize that by now anything is possible. Even a Pakistani spy. My contemplation is interrupted minutes later by a telephone call.

"Hello, Mr. Phillips?"

"Yes?"

"This is Gilbert Hill. I just got off the phone with Mike Michaelis—"

"It's the C.I.A. man," I whisper to Josh and David.

"Mr. Phillips, when I was with the C.I.A., one of my main concerns was the anti-nuclear proliferation field. Now, I understand that you are about to be contacted by a gentleman who says he works for the Pakistani government. Mike told me that he wishes to obtain the documents concerning your atomic bomb."

"Yes, as far as I know, that is correct."

"Could you start at the beginning, please, and tell me the whole story?"

"Certainly—"

As I'm describing the story to Hill, Ralph's girlfriend Florence walks in the room and says hello in her habitually cheery manner. She is shushed by David and Josh.

"What's going on?" she whispers.

"J.P. is talking to the C.I.A.," says David.

"Pakistani spies! Shhhhh!" hisses Rafner.

Florence looks completely bewildered. I smile at her. I continue talking with Hill. When I'm finished telling him the facts, he says he will check with some people at C.I.A. headquarters in Langley and call me back. I hang up.

"What's happening?" asks Rafner, practically falling out of his chair.

"Not much. It's confidential," I say, winking at him.

"You're such an asshole, Phillips."

Before I can tell them what was said, the phone rings again.

David lunges and beats me to it. ". . . Yes . . . who's calling? . . . I see, just a minute. . . ." David puts the phone against his chest. "It's for Florence. It's the F.B.I. calling."

Florence's face loses all muscle tension for a second. "What? *Me?*"

"Who is it?" I ask.

"For you," says David. "It really is the F.B.I. No joke."

I take the receiver.

"I hate you, David," says Florence.

"Hello, Mr. Phillips?" says a voice.

"Speaking?"

"My name is Robert Underwood. I'm with the F.B.I. in Washington. Ron Tammen at Senator Proxmire's office just called and told me the whole story. Until further arrangements are made, we'll be working on this thing with the Senator's office."

"The F.B.I.? How serious do you think this all is? I mean what are *you* guys going to do?"

"We're not entirely sure yet. But we want you to take the first step." He says this in an ominous way.

"How's that?"

"We want you to get the Pakistani's name when he calls you. I've talked with the secretary at your Dean's office and she said the man was most reluctant to disclose his name."

"That's right."

"There's a very simple way of getting it. When he calls and asks you for your design, tell him you would be glad to send it to him if he would only give you his name and address. Follow me?"

"What if he gives me a false name?"

"We don't think he will. But in the eventuality that he does, we will still have some leads. Do you think you can do that for us."

"I can try."

"Good. Let's hope it works. We're sending an agent up to Princeton to speak with you in person tomorrow morning. He'll explain everything more completely."

"You're sending an F.B.I. agent?"

"Nothing to be alarmed about. We don't believe that you are in any physical danger, but just the same, it's a normal precaution."

"Okay, I'll be expecting him. How will I know what he looks like?"

"You'll know," says Underwood.

"All right. Whatever you say. Thanks for calling. Good-bye."

David, Josh, and Florence are all waiting to find out what the F.B.I. has to do with all this. Rafner looks like he's ready to swoon. I begin to explain when the phone rings again.

"Hello?"

"Johnny?"

"Can you call me back in an hour. I'll explain."

"What's going on down there? Are you okay?"

"Yes. I'll call you back."

When I hang up the phone, all three of them say in unison, "Who was *that*?"

"My mother."

"Good old Bessie," says David. "Maybe we should get her down here to speak with the Pakistani. She'd have him confessing everything in a matter of minutes."

We all decide it's time to have something to eat. But midway through the sandwiches and beer, the phone rings again. This must be some kind of record for consecutive phone calls received in one afternoon.

"Mr. Phillips?"

"Yah?" My mouth is full of sandwich.

"Gilbert Hill calling. I've just talked with Langley. They feel that this case should be under F.B.I. jurisdiction, so they're notifying the F.B.I.'s Washington bureau."

"Too late. The F.B.I. just called me."

"I see. Very well, then, you're in good hands. Good-bye and good luck."

"Thanks for your trouble. Bye."

David brings another bottle of beer from the kitchen. "Who was it this time?"

"Your father's C.I.A. connection."

"Connections. Connections. The C.I.A., the F.B.I., Proxmire . . . Everybody and his uncle has called this afternoon. Except the Pakistani. I hope for your sake he calls soon. Ever heard of the boy who cried spy?"

"You're giving me the willies. Pass me that beer."

The next morning, I hear the telephone ringing. It is

eight-ten. I crawl out of bed and walk down the hall to the phone. The heat in the room has been turned way down. I shiver when I put the chilled receiver to my ear.

"Hello."

"Yes, hello. May I please speak with Mr. John Aristotle Phillips?" The words are enunciated precisely, but there is an elastic lilt in the voice. It is the Pakistani. His accent is very strong. His words seem carefully chosen. The tone of his voice is at once polite and cautious.

"This is he. Who's this?"

"Mr. Phillips," he says in a merry sort of way, completely ignoring my question. "Ah, it is so good to talk with you. I have been seeing many, many articles about you in the news journals, and I have been following the story of your success with great interest. Allow me to first congratulate you on your achievements."

His expansive tone makes him sound like a maître d' in a very lavish restaurant. "Thank you, Mr.—what did you say your name was?"

"Mr. Phillips, I am an employee of the Pakistan Embassy in Washington, D.C. As you may know, my government is terribly interested in developments in the field of *peaceful* nuclear energy." His emphasis on "peaceful" is a dead giveaway. He continues, "I would therefore be very appreciative if you would forward to me one copy of the brilliant design that I have read so much about."

"I'm afraid that's not possible."

"Surely, Mr. Phillips, you could spare just *one* copy."

"You miss the point. I am not giving out copies of my bomb design to the general public. I don't even know your name."

"But I just told you. I am not a member of the general public. I represent the Pakistan government. Surely it would not be a great inconvenience to forward a copy for our Embassy library."

I pause for a long moment, pretending to be considering the matter carefully. Embassy library, indeed.

"Mr. Phillips, are you there?" he asks.

"Yes, I'm thinking."

"Please, you can be assured there will be no danger involved."

I take another long pause. "All right, I will send you a copy. To whom do I mail it?"

"Oh, thank you so much, Mr. Phillips. You may send it to me, Ali Zai, in care of the Pakistan Embassy in Washington, D.C."

"I'm sorry. Could you spell your last name?"

"Of course. Zai. Z-A-I."

"Thank you. Now, Mr. Zai. Could you please tell me why a government which professes an interest only in peaceful nuclear energy should be so interested in obtaining an atomic bomb design? It seems to me that there is an inconsistency here."

"No inconsistency, I assure you," he says. His voice has raised a half octave. "My government is interested in *all* developments in the field of peaceful nuclear power."

"Have you eaten any grass lately, Mr. Zai?"

"I do not think that that is funny," he says in a tight, acid voice.

"I do not think that an atomic bomb design can be used for peaceful purposes, Mr. Zai."

"Are you implying that you are not going to send me your paper?"

"I'm not implying anything. I'm telling you that you won't be getting anything from me."

"Mr. Phillips, it will be worth your while to cooperate."

"My design is not for sale, Mr. Zai."

"You gave me your word of honor," he says in a very high-pitched voice.

"Good-bye, Mr. Zai."

"Wait. Mr. Phillips. One moment please." He sounds feverish. "We will make it worth your while . . ."

"Good-bye, Mr. Zai."

I hang up and then take the phone off the hook. I lie back on the sofa and look out the window. It is a fine, clean morning. The kind of morning when, before all this bomb business, I might have gone for a long motorcycle ride on an empty country road. I would have wrapped a long scarf around my neck and felt the cold air prickle my nostrils at 60 mph. But this morning I have to wait for the F.B.I. agent to arrive.

# 38
## Curiouser and Curiouser

The man from the F.B.I. calls at eleven, and the Pakistani Affair, as David has dubbed it, takes yet another turn for the perverse. All morning, I've been wondering what my G-man is going to be like. Will he come on like Efrem Zimbalist, Jr., with a cool, steely look in his eye? Or will he resemble a dry-look football coach in double-knits? Could he be a double agent employed by the Pakistani intelligence network to kidnap me? (Will I have enough time to pull that goddamn fire alarm?) Will he flip open his wallet, revealing a badge, and say: "F.B.I. . . . Act One" when he strides in the door? Does he carry a .38 Special in his shoulder holster? Given the circumstances, I must admit that I am secretly, deep down inside, enjoying every minute of this cloak-and-dagger intrigue. At least it gives me a good excuse not to study for my exams. I can imagine writing the Princeton honor code pledge at the end of my physics exam: *I pledge on my honor that during this examination I have neither received nor given assistance to the Pakistanis.*

The phone rings, interrupting my reveries.

"Is John Phillips there?"

"Yes, this is he."

"Mr. Phillips. I'm with the F.B.I. I believe you've been expecting my call."

"Yes."

His voice suggests a heavyset man who is possibly from the Midwest. But I can't be sure. He speaks evenly, giving away nothing. "I've just arrived in Princeton," he says. "I'd like to get together sometime this morning."

"Sure. Why don't you come up to my room. I live in 67 Spelman Hall."

"I think it would be better if we meet somewhere else— not on the campus."

"Why is that?"

"Well, the F.B.I. isn't too popular on college campuses these days, you know." He says this without a trace of sarcasm in his voice. Nevertheless, I think he must be joking. How could anyone tell he was an F.B.I. agent anyway?

"I didn't know that," I say.

"Yes, we have found it to be true."

"Look, nobody is going to know you're with the F.B.I."

"You can never tell," he says.

"I don't think anyone will really give a damn who you are."

"All right," he says. But I can tell he's still skeptical. "I'll be over in fifteen minutes."

"Don't worry. I won't tell anyone who you are."

"Check."

Precisely fifteen minutes later, there is a slight tapping at the door. I look out the fisheye peephole and see a man holding his wallet open, showing an F.B.I. badge. He must know that I'm looking through the peephole because he smiles and puts his badge right up to the hole. Even if he is paranoid about college campuses, at least he has a sense of humor. I give a quick glance around the room to be sure my roommates have cleaned up all the roaches, pipes, and other telltale signs of drug abuse. I open the door.

"Hello, John. I'm George Daniels from the F.B.I. May I come in?"

"Of course."

He smiles when he walks in the door. He is wearing a light blue seersucker suit, and he carries a slim attaché case. The knot of his tie is loosened, probably to blend in better with the "college scene." There is something pleasant, even funny, about his manner. But I'm not yet sure what it is. Then a moment later, I realize: He bears an uncanny resemblance to the comedian Don Rickles. His smile is broad and genuine, and I decide right away that even if my F.B.I. agent looks like Don Rickles and is named George, I like him. I don't yet trust him completely, but I do like him.

As I show George into the living room, I scan the chest of his suit for any bulges which might indicate a gun. (I picked up this trick from reading too many Dick Tracy "Crime-Busters" comic strips as a kid.) I see no bulge, except of the midriff variety.

"Have a seat. Can I get you a cup of coffee or something?"

"No thanks. This is a beautiful campus," he says in a perfunctory way, as if indicating that this is all the small talk we will engage in. He snaps open his attaché case and takes out a folder and a pad of paper. He clicks a ball-point pen and begins to write.

"What are you writing down?" I ask.

"Nothing yet. Just background. Now, could you start with the call from the secretary?"

While I'm giving what must be the fiftieth rendition, I

have the distinct impression that he is hearing it all for the second time. When I finish adding the details about the Ali Zai conversation, he puts his pen down and slouches back in the armchair.

"Okay, John. This is where we stand," he says, looking at me intently. "If this Ali Zai fellow really works for the Pakistani intelligence agency, I don't think you're in any danger. But if he's working for somebody else, then it could be serious."

"But aren't the Pakistanis dangerous?" I ask.

He chuckles a little bit, looking even more like Don Rickles than before. "The Pakistani outfit is the laughing stock of the entire intelligence community. Judging by the amateurish way Ali Zai tried to get your design, I'd say he's got to be a Paki. And if our investigation shows that he is a Paki, then you're in no danger."

"He sounded like a Pakistani. Or maybe an Indian."

"Well, the real significance of this thing is political, and this is why Senator Proxmire is keeping close tabs on the situation. As you probably know, our government has been trying for some time to block the French-Paki nuclear deal. The revelation that the Pakis are in fact trying to get your design may just be enough to force the French to call off the deal."

"Great. What can I do to help out?"

"Nothing right away. Senator Proxmire is planning a speech on the subject which he has agreed to delay until we have a chance to thoroughly investigate this Ali Zai character. What do you plan to be doing for the next week or so?"

"When exams are over, I was going to drive to Florida with my roommate. But if—"

"No, that's perfect. But we do want to know where you will be at all times just in case Zai turns out not to be a Pakistani and the threat seems more serious after all. Where can you be reached in Florida?"

"I don't know yet. But I'll get the number for you. What happens if Zai isn't a Pakistani?"

"Well, it all depends on who he really works for and how big a fish he is. We might ask you to pass him incorrect plans, which would delay their bomb-building program. Alternately, we might arrange for you to transfer real documents, and after you have passed him the secrets, we would arrest him on the spot."

This idea doesn't exactly appeal to me. "Just suppose he didn't want to give up without a fight," I say. "I could get shot when you jump out from behind parked cars or whatever it is you guys do."

"Don't worry," says George. "We hardly ever lose anyone."

*Lose anyone?* I don't want to get lost. I can already see the look on my mother's face when George tells her I was lost in an espionage game.

"By the time you return from Florida, we'll know who this guy is and what he's worth," says George, full of confidence. "In the meantime, if for any reason you have to get in touch with me, call this number." He hands me a small slip of paper. "When you call, leave the name 'Aristotle' with the secretary. That will be your code name."

"Aristotle? Oh come on . . ." I start to laugh. George looks peeved.

"No seriously," he says. "I think it's a rather nice code name. I thought of it myself. Besides, you're going to need it. And don't forget to use it either, because you can assume that your phone is bugged."

"*My* phone is bugged?"

"Probably. The line I call you back on after you've left your code name will be one that is electronically cleared. It's interesting to what lengths the Soviets and others will go to find out what's being said over the telephone. Not too long ago, some kids in Norway saw a limousine pull up to one of those fiords. A man inside tossed a small briefcase into the water. The kids went down after it, found it, and brought it to the local police. It was turned over to the American Air Force base in Oslo, and inside the case, our security personnel found a lot of electronic gadgetry and a dial like the one on any telephone. It was made in the Soviet Union, and simply by dialing any number, the owner could listen in on any conversation being held over that line."

"Incredible. But who would be tapping my line?"

"You never can tell." He cracks a smile. "Maybe some sorority girls." He laughs at his own joke. "Well, John, I've enjoyed meeting with you and we'll be in touch soon."

"Right." I walk over to the door with him.

"Oh—one more thing," he says. "If for some reason, you call to tell me something about Florida, don't say Florida. If someone is trying to track you, we don't want them knowing where you're going to be, so just refer to Florida as 'Sunny.' For example, say, 'Aristotle calling from Sunny.' Okay?"

"No problem."

"Oh, and by the way, I nearly forgot. Refer to me as 'Curious George' when you call. Curious George. Got that?"

"Sure. Curious George."

"I thought of that one, too," says Curious George, smiling as he goes down the stairs.

Ten days later, I return from Florida with the inevitable sunburn, and sand in every corner of my suitcase. I've intentionally put Ali Zai and Curious George out of my mind, but the first night I'm back, I get a phone call: "Checkpoint Aristotle clear," says a voice.

"Who's this?" I ask.

"Curious George here."

"What?—Oh, right, George. How's everything going?"

"Fine. How was Sunny?"

"Sunny. What's going on?"

"Well, our man is a Paki all right, and we've decided to go the original route with him. Senator Proxmire's office will be getting in touch with you tomorrow. He'll be making a speech criticizing the Pakis and praising your good judgment. How do you feel being a national hero for protecting the bomb?"

"A national hero?"

"Sure, why not?" says Curious George.

"Whoopee."

"What?"

"Never mind. It all sounds great. What else do I do?"

"Nothing. Just sit tight and if anything comes up, you know how to reach me."

"Okay, thanks, George. If I get any more kinky phone calls, you'll be the first to know."

"Good-bye, Aristotle," says Curious George.

The next morning, Ron Tammen calls from Proxmire's office.

"John, how was Florida?"

"Sunny."

"Good. Listen: The Senator was waiting for you to return from your vacation before he made any statement to the press and actually delivered his speech on the floor of the Senate."

I don't know why, but I suddenly have this crazy image of Proxmire rolling around on the floor of the Senate Chamber, giving a speech.

"Things may be hectic for you in the next couple of days," says Tammen. "But you should know you're doing a service for your country and the world."

"What can I say? Let's hope it works."

"Okay, good. That's the spirit. The Senator will be making a statement to the press tomorrow morning and then delivering his speech from the floor in the afternoon. The press

203

will probably catch up with you in the afternoon, unless they get advance notice. Remember now, smile and enjoy it."

"I will."

An hour later, I'm sitting at my desk, playing with the design of a new motorcycle crash-protection system that I've been working on in my engineering class. The problem is that I'm trying to make the design so simple that a Hell's Angel wouldn't be embarrassed to use it. But what I'm really doing is contemplating whoopee. It looks as if the whole thing is going to blow up one more time. I don't believe it. Whenever I think it's over, the whoopee second-guesses me. It's got a life all its own.

The phone rings. I don't hurry to answer it.

"Phillips, this is Phil Gould. How are ya?"

"Fine. What's new in the invention business?"

"Listen, I have a great new idea," he says.

"Is it like that last one?"

"Phillips, wait, you haven't even heard it yet," he says. "It's even better than the Gary Gilmore Yo-yo."

"I hope so."

"You've heard of the Pet Rock, right? Well, this is far superior. This is a real class item. We'll start out selling it at Tiffany's."

"What is it?"

"Okay. Visualize a business executive's office at Christmastime. He walks in the door, and there on the floor is a gift from his secretary. It's a three-foot gold-plated cube. Written on the side in big letters is: STUMBLING BLOCK—AN INVITATION TO ERROR!"

Gould pauses the way he always does, waiting for me to say something.

"A stumbling block?"

"Phillips, it's going to sell a million. And I haven't told you the best part."

"What's that?"

"After the Stumbling Block, we'll manufacture a whole line of gold and silver cubes for executive desk tops. First comes the Mental Block, and then a smaller version for writers—the Writer's Block, and so on, down the line to the Pet Block . . . We're going to make a fortune."

"How about a Stumbling Block ice bucket for block parties?" I suggest sarcastically.

"There. You're getting the idea. Now, listen: I have it all figured out. We'll go in on the patent fifty-fifty and then you'll start plugging it on talk shows and in the papers when they interview you about the bomb, and then we'll—"

"Sounds good. Let me think about it. But at the moment, things are a little hectic," I tell him.

"Did I get you out of bed, or what?"

"No, nothing like that. I just can't deal with blocks right now."

"Okay, Phillips. We'll talk later. But remember, if the Pet Rock can sell, so can we."

That evening, I call home. I explain to my parents that Proxmire is going to give a speech denouncing Ali Zai. Bessie is predictably worried. She thinks that with the new publicity, all the terrorists in the world will band together at some monstrous kidnappers' convention to nominate me as the kidnapping candidate of the year. I reassure her by saying that Curious George thinks I'm in no danger.

"Do you think we should go down to Washington to hear Proxmire's speech?" my father asks.

"Definitely."

"Are you taking your vitamins?" asks Bessie.

"Mom, please."

Late that night, I have a nightmare about being kidnapped:

# MUSHROOM

In the dream, I am lying in the back of a small U-Haul trailer, bound and gagged. I am the prisoner of a terrorist group led by Ali Zai. The entire trailer is filled with green grass. It is freshly cut suburban grass. The Pakistanis love it. I sit up and look out. Ali Zai is sitting there on the ground. Set in front of him on the ground is a platinum cube with words written on the side. They say: NUCLEAR BLOC COUNTRIES—AN INVITATION TO TERROR. Phil Gould has sold Ali Zai several million Nuclear Blocs and Stumbling Blocks. Phil Gould is rich. Ali Zai has a typewriter set up on top of the Nuclear Bloc. He is trying to type a ransom note to my parents. From time to time he walks over to the U-Haul to get more grass to eat. He offers me a handful. I decline. He insists that I have just a taste. I hear myself telling him that grass is vitamin deficient. He gets angry and threatens me with crabgrass. I say nothing. Ali Zai returns to his typewriter on the Nuclear Bloc. He announces that the ransom has been set at two million milligrams of vitamins. Following the terms of the letter, Bessie is supposed to drop a briefcase into the Tidal Basin in Washington. The briefcase will contain a telephone dial and two million milligrams in low, unmarked denominations of vitamins A and B. Ali Zai is pleased with himself. Pakistan will get vitamins. He has a stack of magazines in his hand. He brings one over to me. He opens it. It is the Pakistani version of *People*. There is an article about me in it. There are three pictures. In one, I look like Bruce Lee. In the second, I look like David. In the third, I look like Ali Zai. I turn my head away. I smell the grass. Ali Zai laughs.

# 39
## Falling Down the Whoopee Hole (Again)

Morning. I remember the dream while standing in the shower. Usually I don't remember my dreams. But as I'm washing my hair, Phil Gould enters my consciousness, and I remember the Nuclear Bloc. The rest of the dream comes back in color images. I dismiss it, get dressed, and walk over to Ivy for breakfast. When I get there, the steward, Ed, tells me that four reporters have already called, asking for interviews about Proxmire's speech. One of the reporters is from the CBS Evening News. Jesus. Cronkite is picking up the story. It's going to be another red-letter day in the annals of Whoopeedom.

The dream has left me in a strange mood. I feel stuck inside my role as the A-Bomb Kid again. There is nothing I can do except wait for the whoopee to begin. But I don't want this to be more lame-duck whoopee. I want to drive home the point about stricter safeguards on nuclear materials. What I need is a strategy by which I will be able to actively manage this phase of whoopee.

Before leaving Ivy to go to my European Intellectual History lecture, I decide upon a one o'clock "press conference." This will prevent the whoopee from dragging on all day, all week, all semester, as it did the last time around. I leave word with Ed to tell reporters about the press conference. There is only one flaw in my strategy. I should know by now that whoopee cannot be limited or managed. The very nature of whoopee is that it does what it damn well pleases.

I find David at the history lecture. We try to pay attention to Professor Schorske, but I keep leaning over to tell David about my new strategy. He is at first amused, then irritated at me.

"*Press* conference? You're turning into a goddamn prima donna," he says.

"What do you expect me to do?"

"Aren't you sick of the bomb?" he asks.

"Sure. But what can I do?"

"Get back to your other work. What about the patent on that motorcycle crash-protection gizmo?"

"I'll finish it when all this is over," I tell him.

"I'm beginning to think it's never going to end," he says.

"So am I. It's like beating a dead horse—"

"A dead racehorse named Sir Whoopee," says David. Simultaneously we both start giggling. Heads swivel around. I have this macabre image of a pack of reporters thrashing Sir Whoopee at a race track while CBS News cameras are running. I look over at David. Apparently he is fixed on a similar image. *Sir Whoopee.* Another character is born. The more people turn around to see who's giggling, the harder it becomes to stop. Professor Schorske is trying to ignore us. Before too long, the lecture is over. On the way up the aisle, I ask David if he wants to join me at the press conference.

"Didn't I tell you?" he asks. "I'm going up to my old stomping grounds in Cambridge. They've never heard of whoopee up there."

"You don't want to be filmed by CBS News?" I ask him.

"Are you kidding?" He puts on a look of mock disgust. "My conscience dictates against taking part in unnatural acts. And that includes beating dead horses."

We walk out with the flow of other students into the bright sunlight. Someone shouts, "There he is!" I look up and see a bunch of guys huddled around a camera with the ABC News insignia on its side. Most of the other students turn to look at me with perplexed expressions.

"What the hell? . . ." I mumble.

"Smile, Oscar," says David. "An impartial assessment of the situation would say that the camera is pointing at you."

"How did they know where I was going to be?"

"There's your answer," says David, nodding in the direction of Bob Steeler, a public relations man for the University.

"This way, gentlemen," says Steeler, taking charge as he leads the ABC camera crew through the stream of outgoing students. Steeler is smiling broadly. He shakes my hand.

"Ah, John, I've got some gentlemen here from ABC who are going to film you now."

"Mr. Steeler, look—I wanted to do everything at once, so it doesn't go on all . . ." I break off because Steeler isn't really paying attention to me.

"You may begin now, gentlemen," Steeler announces smoothly. The ABC reporter starts mumbling something to the cameraman.

"There goes your press conference," says David.

"How can you explain the problems of whoopee to a public relations man anyway?"

Before David and I can move, the cameras begin to roll. David turns to me and says: "Smile, J.P., you're on nationwide TV. Let's have that all-American shit-eating grin." I grimace at him. He whispers: "I'm getting out of here. Wanna join me?" I nod. We both turn and start walking away quickly.

The ABC reporter waves at us. "Hey, wait a minute. Where's he going? Hey, kid! We're not finished yet—"

David and I pick up the pace. We walk up Washington Road to the intersection of Prospect Avenue. At the corner, David begins to turn right. "This is where I jump off the Whoopee Express," he says, grinning.

"You're leaving?"

"Got a train to catch."

"Just when things were getting fun."

"I'll make sure to drop in at Off-Track Betting to put my money on Sir Whoopee," he says.

We laugh at each other. David turns to leave. For some reason, I'm sorry to see him go. Having him to laugh with puts this new phase of whoopee in perspective. He senses what I'm thinking.

"Remember, Oscar, they're only shadow catchers."

"I know. Have a good weekend."

"I will. Don't beat any dead horses while I'm gone." He waves, smiling just around the eyes the way he always does.

"Later," I say.

"Much," he yells, crossing the street and trotting up through the 1879 archway.

I walk down Prospect Avenue to Ivy. Just as I get to the gate, I see a CBS News camera crew heading in the front door. I decide to go around to the back entrance. The first person I see inside the club is Preston Longino, a senior member. He comes up to me and says, "Phillips, will you please tell your guests to hang up their coats."

"What guests?" I ask him.

"Those guests." He points to a small crowd of reporters lounging around on the sun porch, drinking coffee, smoking, and shooting the breeze. Longino is furiously scratching his beard. "Could you tell those slobs to hang up their coats. I mean, show a little respect for the club once in a while, Phillips."

"Okay. Relax. I'll see what I can do."

I walk onto the sun porch with no intention of having anybody pick up their goddamn coats. The newspapermen all rise at once to introduce themselves. Joseph Sullivan from *The New York Times* is the first one out of his chair, followed by the U.P.I., A.P., and *Philadelphia Inquirer* reporters. The CBS camera crew is busy setting up its equipment next to a backgammon table. Just as I'm about to suggest that we begin, the ABC crew comes onto the sun porch with WOR-TV–Channel 9 from New York picking up the rear. The room is beginning to fill up with Ivy members coming out of the dining room. Preston Longino is prowling around, looking as if he's about to take all the reporters' coats and donate them to the Salvation Army.

Taking a seat, I decide to get the show on the road. The last thing I need now is for Longino to start ordering the press to hang up their coats. The lights for the television cameras suddenly flood the room in a naked glare. I can hear the *whizssh* of the A.P. photographer's motor drive. I like the moment of anticipation just before an interview starts. Preparing for an interview gives me a case of nerves, but once the cameras are rolling and the questions are thrown out, I relax and have a good time. I take the first question from *The New York Times.*

"Mr. Sullivan?"

"Mr. Phillips, whatever gave you the idea to design an atomic bomb?"

"I don't know, I guess it just seemed like an interesting thing to do." Some of the reporters laugh. The Ivy guys hoot. One of them yells, "So we could use it against Yale!" Sullivan chuckles and scribbles something down in his notebook. I continue, "More seriously, I wanted to point out the need for stronger safeguards on nuclear materials, specifically plutonium and uranium."

Sullivan raises the proverbial eyebrow. "How do you know your bomb would work?"

"I don't. As with all such devices, the design has to be tested for certainty. But I might point out the fact that everyone who has ever attempted to build and explode an atomic bomb has succeeded on the first try."

"What did your professors say when you handed in the design?" asks a U.P.I. reporter.

" 'Nice job, John.' " The Ivy guys laugh at this.

"That's all?"

"Well, when I returned to pick it up, they said I'd gotten an A, but they wouldn't let me have it back." More laughter.

"Who has copies of your paper now?"

"The Physics Department has one, my advisor has one, the F.B.I. and the C.I.A. each have one, and I keep a copy in a safe deposit box."

The *Philadelphia Inquirer* man is looking at me very pointedly. "Are you a genius, John?" he asks.

"No. Definitely not."

"Well, then, what sort of grades do you get?"

"Not the kind I'd want to talk about. Truly."

Sullivan gets a bang out of that. "Now is it true that you were contacted by Pakistani spies who wanted your design?" he asks.

"That's why you're all here, isn't it?"

"What did the Pakistani say?"

"He told me it would be worth my while to pass him a copy."

"And what did you do?"

"I notified Senator Proxmire, the F.B.I., and the C.I.A."

"Has anyone else tried to get the design from you?"

"There was a gun collector from Texas who wanted to add a bigger bang to his collection. I had to turn him down as well."

"John, in a speech on the floor of the Senate this morning, Senator Proxmire called on the French government to cancel its proposed sale of a reprocessing plant to Pakistan. Do you agree with this position?"

"Absolutely. Up to this point, the French have claimed that there is no reason to call off the deal because the Pakistanis have promised that they do not want to build an atomic bomb. In light of the recent attempt by the Pakistanis to obtain my design, there can be no doubt about their intentions. If the French proceed now, they must bear the moral burden of arming a less than reliable regime with the means of mass murder, and the potential for starting the third world war."

There is violent applause from the Ivy guys. Someone yells, "Who's your running mate for '84?" The reporters crack up over this.

"Next question? . . ." I ask.

That evening, the TV room at Ivy is jammed. Everyone is looking at me with strange expressions, as if they don't really believe that I'm going to be on the news. I don't quite believe it myself. Despite the fact that I've spent the afternoon with the ABC and CBS camera crews, being filmed at various locations around campus, it seems so unlikely that the images recorded then will now appear on the news programs that I've watched since I was a kid.

Ralph Taylor jumps up to the TV set as the *ABC Evening News With Harry Reasoner and Barbara Walters* logo is flashed on the screen. Ralph jiggles the knobs on the set, but the reception becomes worse. A howl goes up from the sixty-two Ivy men who are crowded around the tube. Taylor fixes it and sits down. There is a brief round of applause. A silence comes over the room. I feel a dryness in my throat. The camera zooms in on Barbara Walters. Her brown hair is coiffed and Plexiglassed, and she is wearing a designer suit and a scarf around her neck. She emanates pinkness. When she opens her mouth, there is dead silence in the room.

"Good evening. Our top stowries tonight," she begins, struggling valiantly to conceal the famous Speech Impediment that will invariably triumph at least once every few sentences. "Secwetary of State, Cywus Vance says that there must be black majowity rule in Rwodesia. . . . We'll have a comment by Howard K. Smith on working hawrd and not so hawrd in Washington. . . . We'll see how dwrought now could mean electwical blackouts later in the West. . . . And we'll meet a young man who went to college and taught himself how to build a vewy big atomic bomb. . . . Hawry?"

Each time the S.I. slips out, half the room giggles, while the other half says "Sssssh," leaning closer to the TV in anticipation of the you-know-what story. But with the last S.I. everybody explodes at once, trying to say the phwase "vewy big atomic bomb."

Reasoner first does a story about Rhodesia, but I'm so tense that I hear none of it. My throat gets drier as each news story puts us closer to the one about the university kid who designed the vewy big atomic bomb. I clean my glasses and wipe my eyes over and over again. My feet are hot inside my sneakers. The Ivy comedians who usually comment on each news story every night are amazingly silent. I check my watch to figure how much longer it's going to be. I look at the screen, but the images don't register. A commercial break comes on. Surely my story must be next.

Barbara comes back in all her pinkness—Is this it?—and introduces a story about IRA bombings in Belfast. The images of gray, empty streets in Northern Ireland flip by. This is unbearable. I try to sit still. Harry Reasoner's hound-dog face comes on the screen. This has to be it. The room is suddenly pressure sensitive. No one moves. Harry begins, "What much of the world fears most—nuclear weapons in the hands of terrorists or irresponsible small nations is no longer a farfetched scenario, nor are do-it-yourself atomic bombs. As Jim Walker reports, one university student set out to prove that point . . ."

Someone in the room yells, "And he's sitting right here!" A half dozen others tell him to shut up. The image of Jim Walker in Princeton comes on the screen. The background is somewhere along McCosh Walk. Walker is standing alone, hands in pockets, about ten feet from the camera, barren trees overhead, snow on the ground. Whig Hall is off in the distance. He begins, "John Phillips is a senior at Princeton University, but like a lot of people he is afraid of nuclear war and the spread of nuclear weapons. But unlike other people, he did something about it. He decided to demonstrate the danger in a physics project . . ."

A new image comes on the screen: I am sitting in a chair at the press conference at Ivy. A small cheer goes up in the room. Walker continues, ". . . He worked for five months using published government documents and library books. . . . After all your work, what exactly was it you created?"

My face flashes on the screen. I feel a steamroller in my stomach. But in a way, I am relieved. I really don't look so bad after all. My hair isn't sticking straight up. I don't have food caked in the corners of my mouth. And my fly, if it's down, is out of the picture. My voice isn't so bad either. As I begin to speak it comes out deep and clear. I silently mouth the words as they come out of the TV.

". . . I came up with a design for a crude atomic bomb, much like the one that was exploded over Nagasaki. It would have about half the yield of that bomb and it would be about the size of a beachball. . . ."

"How did you do on your paper?" Walker asks me.

"I got an A."

Walker continues, "John's term paper is now under lock and key. Advice from the F.B.I. His work attracted considerable attention from France, which already has an atomic bomb, and from Pakistan, which does not. Less than a month ago, a Pakistani diplomat called him . . ."

My face comes back on. I am smiling. "He wouldn't identify himself at first, and he asked for a copy of the blueprint, and I declined, I said I couldn't give it to him. I wasn't allowed to. He was very persistent and wouldn't take no for an answer."

Walker goes on, "Pakistan's information minister in this country defended his country's interests, saying it does not want to build an A-bomb . . ."

The image of Iqvas Butt comes on the screen. He is a

215

very fat man, sitting at his desk in the Pakistani Embassy. He speaks in the same quicksilver tones as Ali Zai: ". . . Well, we have a program for the development of nuclear energy for peaceful purposes as a matter of routine. We collect published information—" He is cut off in mid-lie. He has that same look of saccharine sincerity that Richard Nixon had for so many years. For a moment, I wonder what's become of Ali Zai. Did they send him back to the spy academy in Pakistan? Walker's report continues, ". . . But with information to build a bomb readily available, nuclear experts believe that John's term paper only underscores the need for tighter worldwide controls on nuclear explosives such as plutonium . . ."

Senator Proxmire's face comes on the screen. This is actually the first time I've ever seen the venerable senator. He is tall and handsome and has this very concerned expression on his face. I couldn't have picked a better senator to call. Proxmire's voice is very convincing, ". . . I think that the message that comes through loud and clear is that we are in a more dangerous world than anybody thought, and that it is possible, conceivable, that nuclear weapons could be made available to terrorist groups, conceivably, as well as to virtually any country . . ."

The next image makes the steamroller in my stomach lurch into overdrive. The camera pulls back to reveal Bessie and Aris standing next to Senator Proxmire. *What the*? . . .

"John Phillips' parents came to Washington today to hear Senator Proxmire praise their son's work in a speech delivered on the Senate floor," says Walker.

Bessie and Aris look like All-American proud parents. Their smiles are right off the Wheaties box. Bessie's eyes are dancing. Aris looks at once professorial and huggable. The camera zooms in on Bessie. I brace myself.

"Well, I think John has made an effort, I think he's made a contribution. And other people who have positions of responsibility, and who make decisions, can take it from here . . ."

A+ for Bessie. She is so believable. But better than that, she has said something important: The ball is now in the policy makers' court. Bravo Mom and Dad. They vanish from the screen. Cut to a distant shot of me, walking down McCosh Walk past the camera. I shuffle off through the slush as Walker finishes his report, "John Phillips' atomic bomb design was an academic exercise, but it was also proof, once and for all, of what many nuclear experts have feared—that where there is a will, there is a way. . . . Jim Walker, ABC News, Princeton, New Jersey."

The room explodes with applause. Taylor jumps up to switch over to CBS. A shot of President Carter grinning is replaced by Walter Cronkite in New York. The camera comes in on Walter's face, ". . . When twenty-one-year-old John Phillips of Princeton University speaks out on the control of nuclear weapons, people listen. Because John Phillips knows what he's talking about. Don Kladstrup reports."

Walter said my name. Jesus. I exist. There is now a truer sense of reality about this whole crazy project, whoopee and all. If Walter says I know what I'm talking about, then I really must know. I try to ignore the sudden sense of authority that I feel. I look at the TV. An image of me sitting in my room in Spelman comes on. I am on the telephone, speaking to a producer for *The Tom Snyder Show* in New York. I sound massively uninterested. My face has that very bored look that plagues so many postal clerks and very wealthy people. It looks as if I turn down talk-show invitations for a living. Actually, a CBS cameraman advised me to turn down Snyder's offer, saying that his show was a hatchet job. The sound of my conversation with the producer comes on, "Okay," I say into the telephone. "Well, I can't get too specif— It's like a talk show then, right?"

We hear Don Kladstrup's voice-over as the camera pans

around my room and stops on a picture of Albert Einstein sticking his tongue out, "John Phillips has become an overnight celebrity. Reporters want to interview him. TV shows want him as their guest—not because of his exploits as a Princeton cheerleader, and not because of his grades (they're only average). It's because of this: a term paper he wrote for his physics class, a paper explaining how to build an atomic bomb. Modest and unassuming, Phillips says he wrote the paper from material he got from the school library and federal government . . ."

Cut to a very close shot of me walking with Kladstrup down Prospect Avenue. I am looking very collegiate in painter's pants and a Princeton letter sweater. Cut to the Ivy library. I look serious and dedicated.

". . . It took me five and a half months. It was hard for me, but I did nothing else but design the atomic bomb. I didn't go to many of my classes during the springtime of last year. But I—after a good deal of concerted effort and a lot of concentration, and one or two educated guesses, I came up with the design that I did."

"Could anyone with a basic knowledge of physics build a bomb like this?"

"If I did it, just about anybody with a basic knowledge of physics could."

The minute I hear this exchange with Kladstrup, I realize that it is factually wrong. He had asked if anyone could *build* a bomb like mine. And I told him if I had done it, then anyone could. We're back to square one in the Great Build-or-Design-Your-Bomb Game. Now thirty million more people will think that I built a bomb. Jesus. The woes of whoopee.

Kladstrup continues, "The paper earned him an A, but that's not all. Foreign governments were after him for his report. First, someone from the French government called, asking for a copy. Then, someone from the Pakistani Embassy called. Phillips turned them both down on advice from the C.I.A. and F.B.I. Phillips says he wrote the paper to dramatize how easy it is to obtain information on building atomic bombs."

"It's in physics textbooks, and it's available from the federal government. If you're going to stop a terrorist group or criminal organization, or a non-nuclear nation such as Pakistan, from getting their own atomic weapon and building an atomic arsenal, what we have to do is restrict the access to plutonium or uranium."

"Phillips says he undertook his project to prevent scenes like this—" Suddenly, a colossal mushroom cloud is seen exploding. "Scenes which he warns could mushroom unless controls are exerted now."

Everyone groans when they hear Kladstrup's bad pun on "mushroom." Then there is silence. The image of the atomic explosion seems to be sinking in. The mushroom cloud has turned me cold. The excitement of seeing myself on the news is now replaced with the eerie realization of the potential of my design.

"Don Kladstrup, CBS News, Princeton."

There is no applause now. Only silence. Walter Cronkite's face appears. He seems grimmer than usual. Or maybe there is irony in his face. Maybe I'm imagining it. Walter looks at the camera and delivers that immortal line, verifying reality for all of us,

"And that's the way it is, Thursday, February 10, 1977. This is Walter Cronkite, CBS News. Good night."

I don't move. I am still thinking about that goddamn mushroom cloud. I make a feeble attempt to acknowledge the congratulations of Ivy members as they file past my seat and out the door. Ralph slaps me on the back and tells me that I looked like a "prettyboy." His girlfriend, Florence, is grinning and saying, "I don't believe it," over and over again.

Bert Oldman shakes my hand and congratulates me. Wade King does the same. I can hear both phones ringing downstairs.

Someone yells up, "Phillips! Your cousin Ted from Syracuse is on the phone." And then a moment later, "Phillips, it's Stoops from California on the other line. . . . Phillips? Are you up there? . . ."

---

# 40
## Alive at Midday

If Walter is the greatest in TV-land, talk shows are the worst. They're somewhere down there with soap operas, *Star Trek*, and Japanese remakes of *Godzilla Meets the Pterodactyl*. But I didn't always feel this way about pterodactyls and the like. When my brother and I were in elementary school, we worshiped the tube. We genuflected and laid down our lives before its fuzzy black-and-white image.

In those days, watching the tube was as much a part of the daily routine as brushing our teeth. (The Stripe toothpaste commercials were the best.) What compounded my mother's despair during those Wonder years was that Dean and I were usually too hypnotized by the porridge flickering across the screen to even realize that she was in the room. Mom fell into the background as we adhered to the daily afternoon rhythms of *McHale's Navy, Hogan's Heroes,* and *Gilligan's Island.* Wally Binghampton, Ensign Parker, Hogan, Schultz, Colonel Klink, Gilligan, and stupid, sexy Ginger were our playmates. We were chums, best buddies. They were members of our gang.

And then something terrible happened. Our gang split

220

up. Peter "Fats" Repson, the kid who lived across the street and who always had the flashy new toys because his father worked for Gilbert Toy Company, moved away. But worse than that, our TV broke. Our beloved black-and-white Magnavox with the grotesquely distorted picture just gave up and died. It had a case of malignant tubes, and no amount of slapping on the side would help. According to the TV repairman, it was terminal. Dean and I suspected that this verdict had been prearranged by our parents. When we finally got a new TV, years later, our tastes had changed to include only Walter and an occasional National Geographic special on the space program. Our childhood had been salvaged by Mom, Dad, and the crooked TV repairman.

But to this day, I have trouble watching talk shows. They usually put me to sleep before the first commercial. I figure they must be TV-land's contribution to the tortured insomniacs of America. There is always the host, a fashion plate, just off the golf course, always witty, always smiling. When he pays attention to what one of his guests is saying, we pay attention. When he's concerned, we're concerned. When he laughs, we laugh, and when he smirks, we dismiss the guest as a boob. The guests: there is always one guy who is plugging his book, a lobotomized girl who wants to be an actress but who wouldn't be on the air if it weren't for her low-cut blouse intended to keep the audience tuned in, a faded movie star who is trying desperately to make a miraculous comeback from the whoopee cemetery, and a drunk who has no business being on there in the first place, except he or she is the only one who is relaxed on the air. But the drunk is usually so relaxed that he trips over the carpet edge, slouches in his chair, babbles incoherently, and laughs too loudly at the wrong time.

That's my idea of your basic talk show.

I wander around the WNEW-TV studio feeling profoundly lost. I am to be a guest on the New York talk show, *Midday Live*, best known for its popular moderator, Bill Boggs. I am looking for the makeup room. I mull over what I've been told about appearing on television: Speak slowly and clearly. Don't pick your nose or play with your hair. Television always makes you look and sound like the village idiot, so *don't think about it*. The Duke of Windsor said there are two rules to making public appearances: Keep smiling and never miss a chance to use the lavatory.

I finally come upon a door that is labeled The Green Room. I knock and enter. Inside, the walls are yellow, interrupted by several large makeup mirrors framed with little white lights. There are a dozen people in the room scurrying hither and thither. An attractive middle-aged woman with a clipboard bustles up to me. She squeezes my arm. "You must be John Phillips," she says. "I'm so pleased to meet you, and happy that you could be on our show today."

I exchange mindless, TV studio babble with the lady. She continues to squeeze my arm, explaining that her husband is a Princeton alumnus and that it was his idea to have me on the show. She writes something on her clipboard and tells me that she has a zillion things to attend to before air time. She looks at my face carefully and says she doesn't think I need extensive makeup. Maybe just a touch around the eyes.

I sit down and check myself out in one of the mirrors. I thought these things were supposed to be flattering. I'm wearing a cashmere sport coat over a black turtleneck, jeans, and my trusty, beat-up tennis shoes. That much is passable. What alarms me is the bags under my eyes. I try dabbing a little makeup around my eyes. It smears, and I end up making an even bigger mess when I attempt to wipe it off with the sleeve of my sport coat.

I give up on the makeup and take a look around. The other guests for today's show are in various stages of *maquil-*

*lage* around the room. I recognize Isaac Asimov, the scientist-writer. He is sitting in front of a mirror looking extremely grumpy. A woman is standing next to him, fiddling with a bunch of makeup jars. They seem to be having a discussion about what to do with Asimov's face. He has this very unruly gray hair, which the woman makes a half-hearted attempt at brushing. He waves her away and goes back to looking at himself being grumpy in the mirror.

Bill Boggs, the moderator of the show, is standing near Asimov, attempting to give advice about the makeup. Boggs is young and good-looking. Asimov will have nothing to do with his diplomatic advice. Boggs sees me and waves. He says something to Asimov, and nods in my direction. Asimov gets out of his chair, and Boggs ushers him over to where I'm sitting.

"John, my name is Bill Boggs," he says in a deep voice that seems to have been nurtured by commercial interruptions. "I'm very happy to have you on our show. It's going to be a great one." I nod my head. Boggs already sounds like he's on the air. "I'd like you to meet some of our other guests," he says. "First, Dr. Isaac Asimov, whom I'm sure you've heard of."

Boggs steps back, and Asimov and I exchange greetings and a handshake. Asimov attempts a quick smile, but then turns to go back to his mirror where he can be grumpy some more. Bill observes Asimov's reaction, smiles at me, and then drags another gentleman over to my mirror. The man is looking at me with an expression of mixed loathing and apprehension. Boggs' introduction explains everything, "John, this is Mr. Eugene Gatzenhorn, who is a lobbyist for the Atomic Industrial Forum and—"

The man seems very perturbed about something. He interrupts Boggs, "We represent over five hundred business and industrial organizations which have a direct interest in the

223

promotion of safe, clean nuclear energy. And my name is Ganzehorn," he says, looking at Boggs. "G-A-N-Z-E-H-O-R-N. Now, if you'll excuse me, I'll finish my makeup."

He walks off very huffily. Trouble. Not only is this my first talk show, but they've put a nuclear industry lobbyist on the air to refute everything I say about stricter safeguards. I decide that it's time I started getting nervous. I take from my pocket some notes I threw together in my hotel room last night. The presence of the nuclear lobbyist makes it even more important that I have the facts about nuclear energy at my fingertips. I begin studying my two A.M. scrawl. The notes read as follows:

1. Origins of Nuclear Power

• After Hiroshima and Nagasaki, many Los Alamos scientists desperately want the energy of the atom to be harnessed for peaceful purposes. (Guilty consciences.)

• 1946: Atomic Energy Commission is established to promote peaceful uses of the atom, as well as continue weapons development. (Hi-ho.)

• 1950s: Despite AEC promotional campaigns to interest private utilities in atomic energy, not one nuclear reactor is ordered. Atomic energy has bad image. Uncertainties over safety of reactors. Study commissioned by AEC to calm fears does opposite: worst case estimates for accident in reactor predict *3,400 immediate deaths, 43,000 seriously injured* and *several billion dollars in damage.* Insurance companies balk at insuring utilities with nuclear power plants.

• 1953: Eisenhower's Atoms for Peace program: exporting the atom for peaceful purposes. (Impossible!) Technical assistance to scientists of foreign countries includes access to previously classified top-secret information about bomb building, training in plutonium reprocessing techniques. Home front: Ike creates massive giveaway subsidies for reactor purchases by domestic utilities who want to go nuclear. First technological export: "heavy water" to India. This material will later be used in the construction of India's first A-bomb. Learning the techniques of plutonium reprocessing are: twenty-four Indian scientists, seven Brazilians, eleven Pakistanis, five Israelis, nine Taiwanese, eight South Africans, twenty-nine Japanese, and twelve Germans. (Mention Tom Lehrer's song "Who's Next?")

• 1960: Uncle Sam has eased Hiroshima conscience by opening Mushroom Club to virtually anyone who can buy a nuclear reactor. France, West Germany, Canada have also gone into nuclear reactor exporting business.

• 1973: Pakistanis begin eating grass when India explodes first A-bomb, becoming sixth nuclear weapons state. India's explosion demonstrates the link between having a nuclear reactor and having an atomic bomb. Uncle Sam reacts with dismay. Atoms for Peace has become Bombs for Sale.

## 2. The Fuel Cycle and Plutonium

• Uranium supplies are limited. So if nuclear power is to have a future, plutonium must replace uranium. The plutonium breeder reactor—producing more plutonium than it uses—is reactor of future. This would posit tens of tons of plutonium in transit all around world. Plutonium, unless strictly guarded (it isn't yet), could be vulnerable to theft by would-be nuclear nation or terrorist group, who could use to build crude A-bomb like my own. Also, plutonium highly toxic substance. In event of accident while in transport, plutonium would contaminate environment for very long time. (Half-life of twenty-four thousand years!)

• 1977: In response to dangers, Carter Administration announces that it will abandon plans to use plutonium as a fuel. Jimmy says he will "mothball" the 2.2 billion dollar prototype breeder reactor at Clinch River. Intense nuclear industry lobbying against Carter's plans in Congress. Remains to be seen if Congress will go along with Jimmy or lobbyists.

3. The French Connection

• Despite Jimmy's policy to restrict the use of plutonium as fuel, the French have taken opposite route. *La guerre n'est pas finie!* French have promised to sell Pakistan nuclear reactor similar to elaborate reprocessing plant at La Hague. Reactor will instantly give Pakistan capability to build bomb. To hell with Iqvas Butt's bullshit on ABC. Doesn't matter if they say they don't want bomb. They will get it if French make sale.

4. Make last point first. Slowly, clearly. Don't smoke on camera. Negatori on chewing gum also. Try to avoid stupid questions re Tiger masc and 'za agency. Brisk answers. Haggle the reactor issue. But don't come off sounding like a radical shellacked with rhetoric.

Three minutes to air time. The guests are ushered out of the Green Room and down a long corridor to a door marked STAGE/ALL QUIET PLEASE. We enter the studio. The first thing that hits me is how small everything is. When one watches television, one always imagines TV-land to be a big place. But the stage set itself is no larger than a display area in the furniture department at Macy's. There is a brown shag rug, two swivel stools, a glass coffee table, and several tacky easy chairs. Technicians are everywhere, positioning cameras, hanging lights, and testing sound.

A minute before air time, I am standing behind the set. Boggs explains to me that as the "star guest," I'll be going on first. He wants me to sit on one of the swivel stools first; then after the first commercial break, I am supposed to dive into the scuzzy furniture off to the side.

"Are you nervous?" he asks me.

"Yes."

"Oh—am I doing something wrong? It's my job to get you to relax and loosen up."

"I'll be okay once we get started. This is my first talk show and all."

"You'll do fine," says Boggs.

"Just tell me one thing. If that Ganzehorn guy starts to take me apart, can I take a swing at him?"

"I won't let him do that," says Boggs. "But whenever we have someone on the show like yourself, who might say something negative about the nuclear energy industry, the lobby groups insist that it's only fair to have their hatchet man on the air with you. But don't worry about it. The audience will naturally be on your side, so if you relax, you've already won."

Boggs gives me a final wink and a pat on the shoulder. He goes out and takes his place on the set. I can tell he's on my side also. The production assistant with the clipboard comes over and clutches my arm again. She whispers in my ear that we are about to start. Suddenly some Herbie Hancock music floods the set. I can see the red light on the main camera light up. Boggs is perched on one of the stools.

He smiles and says, "Today on *Midday:* John Phillips, a twenty-one-year-old student at Princeton University has designed an atomic bomb. . . . Scientist, writer, and super typist Dr. Isaac Asimov. . . . A lesson on how to use that new kitchen wonder tool, Cuisinart. . . . And that wonder couple Comden and Green. . . ."

227

Boggs swivels around on his stool. The red light blinks on another camera. Boggs smiles again, "You know, I'm amazed at our first guest, because he is a senior at Princeton University, and I, of course, am a Penn man, and there is traditionally a rivalry between the University of Pennsylvania and Princeton—make no mistake about that. 'Course when I was at college, our main concerns were running around at TGIF parties on Friday, chasing the sorority girls, drinking beer, and generally trying to muddle through to get a degree. But this guy has drawn up a design for an atomic bomb, so we know that things have changed. . . ."

Boggs' style is very polished. But he's also genuine. You can believe what he's saying. He rambles on about Ali Zai, the F.B.I., the pizza agency, and the Tiger mascot. "He's a fascinating young man. I'll introduce you to him right now. He designed a two-thousand-dollar atomic bomb based on publicly available information. Here, ladies and gentlemen, is John Aristotle Phillips. . . ."

The lady with the clipboard gives me a little shove, and I stumble out onto the set. Some band music starts up with about fifty trumpets. I feel like King Arthur entering his court. *All bow for the King!* Boggs smiles at me as I sit down on the stool next to him. "There it is, John," says Boggs, "the Princeton fight song!"

"That's it all right," I agree somewhat stupidly, knowing damn well that it is definitely not the Princeton fight song.

The trumpets fade out. Boggs turns to me. "Let's examine some of the details that would propel a college senior to draw up plans for an atomic bomb. Was it for a class?"

"It was for the Physics Department—"

"The war department?" he interrupts with an inane smile.

"No, the Physics Department. It was independent work."

"I thought it was a secret how to make atomic bombs."

"It used to be a secret, but most of the information has

been declassified," I say, seeing a red light blink off to the right.

"I read that you made some educated guesswork on one important process in the bomb. Can you explain your design, or would it be too complicated for a Penn man to understand?" Boggs has this very jocular expression. He is asking the question just for effect, because I've told him that I'm not supposed to go into any great detail.

"I don't know if it's too complicated for a Penn man, but I'm not supposed to get into that."

"Okay. Fine. Tell me something: You just designed the bomb. You don't have one in your basement. Could you make one if you had two thousand dollars and the ingredients?"

"Well, the point of the design was to make it simple enough for a terrorist group to do it." Right away, I could kick myself for not saying that the two-thousand-dollar figure was created by the press after I'd said it could conceivably cost several thousand dollars. I guess "$2,000" will end up imprinted on my tombstone.

"What would the bomb look like?" asks Boggs. "How big would it be?"

"About the size of a beachball."

"As small as a beachball! So you could take it almost anywhere." (I'm tempted to say: That's right, and I designed a tote bag and sunglasses to go along with it.) "You know, this is scary," says Boggs. "I think it's a remarkable tribute to your intelligence. But what about this scares you, John?"

"What I find frightening is that I proved that anyone could design a bomb. That includes physics undergraduates, terrorists, or criminals. And they could in fact build one."

"That's scary. How can we control that? What can we do about it?" At last, Boggs is getting to the point. He is sensitive to the issue, and he's helping me to spoon-feed it in bite-sized pieces to the TV audience.

"Obviously, the information is already out. I proved that.

What we must do now is restrict access to the plutonium and uranium that goes into the construction of a bomb such as mine."

"Now why did the government of Pakistan get in touch with you?"

"According to the F.B.I., the Third World nations are tripping over themselves to get the bomb."

"How about the C.I.A.?" asks Boggs. "What's it like to get investigated by the C.I.A.?"

"They weren't investigating me. They were investigating the other guy."

"Right. Now, John, do you think that as a result of what you did, we could be any closer to a holocaust?"

"It was my hope that my project would prompt a clamping down on the access—"

"To plutonium and uranium—" Boggs interjects.

"Right. And I think that has happened already. It was an issue in the campaign and Carter was elected in part because of his promise to tighten up safeguards."

"Where can you get plutonium?" asks Boggs. "Can you just go out and buy it?"

"No, you can't."

"Not even on Seventh Avenue?" asks Boggs with mock innocence. The studio audience laughs.

"No, not even on Seventh Avenue. I've tried." I pause for effect, but no one laughs. I continue, "But there is a lot of plutonium missing. And if the plutonium breeder reactor is built, there will be tens of tons of the material shipped around the world, susceptible to diversion, or hijacking, or just plain getting lost. According to a recent study by the Rand Corporation, there are the beginnings of a black market in nuclear fuels. A Third World country could certainly get the bomb by purchasing outright the proper equipment under the guise of a nuclear power program."

"That's really something. Now, tell me some things about

yourself. You run a pizza business on campus. What's your biggest seller? Do you have an atomic pizza?"

"No, but the mushrooms are going fast." Why do I make bad jokes like that?

"The mushrooms! That's great. And you're also the Princeton Tiger mascot. What do you do as the Tiger?"

"Run around the field and make a fool of myself."

"And you told me before the show that you want to be an astronaut?"

"That's right."

"Do you want to go to Mars?"

"I'll go wherever they send me."

"Great—John, please stay with us. We've got another brilliant physicist, Dr. Isaac Asimov, joining us in a minute . . ."

The red light on the main camera flashes off. The studio audience seems restless. They probably want to see the commercial that's being beamed out to the audience at home. During the break, I again glance over the notes stuffed in my jacket pocket. I have a fact sheet from the Cambridge-based Union of Concerned Scientists, a group of university physicists, engineers, biologists, chemists, medical doctors, and policy makers who have studied the nuclear energy debate. Their conclusions include the following points:

> • A typical nuclear power plant contains an amount of radioactive material equal to the radioactive fallout from thousands of Hiroshima-sized weapons. The fear is not that these plants will explode like an atomic bomb. But much of this radioactive material is gaseous and could easily be carried by the wind for many miles if accidentally released. And it *can* be accidentally released.
> • One accident—from one plant—could kill as many as forty-five thousand people, cause seventeen billion in property damage, and contaminate

an area the size of Pennsylvania. In the next twenty-five years, the nuclear industry wishes to construct almost a thousand such plants.

• The basic safety system in nuclear plants designed to prevent such accidents has never actually been tested under realistic accident conditions. And when it was tested on small-scale laboratory models, this system consistently failed to function properly.

• The history of the sixty-three nuclear plants now operating in the United States shows many malfunctions of major equipment, operator errors, and design defects, as well as continuing evidence of shoddy construction practices such as poor welding, upside-down installation of critical components, etc.

I read the notes that I have jotted down in the margin concerning one nuclear near-miss, the Browns Ferry accident:

March 1975: Technician at Browns Ferry nuclear plant is checking some wiring with four-inch candle. Causes fire that burns for many hours. Knocks out both emergency safety systems. Results in the shutdown of two largest nuclear reactors in world for eighteen months' repairs. After one-hundred-fifty-million-dollar fire, one official says that nuclear catastrophe has been averted by "sheer luck."

Nuclear power supposed to be safe according to promoters in industry. But if they are so safe, why won't insurance companies insure them? (Inconsistency, my dear Watson?)

The commercial is almost over. I pull out another scrap of paper, on which I have scribbled some notes about the waste disposal dilemma:

• According to Union of Concerned Scientists: "No safe way has yet been demonstrated to dispose of the millions of gallons of lethal nuclear wastes.

These radioactive wastes, created when spent fuel is removed from the reactors, are among the most dangerous cancer-causing substances known to man. Radioactive wastes remain harmful for centuries— a grim legacy from present nuclear plants to future generations."

• Promoters of nuclear energy propose one solution after another, yet careful research consistently shows "solution" to waste disposal is inadequate. Latest example: burying wastes in salt mines. Plans to dispose wastes in Kansas salt mines aborted when Kansas Geological Survey discovered weaknesses in salt formation gone unnoticed by Atomic Energy Commission. Problem getting worse: five hundred thousand gallons wastes from government storage facilities. Some wastes will be lethal for a quarter of a million years!

• Home front: Government recently disclosed that eight thousand pounds of highly enriched plutonium and uranium are missing or unaccounted for. Was it lost? (How the hell do you *lose* plutonium?) Was it stolen? Foreshadowing of what's to come when plutonium breeder reactor is built. Each breeder processes two thousand to four thousand pounds of plutonium a year. Only takes fifteen pounds for use in a bomb like mine.

The red light on the camera blinks on. Isaac Asimov walks on the set looking grumpier than ever. Boggs introduces him to the TV audience as the author of over a hundred books. The two of them discuss his latest book on Mars while I'm sitting over in one of the easy chairs. After five minutes of banter about Mars and Asimov's writing style, we break for a commercial, and when we come back, the discussion begins.

"I wonder about your response to what John was talking about earlier," says Boggs.

Asimov takes a long, philosophical pause and says, "It

shows that the brains in some people are greater than the brains in humanity as a whole. It seems to me so sad that an ingenious product like a bomb should be viewed as a danger simply because the insanity level in human beings is so high. It is one thing to face the danger of a nuclear accident, but it is unbearable to think that some people would deliberately do that to someone on purpose."

"What do you think about the extension of conventional terrorism into atomic terrorism? Is there anything we can do about that?" Boggs asks.

"Well, terrorism has been with us a long time. The difference now is that terrorists have access to high technology."

Boggs turns to me. "John, after this publicity that you got, you said that your parents were worried. What were they worried about?"

"My personal safety."

"I think a lot of people are," says Boggs.

"I'm worried about it right now!" says Asimov. Thanks, Isaac.

"There's very little I can do about protecting myself, so I don't think it makes sense to worry about it. But I'm personally more concerned about all the people who would die, for instance, if a terrorist bomb were exploded in downtown Manhattan." Jesus, sometimes I can really sound like a martyr. There is a moment of silence after which Boggs takes a new and somewhat curious tack,

"Let's assume for a moment that this negative aspect of nuclear energy could be taken care of. What kind of world would it be if we didn't have to worry about some kooks taking the fuels and turning them into weapons of mass destruction?"

Boggs has asked this question to no one in particular, but Isaac is looking ten times more philosophical than I am at the moment, so Boggs swivels toward him.

"If we could have nuclear energy free of worry, as you

say, then we wouldn't have to worry about oil and natural gas shortages for a least a generation. So far it's been pretty safe. The only thing that's worrying us about it now is the possibility of future damage, the possibility that nuclear ash that's been stored will get out, and so on. So it's just too bad we can't take the good without the bad."

As I listen to Asimov, I am struck by two things: He is very knowledgeable about Mars, but he is pessimistic when it comes to doing something about nuclear proliferation. This doesn't really bother me. I'm just a little disappointed.

"And do you have any response to that, John?" asks Boggs.

"Yes." I begin cautiously. Can't sound like a screamy radical, I remind myself. "Let's just assume for the moment that no terrorist ever gets his hands on ten pounds of the thousands of tons of plutonium that will be shipped all around the world to supply these nuclear reactors fifteen years from now. Let's just suppose that never happens—and I hope it never does. Nuclear power is uneconomical. It never would have gotten off the ground without massive subsidies from the taxpayer. Capital construction costs for a nuclear power plant are astronomical: one billion dollars. Hundreds of millions more than the equivalent coal- or oil-fired plant. Add to this the reliability factor. Nuclear plants are shut down for costly repairs on the average fifty percent of the time. And the safety considerations: Not only are nuclear power plants dangerous to operate, but in them we are creating tons of deadly radioactive materials which will remain lethal for tens of thousands of years, or almost four times the length of recorded history. Safe, clean nuclear energy is a myth. There can be no such thing. The technology is flawed and unforgiving. It permits no error. Human beings are fallible. So I don't think it makes sense to speak of nuclear energy as the solution to future energy needs."

After having said this, I am damn glad I made those

notes. I am also beginning to feel as if designing the bomb had some greater purpose outside of whoopeedom. I feel good about speaking out. At least a few of the thousands of people who are listening to me right now will be moved to think about the issue and maybe even do something about it. It is a good feeling.

The discussion shifts to solar energy and alternative energy sources. At one point Boggs says to Asimov, "I always get the sense every time I talk to you, Dr. Asimov, that you're cynical about our future rather than optimistic."

Isaac tries to look hurt, but I think he's really pleased to be called a cynic. "Well, I try not to be," he says. "But when you look at the world and see how much more interested people are in quarreling with their neighbors than in surviving with their neighbors, you can't help but feel cynical. You have the feeling that human beings would deliberately choose death rather than life just to do their neighbors in the eye."

Boggs turns to me, "I wonder about you, John—as a student, are you cynical about the future? Do you *feel* cynical?"

"I'm very optimistic perhaps because I haven't lived as long as Dr. Asimov here. I think we're living in one of the most exciting ages ever. I think we have some problems we must address, and we must confront them head on, and look at our problems scientifically, and from a humanitarian perspective as well."

I really mean what I'm saying. As I'm speaking, I completely forget about the TV cameras and all the tension. So that's the trick of doing a talk show: Mean what you say.

"We'll take a break now," Boggs announces. "We will have a man joining us from the Atomic Industrial Forum, and we'll get into the nuclear energy issue in just a minute when we return."

I've almost forgotten that Ganzehorn is coming on. I reach back into my pocket and take out my notes once again.

I look over a statement presented to Congress and President Ford on the thirtieth anniversary of the bombing of Hiroshima, and signed by more than two thousand biologists, chemists, engineers, and other scientists:

> . . . the country must recognize that it now appears imprudent to move forward with a rapidly expanding nuclear power plant construction program. The risks of doing so are altogether too great. We, therefore, urge a drastic reduction in new nuclear power plant construction starts before major progress is achieved in the required research and in resolving present controversies about safety, waste disposal, and plutonium safeguards. For similar reasons, we urge the nation to suspend its program of exporting nuclear plants to other countries pending resolution of the national security questions associated with the use by these countries of the by-product plutonium from United States nuclear reactors.

I have scribbled more marginalia:

• September 1975: Prestigious panel of scientists, including fifteen Nobel Laureates and twenty-six members of the National Academy of Sciences, addressed the special problems of plutonium as reactor fuel on which the future of nuclear industry rests. They concluded that the use of plutonium is "morally indefensible and technically objectionable."

When I look up from my notes, Ganzehorn is on the set. Asimov has moved over to the tacky chair to my right, and Ganzehorn is swiveling around on his stool, looking massively uncomfortable. Boggs' smile could loosen up a mummified pharaoh. He looks at the main camera, "Joining us right now is Eugene Ganzehorn. He is with the public information program of the Atomic Industrial Forum, which is an international trade association that has more than six hundred organizations interested in peaceful uses of nuclear energy. Its members include manufacturers, utilities, milling and mining companies, and research and environmental organizations." Boggs turns to Ganzehorn. "When you were sitting offstage and listening to John discuss the problems of terrorist nuclear weapons, how did you react to that?"

Ganzehorn gives me what I imagine is a vaguely contemptuous look. "Well, we don't export plutonium normally," he says, "and the fuel used in nuclear reactors is extremely low-grade and can't be used for a bomb. That's first and foremost. A nuclear plant can't blow up, for instance."

"Well, John, explain your concern again."

"Yes, maybe I didn't make myself clear," I say, looking old Ganzehorn directly in the eye. "Correct, a nuclear plant cannot undergo a nuclear explosion except—"

"Just a steam explosion," Ganzehorn interrupts.

"That's correct, Mr. Ganzehorn, an explosion which releases radioactive steam that is capable of contaminating the countryside for hundreds of square miles and causing thousands of deaths. But that's only in the event of a series of highly unlikely circumstances. But that is not the issue to which I addressed myself when I designed my bomb. Your Industrial Forum is interested in the so-called peaceful uses of nuclear energy, but when India exploded her atomic bomb, they also called it a 'peaceful' nuclear explosion. So—"

"Certainly no one is going to call a bomb peaceful," he says.

"Correct, Mr. Ganzehorn, and that's just the point. India acquired the ingredients for their bomb under the guise of a peaceful nuclear energy program. So there's very little difference between atoms-for-peace and bombs-for-sale from a practical point of view."

"Well, there are cheaper ways of making a bomb, as you know," he tells me, completely avoiding the issue. Whoever asked about *cheaper* bombs? But he's hooked on them, "You don't need a power plant. I'm not a scientist, I'm a journalist, so I'm not familiar with the scientific aspects. Power plants are expensive. Of course, I don't know that much about bombs. I'm not a scientist—"

I see a weak spot and pounce, "Which is just the point. The people who are talking about this don't really know what they're talking about."

Eugene has a go-to-hell-you-little-prick expression on his face. I press the offensive, "The link between so-called 'peaceful' nuclear energy and the spread of nuclear weapons is obvious and direct. India did it, and other countries are trying to do it now."

He becomes very haughty, "Well, I don't know exactly what we're talking about. To say you can design atomic bombs is a truism—"

Boggs suddenly interrupts, "Well, I do, and I have a question I'd like you to answer, Mr. Ganzehorn." Is Boggs joining my offensive? "Is there a trade-off?" he asks Eugene. "Is it a two-edged sword? As nuclear energy spreads around the world, are we doing bad as well as good? That's what I want to know." A+ for Bill Boggs.

"Of course it's a trade-off," says Ganzehorn. His voice is edging into a whine. He's beginning to feel outnumbered.

"What's the nature of the trade-off?" asks Boggs.

"We would have lost jobs this winter if there was no nuclear energy. Now is that a good use? Do you want jobs?"

"Well, I don't know," says Boggs, knowing full well that in this instance, public safety is more important than jobs.

"Of course, it's good," Ganzehorn says, scrambling for safe ground.

"Who are your opponents?" asks Boggs. "Who are the biggest opponents of nuclear energy?"

"Well, opposition to nuclear energy comes from a small

group of people," he says. My mind flashes over the list of Nobel Laureates and scientists who signed the protest document. "It's often described as a scientific controversy. I disagree with that because I think that most of the scientists understand the value of nuclear energy and don't want it stopped. Some scientists who are not directly involved and people who call themselves scientists and people who call themselves environmentalists sometimes oppose it." Ganzehorn is pretty worked up by now. "America needs nuclear energy. We must have nuclear energy."

He makes me sick: a nonscientific controversy? A *small* group of so-called environmentalists? That's the spirit, Eugene. When you can't argue the point with the facts, attack your adversary. Make people feel like communists for being against nuclear energy. Make it *anti-American.*

"Why do you think the Pakistanis were interested in John's formula?" asks Boggs.

"I haven't the faintest idea," he says.

I'm beginning to question his intelligence. There is only so much of this kind of idiocy that I can sit and listen to.

"I'll tell you why," I say. "Because they want to use their peaceful nuclear programs and my design to build a bomb. That's why."

Ganzehorn doesn't say anything. He doesn't even do me the courtesy of looking me in the eye. Instead, he ignores me and turns to Boggs, who picks up the ball, "Eugene, if we had an environmentalist sitting here with us, he'd probably bring up the issue of nuclear wastes and the dangers of a power plant to the community in which it is built."

"The discussion of nuclear wastes is a perfectly legitimate discussion," he says. "Perfectly legitimate. What is often overlooked is that the technology exists today—right now—to handle nuclear wastes, which is a minuscule amount of waste. It's a perfectly legitimate concern to wonder what the hell are we going to do with this. But the technology does exist. And in the next ten years, the final high-level wastes will be buried in salt mines."

"Salt mines?" Boggs is incredulous.

"Salt mines. I think. From what I can tell, that's what we're going to do with this tiny amount of waste. Another thing is that the tiny amount of waste would be small enough to put into a building the size of a football stadium. That's what we're talking about."

"A good building to avoid," says Boggs, going lukewarm because he sees the producer's signal that the show is coming to a close.

"Well, you wouldn't put it in a building, of course," says Ganzehorn.

"I was just joking, Eugene," says Boggs, winding the show down. "Eugene Ganzehorn, I thank you for joining us today. Thank you, Dr. Asimov. And John, I wish you good luck, stay healthy, avoid meeting nuclear energy lobbyists in alleyways, watch out for strange phone calls from overseas, and go see Comden and Green on Broadway because they're coming up next."

The red light blips off. There is applause from the studio audience. We all rise at once to go. As everyone is saying their good-byes, Ganzehorn actually comes over to suggest that we get together for lunch the next time I'm in the "Big Apple" so that we can discuss the "real issues." He hands me his card. Asimov says good-bye and wishes me luck. We are escorted offstage while Boggs remains to finish the last part of the show. Before I leave he asks me to wait around until the end of the show.

Fifteen minutes later, he walks into the production assistant's office. I am watching the broadcast on a monitor. Boggs is congratulatory and friendly in a genuine, off-camera way.

"John, you were great! I really think the point got across loud and clear."

"*You* helped me pin the sonuvabitch down."

"I was watching the studio monitor, and you look great on the tube," he says.

"Really?" I need to be convinced.

"Seriously," says Boggs. "Are you interested at all in television, or are you dead set on going to Mars?"

"I'm not dead set on anything just now. That whole astronaut thing got started when reporters repeatedly asked me what the A-Bomb Kid was going to do for an encore, and I got tired of saying, 'I dunno.' "

"Have you been approached by any book or movie companies regarding your story?" he asks.

"No. Why? Should I have been?"

"*I* think there's a great movie in it. A book at least. Look, I don't think you should do anything you don't want, but if you're going to be doing more talk shows, you should really have an agent."

"An agent? How much do they cost?"

"Won't cost you a penny. They work on commission. Here, let me give you the name of my agent. She's very good and she works for International Creative Management—one of the best. Give her a call. See what she thinks."

"Thanks. I'll do that."

"Just tell her I sent you. She might have some ideas."

Ideas? Interesting, I think to myself. I wonder what sort of ideas. Perhaps Sir Whoopee isn't dead after all. Maybe he's just at the starting gate . . .

# 41
## Whoopee ad Infinitum?

Two weeks later, a producer from Universal Studios in Hollywood calls the room, and talks to Ralph Taylor's girlfriend,
Florence. When I return to the room, Florence gives me a big
hug. She is breathless.

"John. Universal Studios called today! They want to
make a movie!" She is semihysterical. "We're all going to be
movie stars! We're all going to be movie stars!"

Florence is jumping up and down. I am calm. I have
pretty much dismissed Bill Boggs' advice that I get myself an
agent. I designed the bomb to prove a point, not to make a
buck.

The man from Universal calls again the next day. He
tells me that Universal is interested in buying the rights to
"my story." The film he envisions would be a combination
*Love Story* and *Paper Chase*. For a moment I wonder what
the hell those films have to do with designing an atomic bomb.
The man says nothing about me acting in the film myself.
Chalk that one up to Florence's imagination. He says he wants
to come down to Princeton to talk it over. I tell him I want
to think about it.

During the rest of the week, I give the whole idea considerable thought. The man from Universal did say that he
knew of several screenplays "already in the works" which
portray a student who designs an atomic bomb. In one of
the scripts, the fictional student even goes to Princeton. If he's
telling the truth, it looks as if movies are going to be made
about me whether or not I sell anyone the rights. With this in
mind, I decide to get myself a lawyer.

243

# MUSHROOM

"I'm pleased to meet you," says Michael Heitner, a specialist in entertainment law. "I read a story about you in *The New York Times* last February. Now, what can I do for you?"

"Well—ah—I don't really know," I tell him. "I got a call from Universal Studios. They want to make a movie."

"Do *you* want them to make a movie?"

"I don't know. I guess it depends on the type of movie."

"That's only fair. After all, your reputation is at stake here. You can't allow them to go off and make a lousy movie. On the other hand, if it's a legitimate outfit, and your interests are protected, you could get your point across and make a little money for yourself. And besides, if there really are other projects developing, someone is going to be making a lot of money off this idea. How do you feel about that?"

"To be perfectly honest, it pisses me off."

"In other words, you're saying that if someone is going to be making money off the idea, it may as well be you."

"Yes, but is there any way I can make sure that the point behind my designing the bomb will get across in the film? The money is enticing, but frankly, I'm really more concerned about the principle behind the thing."

"I think it can be arranged if you play your cards right. The first thing you must do is write down the entire story in detail. It should be a kind of diary. We'll get that copyrighted so that anyone who wants to make a movie will have to go through us. But more important, you should think about this whole thing, decide what you want out of it, and then give me a call."

Two weeks later, the diary is sent over to a literary agent. He thinks there is a very good book in it and agrees to represent me. I begin to live half my life in New York, rushing between the offices of my lawyer and my agent, while spending the other half at Princeton trying to catch up on my schoolwork. Throughout it all I keep David posted on the latest developments. I turn to him and to my parents for advice, for reassurance that what I'm doing is right, and for the confidence needed even to contemplate writing a book.

Over beers and pizza, David and I talk late into the night about what one would say about the entire experience if given a chance. David thinks there is a story to tell, but he wonders if Sir Whoopee hasn't been beaten to death already. We both agree that the serious points about proliferation and safeguards must be made. But the task is gargantuan, and I realize early on that my meager literary talents do not correspond to the caliber of book I want to write. The possibility of a ghostwriter is explored in New York, while in Princeton, David dismisses the notion as the worst form of sellout. He honestly believes this, but I know that he would like to help me write the book. It doesn't take much convincing before I realize that the book would be less superficial if I relied on the talents of my closest friend, whose perspective on the whole story would be greater than a ghostwriter's. Three weeks later, William Morrow offers a contract for the book.

The phone call from Universal and the opportunity to write a book have forced me to make decisions about my life. In recent months, I've been so involved in the daily vicissitudes of whoopee that I haven't given much thought to the future. I don't pretend to know what I will be most happy doing two or ten years from now. I can say with certainty that I will want to do something meaningful, something that benefits my fellow man. There will have to be some adventure and a challenge in whatever I do because I need to encounter new and exciting experiences from which I can learn more about myself and life.

I continue to think about becoming an astronaut, but there are questions. The people who know me best—my parents, Professor Dyson, Frank Chilton, and David—don't think I'm really cut out to be an astronaut. They believe that I would rebel against the rigid restrictions imposed by the people in the astronaut corps. Perhaps they are right. Of course, no one has offered me the lead in a film yet.

---

# 42

# The Three-Piece Whoopee
## (Dress for Success)

Mark Carliner is a producer. He went to Princeton, graduated Phi Beta Kappa in 1960, and flew out to Hollywood shortly thereafter. Although I have never met a Hollywood producer before, I spot him right away in the flood of drab-gray businessmen in the lobby of the Princeton Club in New York on a sunny afternoon in July. He is wearing stylish slacks and a tapered shirt. His loafers click as he walks. He spots me, waves, and clicks over to where I am standing.

"Hello, John! Mark Carliner!"

Some people speak in measured phrase in which you can almost visualize the commas and periods. Mark speaks in exclamation points. As we walk toward the club dining room exchanging banter about Princeton, I can see each exclamation point lit in neon.

I have told my agent that selling the film rights would depend upon my having two things: veto power over the script to insure that the film will not misrepresent the political implications of the bomb design, and the right to play myself in the lead role. My agent had sounded skeptical about the latter, but at least he hadn't laughed out loud.

Mark clicks ahead of me into the dining room. I am dying to find out what he is thinking. If he is really serious

246

about making a movie, will I get the lead? If he says no to the lead, will I be able to stick to my guns? Mark tells the maitre d' that we want a table in the corner where we can "discuss business."

The waiter comes immediately to take our drink orders. Mark orders ice water. Interesting. I ask for 7-Up. Mark looks amused. He unfolds his orange napkin and looks me in the eye. He smiles.

"Well! John!" By the way he says this, the appropriate response would be: "Well! *Mark!*" I smile and say nothing. He drops the napkin in his lap and begins: "I first read the story in the *L.A. Times* last February and then saw the article in *People* and thought, Wow! what a picture this would make! College kid designs A-bomb, gets famous, and is chased by Pakistani spies!"

He is talking a jet streak, which I suppose is normal for a Hollywood producer. And yet, despite all the hype, he seems genuinely enthusiastic. This makes it hard for me to keep him at a distance. "How would you like to become a star, John? Are you psyched to make a TV movie about your life?" Hearing this, I assume that my playing the lead won't be an issue. I am relieved. I let my defenses down a little.

"Yes, I think it could be a fine movie. I'm looking forward to doing it." Something prevents me from directly addressing the question of the lead right away. But then, remembering the advice of my lawyer, I try to sound uninterested: "Of course, it depends on the type of movie."

Mark puts a piece of bread in his mouth and swallows it at once. His tempo is building. "I want you to tell me the whole story, beginning to end. I want the details this afternoon so I can get a feel for the kind of screenwriters I'll want to hire when I get back to L.A. Then I'll fly you out to meet them. The movie will be a rough adaptation of the real story, fixed up in places, if you know what I mean."

\* \* \*

# MUSHROOM

Two hours later. We have moved from the dining room up to the reading room. I am almost finished telling Mark about the Pakistani Affair. He has been interrupting me periodically to inject an enthusiastic "This is *terrific!* You just wait and see!" I have reiterated the political implications behind the bomb design several times. Mark has responded by saying, "When we make this movie, *laws* will be changed!"

As I bring the story to a close, I feel myself getting excited about the idea of a movie that will change people's minds about nuclear proliferation and the safeguarding of plutonium. But my enthusiasm is squelched when I realize that Mark is already talking with assurance about making the movie himself. The intimations of a fait accompli without the question of the lead resolved make the next twenty minutes unbearable. "Now, I spoke with your agent about the contracts," says Mark. His exclamatory notes have been scaled down to a subdued businesslike tone: allegro to largo. "He mentioned that you want to play yourself in the film. All I can say, John, is that I'll see what we can do."

"There are two things I expect from this film," I tell him flatly. "One is veto power over the script. And the other is the—"

"John. I might be able to work something out regarding the veto power to give you some say in what the final product will be. But all I can do regarding the lead is write into the contract that I will do my best to get it for you."

"Mark. Maybe my agent didn't explain clearly enough: no lead, no movie. Those are the only terms under which I will sign away the rights."

"But it's not in my power to guarantee the lead. I am an independent producer. CBS buys the film from me. Everything has to be okayed by CBS, and they can't okay anything until after you've signed the contract. That's the way it works out there. I'll do my best. That's all I can promise in the contract."

248

There is a certain finality in his voice which irritates the hell out of me. When I'm mad, I can get extremely impatient with people who say that something is impossible.

"I'm sorry, Mr. Carliner, but that's just not good enough. No lead, no movie."

"That's impossible, John. Hollywood doesn't work like that. CBS won't risk a million bucks on a kid who's never acted before."

"Don't tell me what's possible and what's not. I designed an atomic bomb."

Even as the words come snapping out, I am aware of their arrogance. But in a funny way, I am not ashamed of them. I figure that one of the few things Mark will respond to is bullishness. He responds by calling me "kid." "There's a big difference between designing a bomb and making a movie, kid. All I can do is promise to do my very best . . ."

We storm on in this fashion for another hour. Mark ranges up and down the scale, alternating between the Sonata of the Unmade Flick and the Ballad of the Independent Producer (at the mercy of the CBS *Fledermaus*). Finally, I weaken my tune and agree to think about his terms. Carliner tells me I am being sensible. He smiles and says that he will see to it personally that I don't sell away the rights "for a song."

I call Mike Heitner on the phone.

"Do their best—bullshit! It's typical of these Hollywood types. You're not going to sign any contract unless it's got the guaranteed lead written in. Otherwise they'll get the rights and forget about their promises. They'll spit you out like a plum pit. We tell them no lead, no rights."

"Somehow it sounds more convincing when you say that," I tell Heitner.

"If you don't want to tell Carliner, then I will. But since he wants to fly you out there, it's only fair to let him know what your conditions are before he goes to the expense of getting you together with the screenwriters. Then, if he still wants you to fly out, fine. You can enjoy all the things Hollywood producers do for people from whom they want something. But we have to tell him now that you won't sign anything."

"Okay, I'll call him tomorrow when he's back in L.A."

When I call Carliner's office the next day, his secretary answers and immediately asks me what flight I'd like to be booked on. First class, of course.

"The flight won't be necessary."

"What?"

"I said that it won't be necessary."

"You mean you're not coming out?"

"I don't think so. Listen, if Mark is busy, he can call me later."

"No, wait," she says. "I'll find him."

A minute later, Mark gets on the phone. His voice has an edge of panic in it, "What do you mean you're *not* coming out?"

"My final position is no lead, no rights, Mark. I'm just trying to save you money. It would be a waste flying me out because I'm not going to sign anything that doesn't give me the lead." There is a long silence. My bravery wears thin. I add, "My attorney won't let me."

Mark short-circuits, "John, you're crazy! If those are your final conditions, you've blown the deal! There's no way they're going to use a novice in a million-dollar film! You're going to blow the whole deal!"

"I know." I try to conceal the disappointment in my voice.

"You're making a big mistake, kid. I'll go in and tell the CBS brass that unless we guarantee you the lead, you won't sell us the rights. Is that what you want? I'll go in there right now, and I can tell you ahead of time they're going to laugh me right out of the office. Is that really what you want me to do? Are you sure?"

At times, Carliner can be very convincing. I almost tell him to forget it; that I'll be out on the next flight. I resist the temptation. There is a long silence.

"John? . . ."

"Call me when you get their decision."

"Okay, *kid*," he says sarcastically, slamming down the phone.

An hour later, the phone rings.

"Well, kid, I told you. You've blown the deal. They laughed me right out of the office. You've really blown it, kid. Now nobody's going to make your film."

"That's my problem, isn't it?" I'm beginning to get a little sick of Carliner's patronizing tone.

"Nobody's going to touch your story. Maybe if you're lucky, the Triangle Club will accept it for the spring comedy."

"If they give me the lead, I'll sell them the rights."

Now it's my turn to hang up in a fury. But when I slam down the receiver, it makes me more angry than before. I am massively bummed. I begin to hear the distant screaming of a colony of rhubarbs heading in my direction.

The next afternoon I am standing in front of a triptych mirror at Paul Stuart, trying on suits. The salesman is trying to convince me that I look "distinguished" in a three-piece gray herringbone, when I see David's reflection in the mirror. He has been working on the book up at his apartment, but he is now running full tilt across the floor. He shouts something to me, and I figure he's come to give me shit about "tacky" suits.

"Could I see that tweed one again?" I ask the salesman.

David pounces on me. He starts talking at 78 rpm,

"J.P., you don't understand. Carliner just called. He said he convinced the CBS brass to risk a million dollars so you can play yourself."

"Very funny. What did he say?"

"I'm not kidding. Carliner did it. He's very proud of himself. You've got to get out to Hollywood by Sunday. He told me to tell you that you absolutely can't stutter or stammer because he's stuck his neck way out."

"Are you serious?"

"Perfectly."

"Hot damn!"

We leave Paul Stuart and walk up Madison Avenue. I let out a whoop. "I thought you were coming to give me shit about the suit."

"No, I wanted to tell you right way. I looked everywhere. Brooks. Abercrombie. Tripler."

"Unbelievable. Listen, I have to meet my mom at Tripler's right now."

"Okay, I'll meet you back at the apartment. Oh, J.P., one more thing. That gray suit was truly tacky."

"Okay, David, later."

"Much," he says, crossing the street. I walk into Tripler's. I hear David yelling something. I stick my head out the door. "Dress for success, pal!" he shouts, referring to the manual of the same title which my mother gave me when I started looking for a three-piece suit.

# 43
## Sic Itur ad Astra

"Welcome to the Beverly Wilshire, sir."

The doorman holds the car door open. I step out of the Mark Carliner Productions limousine into the brilliant California sunlight. Three porters immediately rush over to carry my one suitcase. I walk into the hotel, an ornate extravaganza designed for the very rich and the heavies in the movie industry. Just before I get to the desk, I hear a muffled whisper behind me. I turn around. The porter is staring at me.

"Are you in the business?" he asks in a secretive tone.

Not knowing what to say, I make a half-turn to the blond girl at the desk. "Your name, sir?" she asks.

"Phillips. John Aristotle Phillips."

She looks at me blankly.

I clear my throat. "I'm here with Carliner Productions."

"Mark Carliner Productions? *Yes, sir!*"

As soon as I get my things into my room, I change and find a cab outside the hotel.

"CBS headquarters. Studio City, please."

"Yes, sir," says the driver. We ride along in silence for a few minutes and then the driver says, "You an actor or something?" Before I have a chance to say anything, he says, "I been in a coupla flicks myself. TV shows and all. Mostly extra parts is all though. I get work now and again." He looks at me in the rearview mirror. "Let's see. You're a writer? Am I right?"

"Ah, sort of. I guess."

"And CBS digs it, huh? Hit 'em for all they're worth. If you have faith in your story, don't settle for anything less. Be smart. I'm a writer, too, ya see. I write some pretty good stuff. You should let me show it to you sometime."

"If you're a writer, what are you doing driving a cab?"

"Got to eat sometimes. But I'm really good. In fact, I make this run over to Studio City once, twice every day. Network execs mostly. I got a copy of my script here in the cab. I show it to some of 'em. You wanna take a look? Maybe you can take it around to a coupla producers or something."

"Listen, I'm really a nobody. I have no connections and it would be a waste of paper giving it to me. Honest."

We ride in silence through the gate of CBS's Studio City. Since I can do nothing for him, he's got nothing more to say to me. I get out in front of the CBS headquarters, a four-story poured-concrete pill box.

Mark's secretary, Anne, a statuesque redhead, greets me warmly and fixes some coffee. She's nice. Friendly. Genuine. I like her.

Mark is warm and enthusiastic. He leads me into his inner office. The first thing I notice is an orange-and-black Princeton beer mug on a table. Mark sits down behind a huge desk.

"You know, John baby, I never thought all this would happen. But I went back in with the CBS brass and—I don't know how I did it, but I convinced them that they had to take a look at you. Can you believe that? You're going to be a star."

We both become aware of a light melody drifting through the walls. There is the sound of many people applauding while a woman sings. She trills up the musical scale, straining for the high notes. All of a sudden she is interrupted by the sound of boots pounding pavement, a command barked in German, and then the rattle of submachine-gun fire. A few seconds of hysterical screaming follows.

Mark jumps up and puts his ear against several places

on the wall. He is baffled. "Anne! Anne!" he shouts. "Could you please find out what that is. I can't work in here with that holocaust going on next door."

"I already checked," she calls from the outer office. "They're screening a new Nazi war series upstairs."

"Good Christ!" says Mark, throwing his hands up in the air, and returning to his desk resigned to the intrusion. Ah, the woes of Hollywood, I think to myself. Mark fires off some last-minute instructions to Anne regarding the preparations for tonight's party at Mark's house to celebrate his birthday and the beginning of the "Mushroom" project. Anne shows Mark a list. "Yes, tell him he can come," says Mark. "Who's he? . . . No, he can't . . . oh, to hell with it . . . sure, send him an invitation, too. . . . And Anne, could you phone Ross Brown and ask him to please come down and take a look at the Kid." Anne leaves.

"Ross is one of the top casting directors in the business," explains Mark. "I asked him to take a look at you. CBS is going to want to give you what is called a "personality test.' It's like a screen test only not as tough. It's scheduled for Wednesday afternoon, and after the CBS brass take a look at it, they'll make final decisions."

Five minutes later, Ross Brown strides into the room. The first thing I notice is that he has a tremendous amount of presence: attractive, big, and yet not showy. He has that peculiar something that would make him stand out in a crowd. He is solidly built, but he doesn't seem at all athletic. A small, thin cigar resides comfortably between his teeth.

"Mark," he says, nodding. There is a trace of an accent which I guess is Australian. He turns to me, "I'm Ross Brown, and you must be—" he pauses, smiling with his panda bear eyes, "the Kid."

I have been getting thoroughly sick of that label, but somehow when Ross uses it, the phrase takes on a special, humorous quality. There is a sense of directness and perspective in his voice that blends together with a distinct self-confidence. Right off, I can tell he has an excellent sense of humor. His eyes show that he can laugh at himself. I know I'm going to like him.

We sit: Mark behind his desk, me on the couch, and Ross in a swivel chair directly across from me. And I mean *directly* across. He immediately hunches forward, puts his chin in his hands, and squints at me. It is a cold, judgmental, absolutely professional squint. But there is an honest intensity in his face that is completely different from that of anyone else I have seen in Hollywood. "What exactly do you do around here?" I ask him.

There is silence. Rather than answer my question, he cocks his head to one side. His gaze intensifies.

"What do you want?" he asks me.

I think about it for a second. "What's available?"

Mark is taken back by my response. "Ross, what do you think?" he asks.

"Well," says Ross, "his nose is too big, he's got a gummy smile, and his voice is a little flat . . . But I *like* it." Then, almost to himself, "I *like* the effect— Can you act?"

"No."

"He's honest too. The acting can be taken care of. I'd like to send you over to see Vincent Chase. He's an acting coach and he's *good*." When Ross emphasizes certain words, I can tell that he really means them. He is not excessive with his speech. I am again struck by his honest and straightforward manner.

After they make arrangements for me to see the acting coach, I walk with Ross up to his office on the fourth floor. We enter the room and the first thing that grabs my attention is a tiny, plastic Christmas tree with blinking lights set against the bay window, catching the August sunlight. Ross smiles. It is a smile that indicates his awareness of the absurd side of life. Ross sits down, slowly unwraps a fresh cigar, and lights up. Taking a puff, he turns to look at me.

"Now, what did you say you wanted?"

"I need someone I can trust." I say this without having thought about it beforehand. Having said it, I realize that I have never opened myself so completely to a near-stranger before. Curiously, it feels good.

Ross blows a cloud of smoke into the air and continues to regard me. He smiles slowly. "Fair enough." He extends his hand. We shake. Just like that. I know he's going to play straight with me. I just know.

"Hollywood is a wunnnderful place," says Ross, elongating "wonderful" to make it sound like a crazy roller-coaster ride.

"It seems hard to trust people out here."

Ross thinks for a moment. "Fair enough," he says. And then comes the laugh: a deep, genuine, lunar laugh that makes you want to laugh with him. While I'm enjoying this moment with Ross, I think: This is the first time I've had a good laugh since I arrived in this strange world. I guess I eventually had to find someone to laugh with in Hollywood.

A call comes from Mark's office: A meeting has been called so that the head honcho at CBS can meet me. Ross and I share another smile. This could be it.

Entering Paul Monash's office, I glance at posters of Monash productions: *Carrie, The Exorcist, Butch Cassidy and the Sundance Kid,* and others. The Great Monash—gray-haired, intense, Napoleonic—is seated behind his desk. He rises, shakes my hand assertively: testing. He smiles slightly and sits down. Looking at Monash's desk, I make a mental observation: Out of all the desks I have seen in the CBS headquarters, Mark Carliner's is the biggest.

There are others in the room. Mark looks anxious. Ross

looks confident. Jerry Adler, the number-two man at CBS, looks intrigued. I sit down on the couch, remove my panama hat, and balance it on my knee. Monash begins in an authoritative manner:

"You designed an atomic bomb, did you?"

"I did."

"And now you think you can play the lead in a million-dollar movie?"

"I do."

"Have you ever acted professionally?"

"Never."

"And you won't sell us the rights until we give you the lead?"

"Those are my terms." I figure that at times like this, the less said, the better.

Monash continues, "We cannot guarantee you the lead in a two-hour TV movie unless we know that you can act."

"Well, then," I say, "we'd better find out if I can act if we're going to talk business, hadn't we?" Right after I've said this, I get up, put on my hat, and turn to leave. The room is electric.

"Wait a minute!" says Monash, also rising. He is smiling now. There is a long pause.

"I like you," says Monash, pointing at me with his forefinger. He pauses again. "You've got the lead."

*Wham.* Just like that.

Mark is incredulous. Ross is laughing. Monash says, "How did a goddamn Princeton senior get in here anyway? You know, I think we're sitting here with a fucking genius."

When we get outside the office, Mark is ecstatic, "I can't believe we did it!" he marvels.

"Congratulations, kid," says Jerry Adler, shaking my hand. "You've got balls."

Fifteen minutes later, I am downstairs in the Carliner

Productions office. Mark is still on the fourth floor. Ross calls and whistles the Cole Porter tune, "Another Op'nin', Another Show."

"It's final," he says. "They even canceled the personality test. Congratulations—*kid*."

A minute later, Mark comes bursting into the office. "They called off the personality test!" he shouts. "We're going to make you a star, kid. I don't believe it!" He laughs. "You know," he says, "what gets me is that you're handling all this exactly the way I would."

An hour later, I am at Vincent Chase's studio. Vincent's life is the actors who come to him. He has worked with the best, transforming an impressive number of amateurs into stars. He is a very kind man who is both supportive and critical.

He has me read a short script first. Then he puts me in front of a video camera to read it again. When I am finished, he turns out the bright spotlights, and reviews the tape on a TV monitor.

"I thought so," he says.

"What?"

"Ross was right. You've got a certain quality and it is captured beautifully on the screen. It's a kind of innocence, honesty, and attractiveness that others would give their right arm to possess. I would say you're a natural. You should consider yourself lucky. I train actors for years to imitate what you just demonstrated."

I could almost believe him if I saw something special when I watched myself on the video screen. Instead, all I can see is me being myself and saying some lines rather awkwardly. It is not a riveting performance.

"Of course you'll need professional training. You obviously don't know how to act, and even in a film in which you'll be playing yourself, you're going to have to act."

# 44

## Twinkle, Twinkle in Tinseltown

That night, I am walking up the long red gravel path to the party at Mark's mansion. I pass a string of parked chauffeur-driven limousines and manicured bushes where the bright light from the house is shining on the leaves. I can already hear the sounds of the party rising and falling in a roller-coaster rhythm. The closer I get to the front door, the more I feel like an outsider. I'm excited about watching the follies of a Hollywood party, but I am apprehensive. I remind myself of Mike Heitner's admonition, "Enjoy all the things Hollywood producers do for people when they want something, but don't let them get you drunk so you'll sign it all way." Right away, I resolve not to touch a drop of booze.

Enter John the Mormon.

Inside, I make my way through the crush of well-tanned, expensively garbed bodies. There are dozens of people linked together in shiny groups where gold earrings, silver cigarette cases, and ice cubes catch the light. All these people seem to be beautiful for a living, or at least they seem to relish the fact of being beautiful together. Strolling through these clusters are gypsy mandolin players, palm readers, and a small army of white-jacketed butlers presenting little snips of this and that on silver trays.

I step out onto the garden through sliding glass doors. Small linen-covered tables illuminated by torches are set along the slope leading down to the pool. Like the storage pools where highly radioactive nuclear fuel rods are kept in an atomic reactor, Mark's pool radiates a dazzling blue-purple light. It somehow looks too pristine, and I entertain the image of it being filled with wild, half-dressed revelers before the night is over. Mark's voice startles me.

"John! What took you? I was worried you might not come."

There is again the element of hurt in his voice, echoing from this afternoon at the screening room. I can tell he seriously thought I might not come on purpose. Twinkle, twinkle. Mark has a young, blond girl dangling off the right sleeve of his pearl-white dinner jacket. She is quite sozzled and seems to be using Mark as a kind of lamppost. Mark explains to her that he wants to introduce me to some "important" people. She gives an alcoholic nod and burbles off into the party. Mark puts his arm around me, snaps up a glass of champagne from a passing tray, and hands it to me. I hold it, but don't drink.

Everyone I meet is either a producer, a director, or a screenwriter. The comments I get are similar in every cluster we enter: "Oh! So *this* is the A-Bomb Kid!" or "Congratulations, kid. I heard you gave CBS a run for their money," or my all-time favorite, "*You're* the guy who designed that bomb? What the hell are you doing in Hollywood?"

After a half hour of this, Mark takes me aside near the food table and says, "Get used to this crowd, John, because after you become a star, you'll be working and playing with a lot of these people."

The only people I'd really like to see right now are Ross and his partner, Hank. God, would I like to talk with them. Just as I'm thinking this, I see Mark's birthday cake on the table near me. It is a huge cake with yellow frosting, but it has a funny shape. I move a step closer. A mushroom! The goddamn thing is shaped like a giant mushroom. There is lettering on the top: SITTING ON A MUSHROOM [the proposed title for the film] HAPPY BIRTHDAY MARK! I control my immediate urge to sit on the cake.

Suddenly I start to laugh. If anyone had told me a year

ago that I would be a guest at a Hollywood party prior to my acting in a film called *Sitting on a Mushroom,* and that the film would be my autobiography at age twenty-one, I would have told him he was crazy. Or I would have laughed. Which is what I'm doing now.

An hour later, I am sitting at a large table in the house. Ross and Hank found me laughing next to the birthday cake, and, overruling my violent protests, they have dragged me into the party to have my fortune told by Madame Zenobia, a tarot card reader.

Madame Zenobia is an enormous woman, garbed in flowing, colorful robes which reach out a full two feet on either side of her chair. Her bust is enormous, and her face is so made up that it looks as if she stuck her face into the birthday cake. Her eyelashes are enchanting. Most people have ten toes and ten fingers. Madame Zenobia has ten eyelashes: five long hairy things pasted on each eyelid. She bats these laboriously from time to time. A good wind would blow them down into the pool. She is delightful.

Ross introduces me to her and forces me to sit down at the table where she is turning the cards for her unfortunate victims. Twenty people crowd around the table.

"I'm looking forward to reading your cards," says Madame Zenobia in a thick Brooklyn bark.

(A brief word about astrology is necessary here: Astrology is bullshit.)

I'm about to tell her no thanks when Ross interjects: "He'd be delighted." I glare at Ross. He is smiling with a cigar between his teeth, looking more panda-bearish than ever. Mark is standing among the crowd around the table. We exchange grins. Standing next to Ross is an unspeakably beautiful girl, named Kathy Davis. She is a twenty-four-year-old fashion model who wants to be an actress. It is painful to look at her. Her styled blond hair ripples around a face that is at once intelligent and coolly sexual. She is wearing a black Halston gown and her body is sculpture. I smile at her. She winks at me.

Madame Zenobia squares the deck. She turns to me, batting her eyelashes.

"What's yer sign?" she asks.

"My sign?"

Mark announces: "We're all Leos here!"

"A Leo. I shoulda known," says the Madame. She flips through the deck once, then a second time. She looks perplexed. Sticking out her jaw, she resquares the deck. Her eyelashes stop fluttering. "That's strange," she says. "I can't find the Leo card . . . I'll just have to use the top card on the deck." She shuffles the deck a third time, and lays three rows of six cards face down on the table. "Now we begin," she announces.

With a twist of her wrist, she snaps the first card over, showing a picture of a relatively docile lion yawning in a lavender field. A murmur comes from the crowd—no doubt astrological buffs all. Madame Zenobia's eyelashes are about to fly away.

"That's like interesting," she says. "Your missing Leo card reappeared as the first card. You are a very lucky person." I smile politely. I do not believe in luck, especially the foretold variety, so I say nothing. Getting no reaction from me, she turns over the next card: the Ten of Cups. "You're going to make a lot of money in your lifetime," she states. "Lots of money." As the third and fourth cards are turned, I maintain my polite smile. I feel the crowd getting bigger around me.

"Oh, wow!" says Madame Zenobia. "This is like unbelievable. You're going to make so much money you won't be able to count it. Everything you touch in the world will be so, like, so beautiful."

It's that Midas touch, I tell myself. She flips over the next few cards in a hurry, as if searching frantically for connected meanings. She is either faking it very well, or she really believes this crap. I am intrigued by people who can lie effectively—something I've never succeeded at. The Page of Pentacles, the Wheel of Fortune, and the Ace of Pentacles go by. Madame Zenobia tells me that I have a creative, innovative mind and that I will make all my money before I'm twenty-five. The Four of Pentacles reversed is turned over. Her mouth twitches. She tells me that I am also going to lose millions of dollars. But when the Nine of Cups comes up, her eyes splash around under their great awnings. "The money you lose won't matter," she says, looking relieved. "You'll have so many millions, it'll just be a drop in the bucket." Someone laughs.

"The Emperor," she announces with a flourish. "You've got a brilliant, inventive mind." And then, "The Sun—You are so lucky! You're almost—like you're almost *enchanted*." I thought she was supposed to be the enchanted one around here. The next card is the Magician, a serious little guy with tiny stars around his head. "There's a certain magic in your life . . . let me see . . . a magic which goes along with your brilliance . . . but—but like you weren't bright in everything when you were a child . . . like you weren't good with girls or like taking tests or something . . ."

Her voice trails off. She wants me to affirm this conclusion. I remain silent because I really want to test her "powers." It is true: I never did well on tests.

The next card is the Ace of Wands. "You'll be doing unimaginable things . . . it's you against the world . . . you against the odds." The Eight of Wands comes up. Madame Zenobia is concentrating intensely. I expect her to say something very prophetic about my future. Instead, it is another "you are a very lucky person."

"I don't believe in luck," I tell her.

"Oh," she says, looking a little peeved. There are giggles

around the table. The Chariot is turned up. Madame Zenobia stares blankly at the card. She squeezes her eyes closed, welding her lashes together as she communicates with the beyond. A few moments pass in silence. Finally, her mouth opens, trembling. With her eyes still shut, she says in faltering tones, "Forgive me . . . this doesn't make any sense . . . but . . . I see . . . I . . . I see . . . *equations?*" She opens her eyes, bewildered. "I see your first success coming from equations."

There is a collective gasp around the table. Ross and Hank respond to my accusatory glance with looks of innocence. Mark must have told her. He is just now leaving the table. Maybe she read about me in the papers. Madame Zenobia searches my face for signs of gullibility. Satisfied that she's made a believer out of me, she turns over the next card.

"The Hermit! This means that a contract may soon be signed."

Madame Zenobia turns over the penultimate card: the Page of Wands. She thinks for a moment. "You are very creative, very bright, but you need someone—like almost an older brother to advise you." I look directly at Ross, whose head is thrown back in the midst of his lunar laugh. I scowl at him. Madame Zenobia turns to me, satisfied that she has done a tremendous job. She asks if I have any questions.

"Yes, what's the last card?"

She is flustered. From under her arm she takes the card she has overlooked and turns it over: the Three of Pentacles. "Yes, yes," she says. "You're a very lucky person, and . . . ah, and . . . a contract is definitely going to be signed in the near future."

Despite feeling a little like Dorothy finding the Wizard of Oz behind a curtain, I thank Madame Zenobia and turn to go. Mark is standing behind me, grinning. "Hey? What did I tell you," he says.

"Come on, Mark."

"What's the matter, kid?"

"Level with me. How much did you tell her and how much did she read in the papers?"

"Nothing. Honest." He is trying to look shocked that I would even ask.

I smile at him. "All right, you bastard, then you're going to have a drink with me. I'll get it out of you before the night is over."

"You saw the cards, John. The Kid is going to be big— *very* big!"

We laugh together.

# 45

## No Tongue

Wednesday is an extremely Three Stooges kind of day. It starts when the maid kicks me out of my room at the Beverly Wilshire because my reservation has expired. When I arrive at Mark's office, I am introduced to two young screenwriters who have been assigned by CBS to *Sitting on a Mushroom*. Mark had told me earlier that he would try to persuade the CBS brass to hire a highly regarded, veteran screenwriter named Phil Reisman, but for the moment we are stuck with the young screenwriting team because CBS is convinced that only young writers can "relate" to a story about the A-Bomb *Kid*.

I sit down with the screenwriters and begin to tell them the story. Right away, I can tell they aren't right. They both ask questions about "the love interest" and "the father figure," as if they're trying to fit it all into an unbeatable formula.

Every time I flash an aggrieved glance at Mark, he gives me a "bear with it" look. So I am forced to spend the next two hours telling them about my first impressions of Princeton, the Tiger mascot, the pizza agency, and the implications behind my bomb design. By noon, I haven't even gotten to Ali Zai. Just before we break for lunch, one of the screenwriters asks me where I keep my bomb hidden.

Jesus.

I race up to Ross' office during lunch and receive some bad news. Ross tells me that CBS has changed its goddamn corporate mind. The top brass balked and now they want to see me in a screen test before they give final go-ahead. I can't believe it. How can CBS renege? Angry alternatives for revenge race through my head. Ross convinces me that it would be damaging to go storming into Monash's office. I am forced to sit and stew. Ross tries to brighten me up.

"Did I ever tell you about Hermione Gingold's wig?" he asks.

"No. Who's she?"

Ross' face lights up. He is warming to a good story. I have never met a man who takes such pleasure in telling stories. (Ross also gets infinite pleasure from thunderstorms, panda bears, and Coney Island hot dogs.)

"Hermione Gingold is an actress," he tells me. "One night after a show on Broadway, she walked out of the stage door into the pouring rain. A gust of wind took her wig off and blew it down the alley. Two young men passing by began to pursue the wig. They chased it all the way down the alley and finally got it. One of the young men took it back to her and said, "Madam, I'm very sorry. Your little dog has drowned.""

We both start laughing. The phone rings. Mark is desperate: "What am I going to do, Ross? The Monster will get on a plane and fly home when I tell him. He'll think I screwed him." Ross tells Mark not to get excited. The "Monster" can probably be convinced to go through with the screen test. I grimace monsterlike at Ross. He blows a puff of smoke in the air and gives me an everything-is-going-to-be-okay look.

By Thursday, I am less angry at CBS, and more worried about myself. The screen test is tomorrow, and let's face it, I can't act. I've worked with Vincent Chase for two days on vocal projection, relaxing on camera, picking up cues, and so on. Vincent is doing his best, but I'm beginning to think the whole thing is hopeless. That morning, the screenwriters drop off a script to be used for the screen test. It is a scene between me and Mary-Lee where I am trying to seduce her in my dorm room. It is so far from the real me and the real Mary-Lee as to be laughable. Every time I say one of my lines, I sound like Wally Cleaver talking to Beaver. Vincent and I read it over and over again. It does not improve.

That afternoon, Ross sends over several girls to try out for the role of Mary-Lee in the screen test. The first one who appears is named Sandy. She's an attractive girl. A bit nervous. She thinks she is trying out for a part in the actual movie. I show her the script and ask her if she thinks anyone would make a movie out of this junk. She looks at it and laughs. But not because she thinks the dialogue is bad. She thinks the part about a college kid designing an atomic bomb is ludicrous. Vincent signals us to start reading. I try to act as if I know what I'm doing, but it's painfully obvious that I don't. It all becomes very awkward when we get to the kiss. The first read-through is rushed, so we don't actually kiss. The second time is slower. The dialogue sounds just as bad, maybe worse. The kiss is pathetic: tight and clinical. No Rhett Butler and Scarlett O'Hara on the stairs of Tara here. By the third time around, I've discovered that if I pretend she's a real girl and not an actress, the kiss works better. I'm about to try it again, but Vincent thanks Sandy and shows her to the door. She wants to know if she got the part.

Sandy isn't gone two minutes before the next girl knocks on the door. In walks Julie, a brunette, tall, cute, but condescending. I immediately realize she's wrong. She is older than I am and I feel like a kid next to her on the couch. We run through it several times without any success. I thank her and she leaves. Vincent asks me what I thought of the first two.

"The first one was too nervous, and the second was better, but she was too old for me. I don't know, Vincent."

"Why did you like the second one?" He walks to the door to let the next girl in.

"She was a better kisser," I tell him.

Vincent opens the door. Patty is tall, blond, and beautiful. Feeling as if I'm finally getting the hang of this, I give her the script and tell her what's going on.

"Ready?" I ask. She nods, positioning herself on the couch. She smiles at me and licks her lips. I sit down next to her and slide my arm around her back. We launch into the script. I hear the cue for the kiss and begin to turn her toward me. For some reason she won't budge. Trying to stay in character, I apply a little more pressure, thinking about her as a girl, not an actress. Reluctantly, she turns to me. I take her chin in my hand and try to kiss her. Our lips have barely touched when I hear a mumbled sound. I ignore it, bending into the kiss. I hear it again. Her eyes are wide open. She seems to be saying, "No tongue."

"What did you say?"

"No tongue. I have a boyfriend."

"Oh, that's nice," I say idiotically.

"That's enough," says Vincent. "Thank you, Patty."

She gets up and walks huffily out the door. I start laughing. I suddenly think about what a bang David would get out of this whole weird scene. It reminds me he's in New York working on the book. I make a quick note to call him about "the Hollywood chapter." Vincent is fiddling with the camera, remarking to himself, "You'd think she was being raped or something."

"She seemed really uptight. Was I doing something wrong?"

"Don't worry about it. The next girl who's coming over could be just right for the scene. I've worked with her for a couple of years now. She's very talented."

"I hope so." At this point I need massive injections of reassurance: enough to cause cancer in rats.

The next girl is just what the doctor ordered. She literally skips into the room, introduces herself as Doani, does a little shuffle-stamp on the hardwood floor, and flops down on the couch next to me. Doani possesses infinite energy and a fantastic smile. We read through the script. She's the first girl I click with, which is fortunate, because she is also the last Ross sends over. She's very relaxed and confident, and as we go along, some of this rubs off on me. We work well together, giving each other help on the more moronic lines. We spend the rest of the afternoon rehearsing the script. Slowly, it gets better, but we all realize that it has a long way to go before the screen test tomorrow afternoon. Despite Vincent and Doani's encouraging remarks, I get more and more depressed.

That night, Ross picks us up and takes us all out to dinner at a restaurant on the shore north of L.A. The mood during dinner is gloomy. All I can think about is how hollow my lines sound. I look out at the waves breaking on the beach, willing the screaming rhubarbs to stay away until I finish the screen test. Later that night, since I have no place to stay, Ross offers to put me up for the night. His generosity never ends: Overruling my objections, he gives me his bed while he sleeps on the couch. The man is a saint.

The bed is useless, however. I could be at a boxing match for all the sleep I'm getting. After an hour, Ross walks into the room.

"John, wake up."

"I'm awake. I can't sleep. I guess you know why."

"I know. I've been sitting out there trying to figure a way out of this." He lights up a three A.M. cigar.

"It's just not going to work," I tell him.

"Now stop that nonsense. Tell me, with whom could you do it better? Can you think of anyone?"

I think about Kathy Davis right away. I know it's a ridiculous idea, but I throw it out anyway.

"Hmmm," says Ross, puffing. "*Yes*. That just might work. I wonder." He thinks for a few minutes, and then announces, "Okay, I'll get the screen test postponed until Monday, and I'll get Kathy Davis for you. I know her agent and he'll do it for me."

He says this with such authority that I don't ask if he's serious. He is. Five minutes later I'm asleep.

On Friday, word comes down from the CBS powers: The screen test has been postponed until Monday. Early in the weekend, it becomes evident that Mark can make me work for him. He is running the whole show now. Despite the distracting presence of Kathy Davis, he can harangue me enough, make me angry enough, to outdo myself. By some strange chemistry which I begrudgingly acknowledge, and then come to rely on, Mark makes me work until the scene gets better. By Sunday, I know I can do it. Everyone who has been coaching me—Mark, Ross, Hank, Vincent, Kathy, and a professional director CBS has called in—begins to look less worried. On Monday morning, before the test, Mark cancels all further rehearsals.

"I don't want the Kid to overrehearse, to burn himself out on this one. He can do it. I know he can," I hear Mark saying to some CBS brass.

That afternoon, as if nothing special is going to happen at five o'clock, Ross, Hank, and I joy-ride around Los Angeles, ending up in Chinatown, where we avail ourselves of the services of Doctor Wu, an acupuncturist. With two pins in my back and two in my legs, Doctor Wu relieves a severe back pain I've been suffering from for two weeks.

We arrive at Television City before five. I feel wired, but good. The makeup artist erases a zit or two, and puts an Acapulco tan on my face. While the set is being readied, I wander around the cavernous spaces of the studio where soap operas are usually filmed. A studio cop picks me up and detains me for lack of proper identification. ("No, honest, officer. They *are* making a movie about me.") Ross finally finds me, gives me a scowl, and drags me back to the set.

The whole area is flooded with bright light. Three cameras are positioned around the couch on the set. Dozens of cameramen, technicians, and directors rush around. Taking command, Mark banishes everyone from the set. He asks me if I'm ready. I nod my head and walk into the light on the set. Kathy gives me a peck on the cheek. A technician runs out with one of those little clapperboards. The word "Mushroom" is chalked on it.

He claps the top down. "Mushroom. Take one." He withdraws.

"Roll 'em," Carliner says curtly.

The little red light on camera one flashes on, and we start eating up film at one thousand dollars a minute. Kathy and I embrace and kiss passionately. She breaks away, leaving me with my mouth open, my eyes closed.

The first take goes quickly. The lines sound natural. It feels good.

"Cut!" shouts Carliner.

Everyone rushes onto the set at once, congratulating the two of us. Ross and Hank nod approvingly from offstage, letting me know that it went better than any of us expected. That's all the reassurance I need.

We do four more takes, just for insurance against a technical foul-up. In the middle of the third take, on the "Is your room bugged too?" line, Kathy buckles over in hysterics. We start from the beginning. No problem.

As we're walking off the set after the final take, two network officials who had come to see my performance are conferring in the corner. I overhear the conversation:

"Do you think he's got enough?" asks one.

"He's got more than enough. The Kid's got it!"

I get the lead.

---

# 46

# The End of the Parade

When the plane lands in New York, I'm still feeling buoyant, satisfied. At the last minute in Los Angeles, Kathy Davis and I had discovered that we'd be flying to New York at roughly the same time, so we got on the same flight. In New York, we ride into town together, and Kathy drops me off on East Sixty-sixth Street where David has been staying all summer. We make plans to get together the next night.

David comes to the door dressed in a blue bathrobe. He is smoking a cigarette and carrying a manuscript. We smile. It's good to see him.

"Twinkle, twinkle," he says.

"Is that the password?"

"You're looking ballsy," he tells me.

"I feel ballsy. Is that the first part of the book?" I point to the manuscript.

"It's belles litter," he says. "I've been sweeping it into fastidious little piles with my literary broomstick."

"Now I know I'm really back."

"How so?" He smirks.

"I haven't heard the word 'fastidious' in ten days."

We go into the apartment and fix drinks. I've been wondering how I'm going to tell David about everything that went on in Hollywood. There is no place to start. It all seems so distant from New York and our work on the book. In the end, I tell him very little about the whole experience. Instead, we talk about the book late into the night. During the conversation, I sense that something is on his mind that he doesn't want to talk about right away. This is rare for David. He always tells me exactly what he's thinking. The next day at lunch in P. J. Clarke's, it all comes out.

"J.P., there's something we should talk about."

"Okay, shoot."

"I've given our financial arrangement regarding the book a great deal of thought. I don't think the ten percent I'm getting is fair."

"Neither do I. Before I went to Hollywood I realized it had to be changed."

"Good." He looks relieved. He raises his wine glass. "To a fairer agreement."

"Cheers." We drink. "What do you think is a fair split?" I ask him.

"Fifty-fifty, or sixty-forty. Sixty, you. Forty, me."

I had been thinking about a sixty-forty arrangement when I first considered changing the contract. But there is something about the tone of David's voice that disturbs me: It's as if he's *demanding* fifty-fifty. I have to make this decision.

"Fifty-fifty is out of the question, David."

"Why?"

"It's my story."

"I know that, but I'm doing half the work. I should share half the benefits."

"The work has nothing to do with it. A ghostwriter

would do ninety percent of the work and get ten percent of the profits."

"Sure, but I'm doing more for this book than some schmuck ghostwriter. That's why we started working together in the first place. But at that time, your lawyer was pumping you full of crap, telling you that you could do the book by yourself with minimal editing from me. Now the situation has changed. If I do half the work, I should be compensated with half the cut."

David looks rattled. I feel a familiar anger building in my stomach. I thought I'd finished a decade's worth of haggling when I left Hollywood. Now my best friend wants to haggle with me. "You haven't given me one logical reason yet," I tell him. "Give me a good reason."

"Didn't you hear what I just said? I'm doing half the work. This is a partnership. When we went into the pizza business, it was my idea, but we each did half the work, and we split the profits fifty-fifty. And when you stopped working on it last spring because you were still beating Sir Whoopee senseless, I continued working alone, and yet you still got your paycheck every week. I didn't bitch about the inequity. I respected the partnership."

"This is different," I tell him, feeling the anger rising to the back of my head now. "When the idea of a book was first raised, I was the one who had to pay for a lawyer and sell the book to a publisher. This book has been my baby. And the financial decisions are mine to make."

"How can you say that?" David lights a cigarette. "Look, John, it's not the money that's bugging me. I don't want more money per se. It's the principle, the partnership, the—it's this! We've never talked like this to each other before. *This* makes me sick."

"I agree. But you have to let me give it some thought."

"Why should I be left out of the financial decisions if I'm doing half the work?" David is getting hot.

275

I explode, "The work has nothing to do with it! Look: This is my decision and I will make it alone. Drop it, David," I snap.

David is incredulous. "I don't believe it," he says. "You're telling me that I can't talk to you—my friend and collaborator—about the financial side of a project I will have spent six months working on when it's over. Is that what you're saying? Total censorship?"

"I know what you want. Now I need time to think about it."

"What's the matter with you, J.P.? Are you going home to Jerome? What the hell did they do to you out in Hollywood?"

"Hollywood? What's that got to do with—"

"Yes. *Hollywood.*" He spits out the word. "You've been completely different since you got back. You've been—weird."

"Not 'weird,' David. You have no right to press this discussion, no right to even bring it up again. I will bring it up when I've decided."

"Oh, man . . ."

"Listen, I have to go over to my patent attorney's about the motorcycle device."

David says nothing. We get the check. David pays for it. I look him in the eye, "Do you understand?"

"No."

That night, David goes down to the Village to listen to jazz. We agree to meet at the Vanguard after midnight. I want to pick up Kathy Davis at the St. Regis and bring her down for the last set. But the whole evening gets messed up. When I get to the lobby of the St. Regis, Kathy isn't ready to go out yet. I rocket down to the Vanguard hoping to find David. It isn't midnight yet. I can't find him. I leave a message at the door and.head back to the St. Regis. David never gets the message.

The next morning, David doesn't mention the foul-up. In fact, he isn't saying much of anything. I explain what happened. He tells me the music was excellent and leaves it at that. He walks to the study at the back of the apartment. I come into the room. He is looking out the window, smoking. I ask him if he could give me a lift to Tripler's. I have to pick up my suit.

"Sure," he says without looking at me.

"What exactly is eating you?" I ask him.

"It's too long to go into right now. And besides—" He turns and looks me in the eye. "I'm not supposed to tell you what's on my mind. Remember?"

"Are you still stewing about sixty-forty?" I feel the beginings of another anger balloon rising in my stomach.

"Not specifically," he says. "It's more than that. Come on. Let's get the car."

I grab my hat. David wears sunglasses.

We turn off Sixty-sixth Street, heading down Park Avenue. The streets are deserted. The August sunlight gives the city an unreal, empty glare. David guns the engine of the MG, ripping from one gear to the next. I had already decided last night that sixty-forty would be a more equitable split. But David's attitude is really pissing me off. I don't tell him that I've made up my mind.

"What is it besides sixty-forty that's bothering you?" I ask.

"J.P., the older I get, the more I realize one thing: I expect too much from my friends. That bothers me." He is bitter. "Yesterday, I expected you to act the way I would have if I'd been you. I would have said fifty-fifty and left it at that. But I'm learning how unrealistic my expectations are."

I say nothing. The anger balloon is rising as every block goes by. We come to a stoplight. David looks over at me. His face is taut. He starts to say something, stops, throws the car in first gear. We squeal through the intersection. A few minutes pass. David continues, "Last night when I was at the Vanguard waiting for you, I thought about you telling me that I had no right to bring up the subject of our financial agreement again. Frankly, that pissed me off more than anything else you said. I felt totally screwed. I don't *want* to bring it up. I don't ever want to think about it again. I hate this shit. It's—it's scuzzy. But I do want you to know one thing—" He stops talking as we turn onto Madison, heading uptown. "I want you to know that you can screw people in Hollywood, but you can't screw your friends."

The anger balloon explodes hot inside me, "*Screw?* I am not—repeat—am *not* screwing you! And I do not screw people in Hollywood either. Look: Originally I was going to get a ghostwriter, but you convinced me to use you instead. Then you wanted cover credit and I got you that too. Now you want something else and I tell you that I want to think about it—Is that screwing you?"

David's knuckles are fierce on the steering wheel. We pass Tripler's on Madison without stopping. David heads west, then turns down Fifth Avenue. The sun is directly in our eyes.

"You didn't tell me you wanted to think about it," says David. "You told me I had no right to bring the subject up. *That* is screwing me. *That* is telling me that you don't respect what I'm putting into the book. People who pay a writer ten percent to do their work don't respect the writer. Let's not even talk about the writer being your best friend."

"Look, David!" I turn in the seat to face him. "I *did* tell you I want to think about it. This book is my baby. *My* baby! And I have the feeling that no matter what cut I give you, you will always want more."

"Not true. I told you. I'm willing to settle for forty percent of profits."

"David! I thought the money didn't matter!"

278

"It doesn't! It's the goddamn principle. I talked with my father—"

"The whole thing is a foregone conclusion," I tell him.

"What's a foregone conclusion?"

"What did your father say?"

"My father advised me to pull out entirely," he says.

"Well, if you keep this up, you may just push me into deciding to get somebody else." David is momentarily quiet. "Green light, David."

We turn and head east on Forty-second Street. David races down the block and turns up Madison, narrowly avoiding a New York City Police Department parade route barricade. Madison is totally deserted. We scream uptown. I roll down the window.

"How can you show so little respect?" yells David.

"How can *you* be so greedy?" I shout at him.

"Me? *Greedy?*" David slams on the brakes. We are in front of Tripler's. "You're the one who wants to give me ten fucking percent!"

"David! Sixty-forty is a *foregone conclusion!*"

"What?"

Just then we both hear the sounds of a parade coming up behind us.

"There's a goddamn parade back there!" yells David.

"I know!"

"What the hell do you mean it's a foregone conclusion?"

"If you wouldn't push me so much, you'd—I hope you realize that you are using our friendship to get something out of me."

"I am not," he shouts.

"Then why are you pushing me?"

"Why is sixty-forty a foregone conclusion?"

"Christ! I decided last night that you'd get your fucking forty percent."

The oom-pah-pah parade music is louder now. The first

279

wave of marchers passes the car. It seems to be a Sun Myung Moon "God Bless America" parade. No one is on the street to watch. No applause, no ticker tape.

David is shaking his head, "Then why didn't you tell me you'd decided before this thing got so out of hand?—Oh, God . . ."

"Because I don't like to be pushed, David. You better realize that right now! *I don't like to be pushed!*"

David looks at the parade going by. "Then I'm very sorry," he says, turning to me.

I open the car door and jump out, running smack dab into the end of the parade.

Late that afternoon, we decide to take a walk together. Things are cooling down. We head east to the river in silence. The streets seem even more empty now than before. On York Avenue, we look out across the river and see the dark geometry of the Fifty-ninth Street Bridge against the soft afternoon sky. David nods his head toward it. We cut back to Second Avenue to get on the pedestrian ramp. The metal of the bridge sounds good under our feet. We walk out to the center on the downtown side. Silence prevails. Our arms hang marionette-style over the railing.

"How do you feel?" asks David.

"I'm still pissed, but I'm cooling off."

David lights a cigarette. "Wanna talk about it all now—or wait?"

"Now."

"Good," he says. "I've been thinking."

"Yeah?"

"After you got out at Tripler's, I drove around for an hour, figuring things out. I could have kicked myself for not realizing earlier what part of the problem was."

"What?" I ask him.

"Bessie," he says. "The expression on your face in the car was exactly the same one you get when Bessie pushes you to do something. You've never liked that."

I ponder this for a moment. "Maybe. But it was also my decision to make."

"Right," he says. "And you made it yourself last night. So why didn't you tell me this morning before we got into the car."

"I wanted to see if you'd respect my judgment on the matter and not bring it up again."

David looks down at the river. "How could I have respected your judgment when I would have made it fifty-fifty if I'd been you?"

"You aren't me. And the decision was mine. You didn't recognize that."

David offers me a cigarette. We light up and smoke in silence.

"So it was a question of power?" he asks.

"To some extent. And respect . . ."

"Yes, respect. But what about power? What does it mean to you now?" he asks.

"Many things. I can't exactly define it. But I guess it comes from within." David says nothing. "It's knowing your own potential," I tell him. "Right now, I'm stretching my muscles and finding out what I'm capable of doing."

"Stretching your muscles?"

"Testing."

David nods his head. "Do you remember the first time we were up here?"

"Yeah. It seems like a helluva long time ago."

"It was," he says. "We've changed. *You've* changed."

"So have you."

"Do you remember you said you didn't know if you wanted power?"

281

"Yes."

"Well, believe it now," says David. "You do."

I think for a little while. David looks at me pointedly.

"Not *wanting* power," I tell him. "*Having* power. And using it wisely."

# Epilogue:
# Falling Upward

We had changed. The sixty-forty argument had been a test. It strengthened our friendship. We went back to Princeton in September. David was a junior. I was repeating my senior year. I had decided the previous spring that graduate school was not for me. But I wanted another year of academics. David and I moved into Pyne Hall, christening our room Yucca Flats. A sign on the door, taken from an Air Force documentary, as reported in *The Curve of Binding Energy*, stated: *This is the valley where the giant mushrooms grow, the atomic clouds, the towering angry ghosts of the fireballs.* But the angry ghost of this Yucca Flats was our deadline. We gave up everything for the book. Academics went out the window. The Chart of Deadly Sins went back up on the wall.

We took long walks, bouncing ideas off one another. One night we were passing under the window of 42 Little. I caught sight of the enormous map of the world still pasted to the living room wall. David knew what I was thinking. We couldn't resist.

There were four sophomores living in the room. We informed them that as prior residents of 42 Little, we had come back to claim our map. They looked at us, then at the map, then at each other. I told them a deal could be made. One of them wanted the map. The others looked skeptical. They asked us how we would get it off the wall if they didn't buy it. "Map remover," said David. They started smiling. "You've never heard of map remover?" I said. We played out the scene deadpan. "Look, we'll give you a bargain.

Twenty-five bucks not to remove the map," I told them. "Do you think we're suckers?" one of them asked. "Hey, it's a tradition," I said. They conferred among themselves and agreed to buy it. "Send us a check," I told them.

When we were outside, David said, "Remember Patrick James Huston?" We laughed. Huston was the "In Memory of Mom" ex-con in the wanted poster we had put on the wall in 42 Little two years before. Last summer David had found a trashy magazine called *Violent World*. The cover of the magazine showed a photograph of a mutilated body. The pink headline said: EXCLUSIVE: THE PHOTOS THEY COULDN'T SUPPRESS: 344 MANGLED CRASH VICTIMS. Inside the magazine we found an article titled "Vicious Criminals." That same picture of Patrick James Huston stared out at us, as if from our wall. But there was another article in *Violent World* which fascinated us. It helped put whoopee into perspective: Fifteen pages away from Huston's grim face was a picture of me in a Princeton letter sweater. The headline said: STUDENT PUTS SMALL NATIONS IN THE A-BOMB BUSINESS.

In November the book was done. I wondered about the future. The movie would be shot at Princeton in the spring. It would be a crazy time for both of us. During the winter, I took acting lessons to find out how to be myself in front of a camera. When some students at Princeton heard I was taking the lead role in a film about myself, they assumed I was cashing in. I was sensitive to the accusation. I went on a speaking tour of college campuses, taking the serious issue of nuclear proliferation to people my own age. I concluded my speeches, saying:

"Our generation has grown up under the shadow of the bomb. It is embedded in our collective psyche. Who here can't recall the air raid drills in elementary school when the teacher taught us to crawl underneath our desks in the event of an atomic attack? I can. I can also remember when I was seven or eight, the time of the Cuban missile crisis. There was the bomb shelter hysteria, and the parents of a kid I knew down the block tore up their backyard to build an elaborate underground shelter. My family couldn't afford one. The kid took me down there once to show it to me. In the presence of his embarrassed father, he showed me the locks on the door of the shelter which were intended to keep the neighbors out when the bombs started falling. I punched the kid in the nose and that settled it. My family would roast with the rest of them.

"I hated that bomb everyone was talking about. I hate it still. But now, I'm making my voice heard and I'm hoping you'll do the same."

One afternoon in November, David and I took a walk on the golf course near Princeton. We climbed an elm tree. Sitting in the branches, among the yellow leaves and the sunlight, we became quiet for a time.

David looked up into the tree and said, "This sounds absurd, but if I died right now, what object of mine would you want to keep?"

I thought for a while about all the objects that were an important part of David's life: his books, journals, files, photographs, records.

"Your notebook," I said. "The unique way you perceive the world. You are one of the most perceptive people I have ever met." It felt good saying that. It was true. "What object of mine?" I asked him.

"I think I'd want to have those two perfect blackjacks you were dealt the first night we met." He smiled at me. I understood. "I remember you telling me there was no such thing as luck. I didn't believe you."

"I knew you didn't," I said.

# MUSHROOM

"Now I know luck doesn't matter. Luck is for people who need an excuse. It's really a matter of how you play the cards dealt to you. The risks you take."

I nodded my head.

We walked away from the tree and out onto an open fairway. The sun made everything seem alive, brilliant. I looked at David. He glanced back at me. We both knew there was something profound in the air. It was one of those cinematic moments that seem almost embarrassing while they are happening, but are the enchanting stuff of future reminiscences.

We were at the top of a hill of finely clipped grass. A small valley of trees was before us. We had come a long way to this hill. We would be leaving Old Nassau soon. David had just turned twenty. I was twenty-two. We were eager to leave. Princeton wasn't the same now. We were hungry to make a difference in the world. And we now knew that we weren't afraid of making mistakes. And we knew that there was something between us that could never happen again.

We would grow older and find separate avenues. David would go on to write more books. I would star in the movie and find a way to see the curve of the earth by way of NASA or Hollywood. And no matter what happened, I would always seek new experiences, not expecting answers from these experiences. I knew there were no answers. The questions were answers in themselves. I had learned that anything worth believing was worth doubting.

Late that afternoon, on the way back to Yucca Flats, I imagined us meeting years from then, when the seventies would have become part of the amnesia of Americans, who chronicle and devour decades. We would meet in the eighties, or the nineties, or perhaps at the end of the century on a cold New Year's Day. We would meet at the middle of the Fifty-

286

ninth Street Bridge on the first day of the twenty-first century.

We would talk about how the world had changed. And we would talk about how nuclear proliferation had changed the world. And then we would fall silent for a time, the way we had in the sunny elm tree years before.

The river, running to the ocean, and the city would be before us—colossal and complex—but with even more fascination now because we would be older, and we would have seen more of the strange business that goes on behind the myriad closed doors and windows. And we would perhaps fall into a tap-dance step, together once again.

And then we would look at each other and laugh—and, yes, maybe even cry a little. And we would remember how it was in the days when we were young and hungry and falling upward. The days of bombs, and bridges, and whoopee. The days when everything seemed so possible.